The Marketing
Research Process

The Marketing Research Process

MARGARET CRIMP

Prentice/Hall PHI International

Englewood Cliffs, New Jersey   London   New Delhi
Singapore Sydney Tokyo Toronto Wellington

Library of Congress Cataloging in Publication Data

Crimp, Margaret.
    The marketing research process.

    Bibliography: p.
    Includes index.
    1. Marketing research.   I. Title
HF5415.2.C73   658.8'3   81-10720
ISBN 0-13-557710-1 (pbk.)   AACR2

British Library Cataloguing in Publication Data

Crimp, Margaret
    The marketing research process.
    1. Marketing research
    I. Title
    658.8'3   HF5415.2

    ISBN 0—13—557710—1

ISBN 0—13—557710—1

PRENTICE-HALL INTERNATIONAL, INC., *London*
PRENTICE-HALL OF AUSTRALIA PTY. LTD., *Sydney*
PRENTICE-HALL CANADA, INC., *Toronto*
PRENTICE-HALL OF INDIA PRIVATE LIMITED, *New Delhi*
PRENTICE-HALL OF JAPAN, INC., *Tokyo*
PRENTICE-HALL OF SOUTHEAST ASIA PTE., LTD., *Singapore*
PRENTICE-HALL, INC., *Englewood Cliffs, New Jersey*
WHITEHALL BOOKS LIMITED, *Wellington, New Zealand*

10 9 8 7 6 5 4 3 2

Typset by MHL Typesetting Ltd., Coventry
Printed and bound in Great Britain by SRP Ltd., Exeter

Contents

v

Chapter 4   Describing Markets — Focus on Sampling   46

Chapter 5   Describing Markets — Collecting Data by Means of Questions   67

Preface

Marketing research is a wide-ranging subject. It embraces various research procedures, such as surveys, experiments and group discussions to quote those most frequently used. These procedures are applied in a variety of ways to the many different decisions that managements have to make in the course of developing, distributing, selling and advertising products and services.

We need therefore at the outset to decide which of two routes we are going to follow while exploring marketing research:

Route A starts by describing research procedures and then, usually by means of examples, leads to consideration of some of the ways in which the research procedures are applied to the making of marketing decisions.

Route B follows the path taken by a marketing company while developing products or services and bringing these to market, with a stop at each stage en route to consider:
— the kind of data that would be helpful when the decisions are being made;
— how these data are collected;
— how the findings may be used to reduce uncertainty.

This book follows Route B. It is focused on the marketing of goods and services. The research procedures discussed are used not only in this context but are more and more being applied to social marketing, since government departments, local authorities and other social agencies equally need to know the characteristics, motivations and changing habits of those they plan for.

This book, however, concentrates on exploring the relationship between the requirements of 'marketing' and the capabilities of 'research', starting with the location of an opportunity in the market and proceeding

xi

via the stages summarised in Section 1.4 to the monitoring of performance. It will be seen that the process is continuous and circular; the
results of monitoring performance being used to make future plans, and
the marketing research process ends with the monitoring data serving as
inputs to predictive models.

The electronic revolution has made it possible to group data relating
to the buying behaviour, perceptions and attitudes of consumers in
many different ways so that their variety as individuals may be better
appreciated. Indeed 'market orientation' has become orientation towards
the individuals making up a market in a more meaningful way than was
possible when this expression was first coined. This book aims to show
how 'market orientation' and 'marketing research' necessarily hang
together.

Acknowledgements

'The Marketing Research Process' has benefited from the suggestions and criticisms made by:

John Davis, Henley: The Management College;
Geoffrey Faulder, The North East London Polytechnic;
Philip Watkin, The University of Wales Institute of Science and Technology.

They read the book as it developed for the publisher and their comments were especially helpful since they were based on both academic and practical marketing experience.

John Davis's statistical appendix gives the book a statistical authority it would otherwise lack and I am indeed glad he agreed to write it.

Published sources are acknowledged in footnotes throughout the book. I would in addition like to thank the following for the time they spent discussing individual aspects of the marketing research process:

Cyril Ashley, Ogilvy and Mather;
John Bickerdike, Forecast Market Research;
Tom Corlett, J. Walter Thompson Company;
Gordon Heald, Social Surveys (Gallup Poll);
Peter Hoyes, Television Advertising Bureau (Surveys), TABS;
Peter Lagden, Connell, May and Steavenson;
David Lowe-Watson, Esso Petroleum Company;
Tony Lunn, Cooper Research & Marketing;
Brian Pymont, Forecast Market Research;
Graham Read, British Market Research Bureau;
Pam Sellers, The Market Research Society;
Michael Stewart, Beecham Products;
Alan Wolfe, Ogilvy and Mather.

CHAPTER 1

Introduction

1.1 Focus on the Market

It is now generally agreed that the health of a company largely depends on its capacity to interpret the behaviour, attitudes and needs of the individual consumers or industrial users who make up its market. We cannot say that good health entirely depends on effective focus on the market. A company's plans and performance are affected by forces over which it has little or no control, forces such as:

> the economic climate;
> Government action;
> changes in the law;
> technological developments which may make what it has to offer old-fashioned,
> the activities of competitors, who may be quicker to exploit the technological developments.

In a mixed economy, a company's ability to carry out its plans also depends on whether institutions and individuals are able and willing to invest in its shares. Whether investors are able is largely outside the company's control. Willingness to invest will be influenced by the company's market performance, for a decision to invest is often taken on the advice of analysts who study market form.

1.2 Consumer and Industrial Markets

The company's sales will largely depend on the buying behaviour of consumers or industrial users, or of organisations such as local authorities. It may be marketing goods or (and this is a growth area) providing services such as the hire of office machinery, computer facilities or transport.

Consumer goods may belong to the category of those which are used up quickly, or fairly quickly (ice-cream, detergents, toothpaste), in which case they are *fast-moving consumer goods*: or they may be more durable and infrequently bought (motor cars, washing machines, power tools for DIY), and be classified as *consumer durables*.

We shall be interested in the frequency with which products are bought when we come to design market experiments and to build market models. For fast-moving consumer goods *repeat purchase* is an important criterion, as well as getting the product tried (*penetration*). For most durable goods penetration is the criterion.

Industrial goods divide into three categories:

(a) materials (e.g. timber) and parts (e.g. timing devices)
(b) capital items (e.g. generators)
(c) supplies (e.g. lubricants) and services (e.g. advertising).[1]

We are also interested in the frequency with which goods are bought when planning research in industrial markets. Success in marketing goods in categories (a) and (c) depends on repeat purchase as well as penetration, while items in category (b) are infrequently bought by any one customer.

Derived demand. In an industrial market the ultimate consumer may be some stages away: but there are industrial markets in which the ultimate consumer is close at hand so that it pays the company to study the behaviour of consumers as well as that of its industrial customers.

The behaviour of consumers buying motor cars, cooking stoves or washing machines soon affects the sale of timing devices to the car industry or to the manufacturers of domestic durables.

1.3 Feedback and Market Intelligence

If our company is marketing an infrequently purchased industrial good (say machinery used in the manufacture of shoes), to a limited number of customers (shoe manufacture is concentrated in a few hands), with little competition to meet, then we can rely on sales and technical representatives to give early warning of events which might affect our sales forecasts. Most companies trade under rather different conditions. Let us consider the obstacles to communication with its market faced by a company marketing consumer goods, knowing that suppliers of industrial goods often face similar problems.

---

1. Kotler, P. (1980), *Marketing Management, Analysis, Planning and Control,* 4th ed., Englewood Cliffs, N.J., Prentice-Hall, p. 172.

1.3.1 OBSTACLES TO COMMUNICATION

Most companies marketing consumer goods depend on buying decisions made by a large number of individuals spread over a wide area, often in more than one country. The company will only be in direct contact with these individuals if it sells by mail order, or if (like Avon Cosmetics) it operates door-to-door selling. Otherwise, intermediaries stand between the company and those who finally consume its products.

The company may be selling direct to the retail organisations controlling the outlets where its product is bought, or to wholesalers (possibly to a voluntary group of wholesalers such as Mace) who break bulk and pass goods on to retail outlets. The company may sell direct to large retailers, such as Tesco and Curry, and through the wholesale to those with less clout. Finally, in its dealings with intermediaries, and at the point-of-sale to consumers, the company's product meets competition.

1.3.2 WHERE FEEDBACK FALLS SHORT

Feedback from sales representatives is a useful source of marketing intelligence, especially in industrial markets, but information derived from its own sales records and its own representatives' reports will not enable a company to focus effectively on:

— the behaviour, attitudes and needs of the consumers in its market;
— the behaviour, attitudes and needs of the intermediaries on whom it relies to make its goods available to consumers;
— the activities of competitors and the response of consumers and intermediaries to these activities.

'Market research is the means used by those who provide goods and services to keep themselves in touch with the needs and wants of those who buy and use those goods and services.'[2]

1.4 Stages in the Process

Marketing research has two basic purposes:

— to reduce uncertainty when plans are being made, whether these relate to the marketing operation as a whole or to individual components such as advertising;

2. *Guide to the Practice of Market and Survey Research,* The Market Research Society, 1980.

— to monitor performance after the plans have been put into operation.

The monitoring programme has two functions. It helps to control execution of the marketing company's operational plan and it makes a substantial contribution to longer term strategic planning.

If 'research' and 'marketing' are fully integrated, as in the process outlined below, radical and unexpected changes of plan can be avoided: unless, of course, one of the uncontrollable forces mentioned in Section 1.1 comes into play without warning.

We refer from now on to 'product' avoiding the expression 'product or service'. Apart from being clumsy the 'or service' is superfluous. The service offered to consumers by banks, tour operators, local authorities and research agencies (to quote some examples) are the products of these bodies and they are susceptible to substantially the same marketing research treatment as the goods we call 'products'.

The choice of a product field for investigation will depend on the company's financial, technical and productive resources, on its corporate aspirations and management style, and on its marketing experience. A particular product field may look promising because the company is operating in a related field, because it knows the distributive channels serving it, because the brands in the field are susceptible to technological change, or because a company has been acquired, to quote some obvious reasons.

The first research objective is to establish whether there is an opportunity for a *new brand* in this product field.

A 'brand' is a product or service which has been given an identity; it has a 'brand name' and the added value of a 'brand image'. The image is developed in advertisements and in all the other communications associated with the product, including its packaging.

The marketing stages, on which the structure of this book rests, are as follows:

Stages in the Marketing Research Process	*Chapter*
The market is explored	2
The market is described	3—5
The market is segmented	6
The brand is developed	7
The 'message' is tested	8
The media are selected	9
The 'mix' is tested in the field	10
Performance is monitored and the future forecast	11

Let us now consider the content of these stages in more detail.

The market is explored (Chapter 2). All available sources of facts and ideas are consulted with a view to defining the characteristics of buyers and users in the market; the channels through which products reach them; how the products and brands available to them are perceived; ways in which they are used; where they fall short. Some of these data will be in the form of available statistics, others in the form of ideas and these ideas may suggest unsatisfied, or only partly satisfied, wants.

Unless a marketing company is operating in a familiar field, exploratory research is a necessary preliminary to the formulation of research objectives and to the design of more conclusive research.

The market is described (Chapters 3—5). In order to design a descriptive survey of the market we need to know the parameters of the survey population, whether this be a population of households, individuals, firms or retailers. We also need to know how the survey population stratifies and whether some strata (groups) are more meaningful to our purpose than others. If a minority group looks like being significant, the sample must include a sufficient number of its members to justify singling the group out for separate consideration. For an industrial, trade or other 'non-consumer' population, stratification is based on the relative business importance of groups: on volume of production or turnover, rather than on the number of industrial establishments or shops to be found in different groups.

Exploratory research will have suggested what topics should be covered when data are collected and in what detail the topics need to be treated. The method adopted to collect the data will largely depend on the nature of the data required and the characteristics of the survey population. The budget and the time available also influence research design.

The market is segmented (Chapter 6). The object of the marketing process, taken in its entirety, is to locate a target group of consumers or users who have an unsatisfied need which could be met by a branded product. The descriptive survey will probably be so designed that it provides the data for a segmentation study.

There are two basic approaches. Consumers or users can be sorted into groups with 'like' buying requirements according to demographic characteristics, buying behaviour in the product field or beliefs and attitudes held in common (consumer typology). Alternatively, the types of product or brands in the field may be grouped according to the benefits or shortcomings they are seen to share by those who buy or use them (product/brand differentation).

Either way, a descriptive survey of this kind must be carried out on a sufficiently large scale to allow for the sample being broken down for detailed analysis of the data.

A fruitful segmentation analysis defines a target group in the market and specifies the characteristics of a product to suit this group. This focuses product development and the research associated with product development.

The brand is developed (Chapter 7). Ideas, or concepts, for products to meet the need that has been located are tried out on the target group using qualitative methods. Ways of advertising the brand are likely to be tried out at the same time.

This is a weeding-out process. We hope to be left with the profiles of one or two possible branded products but our data, though rich in ideas, lack statistical support. We proceed to set up experiments.

The product as perceived by buyers and users is an amalgam of formulation plus packaging plus price plus communication: i.e. it is a brand. In the experimental programme these components may be tested individually (atomistic approach) or in combination (holistic approach). Both are considered.

We are not yet out in the market, these screening Go/No Go experiments being of a 'lab.' type. Communications research (a large subject) is reserved for Chapters 8 and 9.

The 'message' is tested (Chapter 8). In consumer markets advertising is the most important means of communicating the characteristics of the new brand to prospective buyers and users. Other means of communication are public relations, promotions and, particularly significant in industrial markets, the sales force.

We concentrate on advertising research because here the need to reduce uncertainty is greatest. While advertising can add considerable value to a brand, this added value is achieved at some cost.

We are 'pre-testing' at this stage, i.e. conducting experiments in controlled but unnatural contexts. Post-testing is covered when the 'mix' goes into the field (Chapter 10).

The media are selected (Chapter 9). The advertising industry (advertisers + advertising agencies + media owners) provides a wealth of shared cost data relating to main media categories (television, newspapers, magazines). The 'support media' (radio, outdoor and cinema) are also researched, though less frequently.

Viewers and readers are classified in some detail and it is possible to 'marry' the target group to the audience using the standard regional, sex, social grade, age group, etc. demographic classifications. We may in addition decide to buy shared cost or syndicated research which collects product use and media 'consumption' data from one and the same individual.

The effectiveness of the media plan cannot be measured until the advertising campaign has been launched, and we will then be faced with the problem of disentangling the effect of the media selection from the effect of the creative work and of the other elements in the mix.

The 'mix' is tested in the field (Chapter 10). There are certain important components of the mix which cannot be tested until plans for the brand are sufficiently advanced to allow for a test launch. Distributive, selling and merchandising decisions do not lend themselves to 'lab.'-type experimentation.

Syndicated retail audit data will guide channel decisions with trend data showing the relative importance of different types of retail outlet and how these are being used by competitors.

Penetration and *repeat purchase* data derived from consumer panels enable brand share predictions to be made. The data also show what kind of consumers are buying, and in what quantity and how often they buy.

The ultimate criterion is contribution to profit but the immediate measure of performance is an estimate of retail sales or consumer purchases, and the share of all sales or purchases in the product field these represent.

Sales reflect the impact of the marketing mix as a whole. It is difficult to isolate the effect on sales of individual items in the mix, but repeated and carefully timed surveys enable us to record how consumers are responding to the brand and the image the advertising associates with it.

Tests in the market often require a large financial commitment. This is especially so when a brand is being introduced. In addition, the marketing company's reputation with the retail trade is at stake and competitors are alerted. Micro-market testing (Mini-test

Market), may be used either to shorten the duration of a full market test or to sidestep it and go straight to launch.

Performance is monitored and the future forecast (Chapter 11). After the product or service has been launched, trend data are collected relating to the major components in the 'mix', so that 'own' marketing performance may be compared with that of competitors on a continuous basis.

The immediate task of the monitoring programme is to control the operational plan:

- → to keep track of the passage of the brand along the distribution channel to the ultimate buyer or user;
- — to keep a running record of its market share;
- — to assess the effect of the communications programme and, more particularly, the effect of the advertising campaign;
- — to ensure that the sales force is being deployed as effectively as possible; and, depending on the nature of the product,
- — to record how the brand is being used.

The research procedures used will be those which are also employed to measure the effect of experiments in the field — retail audits, consumer panels, usage and attitude surveys. The data derived from the monitoring programme are used when the future of the brand is being forecast.

The 'marketing research system' is one of four components of the 'marketing information system' (Kotler), the others being the 'internal accounting system', the 'marketing intelligence system' and the 'marketing management science system' (see Figure 33).

The marketing research system makes the major monitoring contribution in consumer markets, but the internal accounting system is critical when marketing costs are related to sales revenue. The marketing intelligence system makes a significant contribution to the monitoring programme of a 'non-consumer' company, while the marketing management science system covers the use of modelling procedures to describe, diagnose and predict.

Sales achievement is, of course, dependent on the marketing support allocated to the brand in terms of sales force time, advertising expenditure and promotional offers: i.e. sales achievement is dependent on marketing costs. The monitoring programme needs to provide data relating to competitors', as well as 'own', marketing costs in order that sales may be forecast and contributions to profit estimated.

The marketing management science system can be applied to this 'chicken and egg' problem inherent in sales forecasting. The data derived from the monitoring programme may be aggregated before they are fed into the computer or the consumers may be represented and processed at the individual level (micro-behavioural modelling). If the individual data are on file, it is possible to treat the repondents as 'electronic consumers' and to simulate their behaviour vis-à-vis the brand.

1.5 The MR Industry

Marketing companies buy research from different types of research supplier and commission research work in a variety of ways.

Syndicated continuous panel services and other large scale shared cost surveys will be bought from one of the 29 (in 1981) companies belonging to the Association of Market Survey Organisations (AMSO). Companies have been amalgamating in this field as elsewhere in industry and the research industry includes some very substantial operators, offering a wide range of research services. (To qualify for membership of AMSO a supplier of research must have achieved a specified turnover, and be equipped to undertake full-scale national surveys. The AMSO companies 'are responsible for some £40,000,000 worth of market research a year'.[3])

Apart from the AMSO agencies, there are suppliers specialising in particular marketing applications, i.e. in product, packaging, pricing or communications research, and the marketing company may have occasion to commission one of these specialist suppliers.

The marketing company may choose to plan its own research programme, then buy fieldwork from a company concentrating on fieldwork. The data may then come back to the marketing company as computer printouts from an agency specialising in electronic data processing (see Figure 1). Translating the data into a report and recommendations is then the sole responsibility of the marketing company. (If one of the AMSO companies is employed, this is likely to be a co-operative operation – see Chapter 3.)

For exploratory and diagnostic work the marketing company may employ a consultant. The consultant may be a psychologist qualified to take depth interviews and group discussions and to interpret the results, or a mathematician with OR and statistical expertise equipped to apply multi-variate techniques to the wealth of data a large marketing company has on file.

The Market Research Society. Most of those who work in MR are members of The Market Research Society. The Society is a professional

---

3. The MRS Yearbook, 1979/80, London, The Market Research Society.

body based on individual membership (not a trade association), and the 3,000 plus members are employed as follows (1981):

in companies buying research	1,397
in companies selling research	1,235
in advertising agencies	252
as academics	141
others, including consultants	163

Members of the Society subscribe to a *Code of Conduct* which puts a premium on confidentiality — anonymity of the respondent is carefully protected.

Practitioners in the 'non-consumer' field may belong to the Industrial Market Research Association. The Code of Conduct is binding on members of the IMRA and the MRS.

Finally, to improve and safeguard fieldwork standards the Society operates the *Interviewer Card Scheme* (Chapter 5).

Sources of Information:
— The Society's *'Guide to the Practice of Market and Survey Research'* is a succinct introduction to the scope of MR and the role of the Society;
— The Code of Conduct is free on request; so is
— *'Organisations Providing Market Research Services in Great Britain'*. This is updated each year and lists the services offered by suppliers and indicates their total turnover. There must be at least one full member of the Society on the board.
— *The Market Research Society Yearbook* (free to members) reviews the Society's activities, lists members, includes some useful demographic data, serves as a guide to the Government Statistical Service, gives 'useful addresses' at home and abroad.

Addresses:
— The Market Research Society, 15 Belgrave Square, London SW1X 8PF (General Secretary: Peter A. Clark).
— Association of Market Survey Organisations, 4 Verulam Buildings, Grays Inn Road, London WC1 (Secretary: Norman Mould).
— Industrial Market Research Association, 11 Bird Street, Lichfield, Staffs., WS13 6PW. 05432 23448.
— ESOMAR (European Society for Opinion and Market Research) Central Secretariat, Wamberg 37, 1083 CW Amsterdam, The Netherlands.

It has been estimated that the total amount of money spent on commercial market research in the United Kingdom in 1979 was about £80–85 million. This compares with a sum of £112,000 million spent by the people of the country in the same year on all goods and services which they bought. So the cost of market research was about 7–8p for every £100 spent by consumers.[2]

CHAPTER 2

Exploring the Market

Introduction

A marketing company is proposing to commission a survey of the buying habits, attitudes and perceptions of the consumers in a market with the object of establishing whether or not there is an opportunity for a new brand in this product field.

Development of the survey is discussed in Chapter 3. Here we are concerned with a necessary preliminary to survey design, exploratory research. Whether the exploratory procedures discussed here are adopted in whole or in part will depend on the company's prior knowledge of the market. Clearly it would not be considering the possibility of entering the market without some prior knowledge, while, if it has reached the stage of commissioning a survey, the research agency may be able to make a contribution based on its experience.

2.1 Why the Exploratory Stage is Important

In order to design a cost-effective survey it is necessary to have available data relating to:

the parameters of the survey population;
the ideas held by this population about the product field; and
the brands available in it.

To put this another way, it is necessary to be informed about the population and topics of interest given the field to be surveyed.

Statistical data are required about the population in order to design the sample. In order to describe the varying habits and attitudes of different groups in the population, for example different age groups, it will be necessary to break the sample down. A minority group may look like being of particular interest. The sample design must provide for the collection of data from a sufficient number of consumers in this group.

Similarly with the topics of interest: in order to design the questionnaire, or any other data collection instrument, it is necessary to have explored consumer behaviour and attitudes with regard to the type of product and brands available and the context in which these are used: motoring, clothes washing, do-it-yourself, etc. The designer of the survey risks two 'sins': the *sin of omission* — not treating a topic in sufficient detail, or failing to provide sufficient respondents in a group which has marketing significance: and the *sin of commission* — collecting data which proves to be immaterial or unactionable, or breaking the sample down to a wasteful extent. It would, for example, be wasteful to provide for a breakdown of the sample into four social classes where two would be sufficient, as in many 'fast-moving' product fields.

In an earlier edition[1] of his *Marketing Management*, Kotler gave a definition of marketing research which takes account of the importance of informed conjecturing in research design:

> Marketing research is systematic problem analysis, model-building and fact-finding for the purpose of improved decision-making and control in the marketing of goods and services.

The key expression is 'model-building', for[2]

> A model is a set of assumptions about the factors which are relevant to a given situation and the relationships which exist between them.

The research planner undertakes exploratory research in order to arrive at 'a set of assumptions' on which to base the research design. Obviously, the more thorough the exploration, the firmer the assumptions.

2.2 The Exploratory Process

In our well-documented society it is difficult to conceive of a market about which there is no information available, over and above the company's own records. Available information is called *secondary data*, while that derived from a new research study is *primary data*. Since search of secondary data takes place before the collection of primary

1. Kotler, P. (1966), *Marketing Management, Analysis, Planning and Control*, 1st ed., Englewood Cliffs, N.J., Prentice-Hall, Chap. 10.
2. Rothman J. (1978), 'Experimental Designs and Models', Chap. 3 in Worcester, R.M. and Downham, J. eds, *The Consumer Market Research Handbook*, Wokingham, Van Nostrand Reinhold.

data, use of the terms 'secondary' and 'primary' can be confusing, and often leads to an elementary mistake in examinations!

Exploratory research includes all or some of the following activities:

Secondary Data Search $\left\{\begin{array}{l}\textit{Internal Sources} \\ \textit{External Sources, including Govern-} \\ \textit{ment Statistics and Syndicated} \\ \textit{Sources}\end{array}\right.$

Consulting Experts

Observational Studies

Consulting People
in the Market $\left\{\begin{array}{l}\textit{Group Discussions} \\ \textit{'Depth' interviews}\end{array}\right.$

Buying into an Omnibus
Survey

Let us take each of these exploratory activities in turn.

2.3 Secondary Data Search — Internal Sources

Internal sources can be divided into two categories: the company's operating records (what Kotler calls 'the internal accounting system')[3] and reports on file, including research previously carried out by the company.

The operating records will cover subjects ranging from the cost of raw materials (if this is a manufacturing company) to sales of the company's output. Transport costs, sales costs, advertising and other promotional expenditures are *marketing costs* to be set against *sales revenue*. Packaging and warehousing costs may also be regarded as marketing costs.

Whether or not the operating records are kept in such a way that they can be used to allocate marketing costs to specific branded products, and to help monitor marketing performance, indicates whether the company is truly focused on the market. Records of this kind were originally designed to enable accountants to account for costs incurred and the sales manager (or sales director) to control the sales force.

The kind of detail and analysis needed for these purposes is not the same as the kind of detail and analysis needed by a marketing director, or brand manager, striving to predict the contribution to profit likely to be made by a particular branded product or service.

3. Kotler, P. (1980), *Marketing Management, Analysis, Planning and Control*, 4th ed., Englewood Cliffs, N.J., Prentice-Hall, p. 603.

Analysis by region. In consumer markets it is helpful if sales records can be related to *IBA television areas*, even if the company is not a television advertiser. Large companies tend to be television advertisers and the data generated by syndicated services (retail audits and consumer panels) are generally presented in this way. So are the statistics relating to readership of newspapers and magazines.

In the case of industrial markets, sales are best recorded by *Standard Region* for comparison with the wealth of information published by the Government Statistical Service.

Analysis by industrial application. Focus on an industrial market is sharper if sales and costs are recorded by the use to which the industrial customer is putting the product. If this happens to equate with a *Standard Industrial Classification*, the figures derived from internal records can be related to a wide (and international) range of statistical data.

Analysis by size? Or by numbers? For industrial and trade customers, how they group by output, sales or turnover is more significant when designing research than how they group by the number of industrial establishments, or the number of shops, in a category. On the other hand, for consumers it is the number of individuals in a particular group that we are interested in.

Where internal records fall short. The company's own sales figures do not tell us

how big a customer is,
how much business competitors are doing with our customer, or
what our potential sales are.

Reports from sales representatives and from staff belonging to technical and professional bodies convey intelligence about competitive activity, but we now need to extend the search to include data deriving from sources outside the company.

2.4 Secondary Data Search — External Sources

We are going to consider this large subject under three headings, Government statistics, other published sources, and syndicated services: and to refer to Appendix 1 (at the end of this book) which lists the more commonly used sources.

Companies operating in industrial markets will rely on the first two when making research plans. Consumer companies are likely to make use of syndicated sources, if they operate on a large enough scale to warrant the cost.

2.4.1 EXTERNAL SOURCES: GOVERNMENT STATISTICS

The most prolific source of secondary data is the Government Statistical Service.[4]

> The Government Statistical Service (GSS) comprises the statistics divisions of all major departments plus the two big collecting agencies — Business Statistics Office and Office of Population Censuses and Surveys — and the Central Statistical Office which co-ordinates the system.

The reference to 'all major departments' reminds us that government statistics are collected for the purpose of government: they do not always fit a particular marketing purpose, but every effort is made to meet business requirements and data additional to that published are often made available on request.

The Business Statistics Office processes returns made by 'firms in industry, retailing and other service trades' and shows itself to be aware of marketing needs:[5]

> You need Business Monitors to . . .
> rate your company's performance with your industry as a whole;
> know what product sales are increasing;
> keep up to date on the industries that supply you;
> show the way to new market opportunities.

There is a Production series, a Service and Distributive series and a Miscellaneous series. The last covers 'a range of subjects varying from motor vehicle registrations to cinemas, finance and overseas travel'. The monitors are published monthly and quarterly.

The validity of the published statistics depends on the care with which businesses make their returns. Anonymity of businesses supplying data is carefully safeguarded. The Business Statistics Office does not tell companies who their competitors are.

Censuses and sampling estimates. The Census of Population is taken every ten years. A sample based on the census is drawn halfway through the decade. The Census of Production is taken at five year intervals. The last Census of Retail Distribution and Other Services was taken in 1971. Its place has been taken by 'annual enquiries' of representative samples (the first was made in 1976).

The CSO regularly publishes updated estimates. In the case of Population, returns made by the Registrars General are used. For Production, Retail Distribution and Other Services, the estimates are

---

4. *Government Statistics, a brief guide to sources*, London, Central Statistical Office.
5. *Business Monitors Give You the Facts About Your Industry*, London, Department of Industry, Business Statistics Office.

based on returns made by samples of industrial establishments, retailers and suppliers of services. It is not easy to compare the government statistics relating to Distribution and Other Services in their new form with statistics derived from the last census. The categories have been reduced from 50 types of outlet to 26. This reflects the way in which retailing distinctions have been blurred in recent years. More to the point here, *this is an example of the kind of difficulty encountered when trying to relate statistical data from more than one secondary source.*

Once a year the OPCS makes the Family Expenditure Survey, the National Food Survey and the National Travel Survey. Surveys are made on a variety of subjects to meet the needs of government departments. It is worth while consulting the regularly updated lists of *Government Publications* available in any reference library.

Exploratory research for a marketing project. The following approach to 'government statistics' may help the business studies student engaged on exploratory research for a marketing project:
— write for 'Government Statistics, a brief guide to sources' free from the CSO (see Appendix 1 for address);
— consult the 'Guide to Official Statistics' published annually by the CSO;
— consult the cumulative and recent lists of Government Publications;
— get familiar with the Monthly Digest of Statistics, Economic Trends (monthly) and Population Trends (quarterly);
— take note of the classifications used for Population, Production and Distribution;
— if there is a Government Bookshop near you, visit it;
— if you are in London, make use of the Statistics and Market Intelligence Library (see Appendix 1 for the addresses of the Government Bookshops and the Market Intelligence library).

2.4.2 EXTERNAL SOURCES: OTHER PUBLISHED SOURCES

Marketing information is also published by banks, stockbrokers, trade and professional associations, media owners, local authorities, and Government sponsored organisations such as the National Economic Development Office. Appendix 1 lists commonly used sources including sources of information about overseas markets.

It would be tedious to discuss these sources individually: books have been written on the subject (see Appendix 1). It might however be helpful to mention the Economist Intelligence Unit's *'Retail Business'*, published monthly. This reviews a wide range of markets (the title is misleading). The articles are based on secondary sources and may provide a useful short cut. Most libraries have the EIU's index to Retail Business, even if they are not subscribers to the publication, and photocopies of articles can be bought.

Ours is indeed a well-documented society, but published data do not always fit requirements and they are often out of date. It is essential to find out how the data were collected.

2.4.3 EXTERNAL SOURCES: SYNDICATED SOURCES

A consumer marketing company of any size is more likely to consult the trend data supplied by the research agencies who operate retail audits and consumer panels. This syndicated research enables comparisons to be made between estimates of own sales and those of competitors, evaluation of performance usually being based on 'brand share'. ('Estimates' because the data derive from *samples* of retail outlets or consumers. A panel is a sample maintained over a specified time so that trends may be observed).

The *retail audit* records sales to consumers through a panel of retail outlets. Auditing is a method of data collection based on observation (see Figure 2). The estimate of consumer sales is arrived at as follows:

| Opening stock for period (checked at last audit) | + | Net deliveries since last audit | — | Stock held at present audit | = | Sales to consumers during period |

The interval between audits is often, but not invariably, two months. As well as estimating consumer sales, the retail audit monitors the distributive, selling and merchandising programmes associated with brands in the product field (see Section 11.1.1). The number of brands recorded in the reports bought by subscribers depends on their individual requirements and on the amounts subscribed above a minimum: i.e. the size of the 'all others' category varies. The A.C. Nielsen Company, Retail Audits and Stats. MR are substantial operators in the retail field.[6]

The *consumer panel* records estimates of consumer purchases, and gives useful information about the characteristics of those who buy and about their buying habits. The data yielded by retail audits and consumer panels are compared in Figure 28. For a survey designed to describe consumers in a product field, consumer panel data makes a big contribution to the making of informed assumptions. Most panels relate to

---

6. *Organisations Providing Market Research Services in Great Britain* (updated annually), London, the Market Research Society.

products purchased frequently but panel data relating to a wide range of durables are available (e.g. The AGB Home Audit). Durables are audited once a quarter. The fast-moving purchases are either recorded by means of an audit carried out by an interviewer once a week, or the data are recorded by the purchaser in a diary designed for easy marking-up and rapid data processing. The reporting interval is four weeks and we need to distinguish between three types of panel:

— *Household Panel*, a record of housewife purchases, the most widely used being The Television Consumer Audit (TCA) and the Attwood Consumer Panel, both owned by Audits of Great Britain (AGB);
— *Individual Panel*, a record of purchases made by individuals for their own use; e.g. the AGB Personal Purchases Index;
— *Special Interest Panel*, a panel such as the Motorists' Diary Panel operated by Forecast (Market Research), a Unilever subsidiary. This panel is devoted to the recording of petrol and engine oil purchases, plus information on accessories, servicing and car insurance.

The range of the data available from consumer panels relating to repeat purchase products is summarised below:

— trends in the *total volume and value* of consumer purchases in the product field;
— the *demographic characteristics* of those buying in the product field, such as age, social class, size of family;
— *buying behaviour* in the product field — average amount bought, frequency of buying, and, since these data record individual purchasing of individual brands (i.e. the data is 'disaggregated'), repeat purchase and loyalty patterns can be established;
— all this information is recorded within *IBA television areas* and by the *type of retail outlet* at which purchases were made;
— *seasonal patterns* can be seen.

But data derived from consumer purchasing panels do not tell us:

— how products and brands are used; or
— how buyers perceive brands in a product field.

Any attempt to collect use and attitude data from the members of a purchasing panel would contaminate the purchasing data. Data derived from new panel members is ignored until they have been given time to settle back into their habitual purchasing patterns.

Finally, for both retail audits and consumer panels 'back data' may be available if the company is not already subscribing. The range of these data will relate to the requirements of subscribers, but important product fields and major brands in those fields will have been covered.

2.5 Consulting Experts

If a company is considering entry into a new product field, the research
planner may feel the need to seek expert advice. Much depends on how
thoroughly he/she has been briefed.

The expert may be on staff, say a research chemist in the R & D
department or a home economist in the test kitchen; or it may be
necessary to go outside to consult a heating and ventilating engineer
or a paediatrician, to quote two possible outside experts.

In a consumer market there is a clear distinction between seeking
the advice of experts and seeking to clothe the secondary data statistics
by encouraging individuals in the market to talk, either alone in 'depth'
interviews or in groups (see Section 2.7).

In industrial markets the distinction between 'experts' and 'buyers'
is muddied by the industrial buying process. The industrial buyer is
often buying at the behest of company experts. Indeed, as we shall see,
determining just who makes the buying decision presents a problem
when designing industrial marketing research surveys. (Who should be
asked the questions?)

2.6 Observational Studies

Strictly speaking, audits and diaries represent data collection by means
of observation (see Section 3.4). Here we consider observation as an
exploratory aid for the research planner.

If the product field is unfamiliar it may be advisable to go out and
observe, say:

— how motorists behave on the forecourt of a filling station;
— how housewives buy bread;
— how retailers shop in a Cash and Carry wholesaler's;
— how customers behave in a DIY centre.

It all depends, of course, on the nature of the product and the planner's
experience as a consumer.

At this exploratory stage we are not collecting statistical data. Our
purpose is to get better acquainted with what goes on in the market as
part of the business of arriving at our 'set of assumptions' (see Section
2.1)

2.7 Consulting People in the Market

If the market is reasonably well documented, the search so far will have
told us what demographic variables are likely to affect the behaviour of
consumers with regard to the product field.

We will have a good idea whether age is a critical variable, or whether social class, having or not having children, living in the north compared with living in the south, going out to work or being a housewife full-time, and so on, are critical criteria.

Who buys and who uses. We also hope to know whether we have to take account of a distinction between 'who buys' and 'who uses' in this market, when deciding what sort of consumers to consult. Electric razors and male toiletries are often bought by women for men. Who determines the kind of holiday the family takes? The model of family car? The kind of bicycle the child shall have?

We need to know as much as possible about consumers, and users, in the market because

> we are going to encourage a limited number of consumers to talk freely and at length about their behaviour in the product field, their attitudes towards what is available in the way of products (or services), their wants and their preoccupations.

We shall either contact them as individuals or bring them together in groups of about eight — a number small enough to encourage general discussion and large enough to make it likely that the group will hold a variety of ideas. This kind of research, which seeks to illuminate the motivation behind consumer behaviour, is described as 'qualitative'; as compared with the 'quantitative' type of research study, designed to produce statistics.

Qualitative research. 'Depth' interviews and group discussions are the two most commonly used qualitative research methods. It would be possible to conduct a sufficient number of lengthy, unstructured interviews to draw statistical conclusions, and indeed this is *sometimes* done. The more cost-effective approach is

> to do enough *qualitative* work to reveal most, if not all, of the ways in which consumers behave in the market and of the attitudes they hold; then to use this rich data to design a *quantitative* study of a sample sufficiently large to allow conclusions to be drawn as to *how many*, and *what sort of*, consumers behave and think in the ways shown by the qualitative study.

Qualitative work is carefully planned. The interviewer will have an inconspicuous checklist of topics, and will have decided how to introduce the subject for discussion. But at this exploratory stage the procedure will be as unstructured as possible. The interviewer's role is that of listener, not question-asker.

In a quantitative study the procedure is structured, data collection proceeds at a much quicker pace and it is possible to process the data electronically.

'Depth' interview or group discussion. They are both clinical methods and 'depth' is in quotes because the interview is shallow

compared with the interviewing technique used in psychotherapy. 'Extended' might be a better description, but 'depth' is still in common use.

'Depth' interviews are used when the subject might prove embarrassing or if it is necessary to avoid interaction between group members. But this is often just what you do want.

A group of consumers with an interest in common, like motoring, child-rearing, taking holidays or DIY, can develop a dynamic so that more ideas are ventilated over a shorter time than would emerge from the same number of depth interviews, however skilful the interviewer may be at establishing rapport.

Designing the groups. The number and make-up of the groups depends on the variability in the consumer market shown by the secondary data search. If the market is not sufficiently well documented a limited number of questions in an Omnibus survey (see Section 2.8) will establish the main variables.

Any variable which is known to be significant is allowed for in the design of the groups, not forgetting regional differences. The groups can either be of like (homogeneous) or of unlike (heterogeneous) types. A mixture of types in each group could reveal a greater variety of experience and ideas: or it could have the opposite effect. In many product and service markets, social grade is no longer a discriminator where buying behaviour is concerned, but in the UK it is still usual to distinguish between middle class (ABC_1) and working class (C_2DE) when designing groups.

Risk of bias. Group discussions are recorded on tape and later transcribed. Statements expressing habits, attitudes and wants are listed verbatim. The lists are cut up into individual statements and the statements are sorted into piles. Then the discussion is summarised, using the respondents' own words as far as possible.

In qualitative work of this kind there is clearly a risk that the results may be biased:

— group members may not be representative of the market;
— the interviewer may influence the course of the discussion;
— the content analysis may not truly represent the experience and attitudes of the group;
— the report writer may impose a doctrinaire psychological interpretation on the content.

Value of qualitative work at the exploratory stage. Depth interviews and group discussions can successfully reveal what counts with consumers, what preoccupies them where this part of their lives are concerned, the words and expressions they use:

— it helps to determine the content of questionnaires;

- it ensures that questions are asked in a language familiar to consumers; and
- it generates attitude statements for quantification by means of scaling techniques.

2.8 Buying into an Omnibus Survey

The Market Research Society's monthly Newsletter carries a regular feature in which research suppliers advertise their Omnibus surveys.

The research supplier draws the sample, administers the question-naire, processes the data, reports results.

The research buyer takes space in the questionnaire, pays according to the number of questions asked and the statistical breakdowns required.

Establishing market characteristics. The number of questions you will include in an Omnibus questionnaire is limited but sufficient to establish basic market characteristics: and your market may be the subject of a *specialist Omnibus*. There are, for example, motoring omnibuses and baby market omnibuses as well as the more *general omnibus* surveys based on a sample of all the adults in Great Britain, or on a sample of all the households.

There are Omnibus surveys relating to the EEC, 'All-Ireland', Scotland, Hong Kong, the Middle East, Malaysia to pick an arbitrary selection from one issue of the MRS Newsletter.

The samples are specified and carefully drawn. The Omnibus survey is an important item in the research supplier's range of products. The surveys are conducted at regular intervals and are relied on for a regular contribution to revenue.

An Omnibus survey would, for example, be a good way of estab-lishing what sort of people are in the DIY market, their DIY equipment, most recent DIY job done.

Effect of the shared questionnaire. This is an efficient and inex-pensive way of establishing the nuts and bolts of a market: but the questionnaire is likely to range over a number of subjects so that it is difficult to engage the respondent's attention in more than a superficial way. This does not apply quite so much to the specialist Omnibus, but the questionnaire still represents the interests of a number of sponsors.

2.9 Importance of Informed Assumptions

It is unlikely that all these exploratory avenues will be followed in any one piece of exploratory research. The objective can be reached by a variety of routes and the objective is sufficient certainty about:

- *the structure of the population to be sampled*, whether this be one of individuals, households, firms or retail outlets; and
- *the topics that are relevant to the marketing problem*

to design a cost-effective research study.

Variation in the population. We need to be sufficiently well-informed about the population to be able to design a sample which takes account of *those variables likely to lead to marketing action*, for example:

> If AB class behaves in a markedly different way from C_1 in this market, then we are going to have to ensure that our sample includes enough ABs for us to have confidence in the representativeness of the AB results. If AB and C_1 behave in much the same way, then making separate provision for AB would be wasteful. But we must avoid the risk of getting results in, finding we want to make recommendations about AB as a separate group: but cannot (or ought not to!).

Topics of interest and level of generality. Here again, we have to avoid sins of both omission and commission. Let us take an example:

> Qualitative work has given us a list of statements expressing motorists' attitudes towards driving a car. We want to quantify these attitudes by putting them to a sample of motorists. Do we need to distinguish between how he/she feels about driving the car when going to work, ferrying children to school, ventilating grandparents; or is it sufficient for our purpose to establish how the motorist feels about driving in general?

The answer will affect the design of the questionnaire, the time taken to answer it (or fill it in), the complexity of data processing and the *cost of the survey*.

Conclusion

This chapter assumes company interest in a particular market and considers how this market may be explored. The time spent on the preliminary investigations reveiwed here will depend on the company's familiarity with the market.

We have seen that there is a wealth of published and syndicated data available. These data, together with some qualitative work, may fit our particular interest so well that there is no need for further data collection. We are, however, more likely to find that the data, while illuminating about the general characteristics of the market and of the distributive channels serving it, are not focused closely enough on the habits, attitudes and requirements of the consumers we are interested in to meet our purpose.

Exploratory research has put us in a better position to define research objectives and to design primary research, tailored to our objectives.

CHAPTER 3

Describing Markets
– Design Choices

Introduction

Exploratory research may yield results that are sufficiently conclusive to obviate the need for a descriptive survey of the market population. In this chapter, however, we assume that:

- exploratory research has put us in a position to formulate hypotheses about the characteristics of the population we are interested in;
- while leaving the extent to which these characteristics of habit and attitude are held open to question.

This chapter is designed to give a general view of the decisions which have to be made, and the choices of research procedure available, when markets are described. Sample design and data collection methods are considered in more detail in Chapters 4 and 5.

3.1 Stages in the Survey Procedure

The order of events from *Review of Marketing Objectives* to *Provision for Monitoring Performance* is illustrated in Figure 1 which shows a good relationship between the marketing and marketing research functions. Marketing objectives are fully discussed with those responsible for designing research and the discussion includes consideration of possible courses of action *before* the research plan is made.

In addition, Figure 1 illustrates a procedure which provides for second thoughts about the nature of the marketing problem after exploratory research has been carried out. Had research been ordered without due discussion of marketing objectives and possible courses of marketing action, the research department would not be in a position to judge whether the research problem could be better defined. Taking the Figure 1 stages in turn:

Exploratory research and the formulation of hypotheses were considered in Chapter 2.

Research objectives are not a repetition of marketing objectives. The marketing objective might be to enter the market for accelerated freeze dried convenience foods and the marketing problem definition of the launch range. The research objectives might then be to establish the

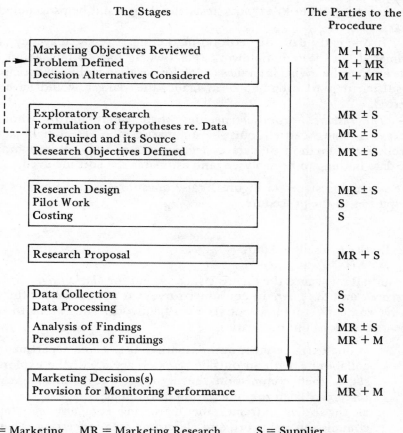

Figure 1. Stages in the Development of a Market Survey

demographic characteristics of those using the main categories of convenience food, to define their attitudes towards products they had tried, how they had prepared them, when they had used them, and where what was available fell short of requirements.

The research design is based on choice of data collection method and of sampling procedure. The possible choices are reviewed later in this chapter. Cost is, of course, an important constraint.

Pilot work is trying out the proposed design — the questionnaire or other recording device it is proposed to use together with the selection of respondents for questioning, or observing. *Pilot work* is not the same thing as *exploratory research*. Exploratory research helps to determine the research design. Pilot work tests the design and helps to determine costs.

In the early days of pet-food marketing, a research agency under-estimated the cost of fieldwork. Pet owners like to talk about their pets and, in the event, interviews took longer than had been anticipated. If sufficient pilot calls had been made, this danger would have been averted.

The research proposal specifies when, where and by whom the survey is being carried out. It summarises the research objectives, specifies the method of data collection, sampling procedure and how the data is going to be analysed, and estimates the cost involved.

The remaining stages in Figure 1 raise questions as to who does what, the parties to the procedure.

3.2 Parties to the Procedure

The initials set against the Figure 1 stages stand for *Marketing, Marketing Research* and *Supplier*. In consumer surveys it is unusual for the sponsoring company to carry out its own fieldwork. The extent to which research work is 'put out' varies:

- at one extreme the sponsor's marketing research department may collaborate with an outside research agency at the exploratory stage, then commission the agency to cover all stages from research design to presentation of findings;
- at the other extreme, the marketing company may merely commission fieldwork and electronic data processing — handing over the questionnaire, specifying the sample and receiving back computer printouts of the analysis.

If the working relationship between marketing and marketing research is a good one, interpretation of the findings will be a joint operation so that the significance of the findings is fully (marketing) and properly (marketing research) exploited.

3.3 Design Choices

The research design will be the product of the choices set out in Figure 2. Selection of data collection and sampling procedures will, of course, depend on the research objectives and the funds available for research.

Data Collection

Questioning	Observing
personal	*by persons*
telephone	*by diaries*
postal	*by instruments*
computer	

Sampling

Probability	Purposive
simple random	*quota*
systematic random	*judgment*
multi-stage drawn with pps*	

Random Location

*   drawn with probability proportionate to size of
     population (see Section 4.2)

Figure 2. Design Choices

In this chapter we are focusing on the use of surveys to describe markets but we might have decided to take a qualitative rather than a quantitative approach. Qualitative work is invaluable, indeed essential, at the exploratory stage. But when market description is going to affect marketing decisions involving substantial expenditures, findings based on statistically significant numbers of cases carry more conviction than those based on small numbers of cases, even though the data yielded by the few may well be richer in ideas and detail than those collected in a large-scale survey.

It is possible to have the best of both approaches: to collect the ideas at the exploratory stage and then to design a survey which quantifies the ideas.

We are now going to review the design choices set out in Figure 2. We will be focusing more closely on sampling techniques in Chapter 4 and on questionnaire design in Chapter 5.

3.4 Questioning or Observing?

In essence, there are two ways of collecting survey data, by asking questions or by observing. As an example of 'observing', from time to time motorists are held up while traffic is funnelled past an observation post. The post is manned by observers with recording instruments and clipboards. The passage of vehicles is recorded and every nth vehicle is stopped. The driver of the nth vehicle is asked where he/she has come from, is going to, purpose of journey and, perhaps, some questions designed to show whether this is a 'one-off' journey or a routine one.

This example illustrates *the strength and limitation of observing as a method of data collection*. The strength is its objectivity. Given that the recording instrument is in order and that traffic is sufficiently slowed down for the necessary observations to be made (e.g. commercial vehicles, passenger cars etc.), risk of bias is reduced to a minimum. The data are not influenced by how questions are asked nor by the respondent's capacity to answer. But the weakness of the data is that they will tell us nothing about the purpose or frequency of journeys unless a sample of commercial vehicles and cars is stopped and questions are asked.

It is sometimes claimed that data derived from observation are more objective than those derived from questioning. This holds good if the data are based on automatic recording by instruments, assuming the sample observed is a representative one. In television audience research meters automatically record whether or not a television set is switched on and the station it is receiving. But in order to know the nature of the audience and who is watching, it is necessary for a diary record to be kept. Diaries are a form of observation but the data are, of course, subject to human error even when the diary is designed to make the keeping of it as painless as possible.

Observation is a useful way of collecting data in retailing studies. The retail audit data (see Section 2.4) are collected by means of observation. *Distribution checks* are commonly made to observe what brands are on sale and the extent to which the retail trade is supporting 'our' brand compared with competitors in terms of shelf space, diplay, special offers. Distribution checks are also used to observe retail selling prices.

The observations may be made by the marketing company or by a research agency offering trade research services. The distribution checks may be made regularly to yield trend data or ad hoc ('one-off'). This use of observation is cheaper than the continuous audit based on a panel and it gives a marketing company the chance to conceal its interest from the retail trade: but the data yield is limited to what can be seen at the point of sale.

Observation is also used on *comparison shopping*. Retailers are as interested in comparing consumer prices as are the consumers themselves. The John Lewis Partnership's claim to be never knowingly undersold is supported by observation research of this kind.

When observations are being made by people, reliability of the record will be affected by whether or not the observer has anything else to do at the time. When self-service was first introduced to the petrol station forecourt the behaviour of motorists was observed to see if they had difficulty in following the instructions on the pump. The behaviour of those being observed may be affected by the fact that they are being watched, however discreetly. When the observer is disguised, say as a forecourt attendant, he is liable to be distracted from the business of recording observations. Hidden cameras get round this difficulty but the rules of The Market Research Society require that the subject be informed before use is made of data collected in this way.[1]

Mechanical apparatuses are used to observe in the development of pack designs (see Section 7.5), the pre-testing of advertisements (Section 8.4) and in the measurement of ITV viewing (Section 9.3). Mechanical observation is dealt with in these contexts.

3.5 Conveying Questions to Respondents

We can ask questions in a personal interview, by telephone, through the post or by computer. The choice depends on:

— the subject of the survey;
— the nature of the survey population;
— the research budget.

Surveys vary in the ease with which the required type of respondent may be contacted and in the length and complexity of the questionnaire. In deciding between personal, telephone and postal interview the criterion

---

1. *MRS Code of Conduct* (paragraph 2.4). The informant's right to withdraw, or to refuse to co-operate at any stage, shall be respected, unless the enquiry is being conducted under statutory powers. No procedure or technique which infringes this right shall be used, except that of observing or recording the actions or statements of individuals without their prior consent. In such a case the individual must be in a situation where he could reasonably expect his actions and/or statements to be observed and/or overheard (though not necessarily to be filmed or recorded). In addition at least one of the following conditions shall be observed:
    (a) All reasonable precautions are taken to ensure that the individual's anonymity is preserved;
    (b) The individual is told immediately after the event that his actions and/or statements have been observed or recorded or filmed, is given the opportunity to see or hear the relevant section of the record and, if he wishes, to have it destroyed or deleted.
The Market Research Society (1976), London.

is the cost of each *satisfactorily* completed questionnaire. This has, of course, to be estimated in advance, the estimate being based on the prior experience of the research agency or of the marketing company and on the results of pilot work (see Section 3.1).

3.5.1 IN A PERSONAL INTERVIEW

For a questionnaire of any length or complexity, satisfactory completion is, generally speaking, most likely to be achieved by administration of the questionnaire in a personal interview. Given proper training, an interviewer has the opportunity to establish rapport with a respondent without biasing responses: while in quota sampling she has an important part to play in the selection of respondents. The Market Research Society's Interviewer Card Scheme, introduced in January 1979, has as a main objective the guaranteeing of standards. (This scheme, and the question of interviewer bias, are dealt with in Chapter 5.)

3.5.2 BY TELEPHONE

It is possible to establish a person-to-person relationship over the telephone and there are skilled interviewers specialising in this field. Over 60% of households now have a telephone and there is evidence that, where fast-moving packaged goods are concerned, buying habits are much the same for those without telephones as for those with them.[2]

In a telephone interview there is no opportunity to sustain interest by showing the supporting material which helps a personal interview along, material such as cards listing all possible answers to multi-choice questions or scales to help respondents rate the strength of their feelings about a subject.

The telephone is a useful means of reaching business respondents. Here the problem is one of deciding who should be asked the questions. Who makes the decisions? The professional buyer? The Managing Director? The chief chemist? A committee? The telephone has a useful screening function and it is also used to put straightforward questions: but in more searching business enquiries the telephone call will precede an interview.

3.5.3 BY POST

The response rate achieved by a postal survey is likely to be low (30% to 40%), unless the survey population consists of members of a special

---

2. See two papers presented at the 1976 MRS Conference: Hyett, G.P. and Allan, G.M., *Collection of Data by Telephone, its Validity in Consumer Research*, and Miln, D. and Steward Hunter, D., *The Case for Telephone Research*.

interest group — e.g. new car buyers, fellows of the Royal Horticultural Society, members of the Wire-haired Dachshund Owners Association. Here we can expect a better than average response to a postal question- naire, provided the questionnaire is about new cars, gardening or wire-haired dachshunds.

. For a subject of more general interest, mailing questionnaires may prove more expensive than anticipated. It is necessary to take into account, when comparing costs with personal interviewing:

— the number of completed questionnaires returned;
— the cost of follow-up letters and other inducements to stimulate response e.g. a ball point pen to fill in the questionnaire;
— the cost of reply-paid envelopes;
— possibly the need for some personal interviews for the responses may add up to what appears to be a biased sample.

A postal questionnaire may be read from beginning to end before questions are answered so that the particular interest of the company sponsoring the research is revealed from the outset, instead of gradually. In addition, we cannot be quite sure that the answers recorded represent the respondent's own habits and attitudes with regard to the subject of the enquiry.

There are, of course, occasions when a family or household response is required and the postal questionnaire gives all members a chance to join in. And it may be necessary for documents to be consulted in order to answer the questions: for example, to consult the log book in an enquiry about motor cars.

There may be a case for *combining data collection methods*. If the questionnaire is long, or if the respondent is being asked to keep a diary record, questionnaire or diary may be placed during a personal interview. The introductory interview will add to the research costs but it is likely to secure a higher response rate so that cost per satis- factorily completed interview may be improved.

3.5.4 BY MEANS OF A COMPUTER

Questionnaire administration by means of computer was the subject of an experiment carried out in 1978.[3] The questions appear on the screen of a Visual Display Unit. For each question all possible answers are listed and numbered. The respondent, sitting in front of the computer, selects his/her answer and presses the button carrying its number. Helpful comments appear on the screen to establish rapport between respondent and computer.

---

3. O'Brien, T. and Dugdale, V. (October 1978), 'Questionnaire Administration by Computer', *Journal of the Market Research Society*, p. 228.

In this experiment 'computer administration' was compared with 'oral administration' of questions relating to personal habits such as bathing. The answers suggest that there may be a case for asking 'delicate' questions via the VDU. Interactive computer procedures of this kind are, of course, used in teaching and in hospital out-patients for preliminary diagnosis.

('Collecting data by means of questions' is the subject of Chapter 5. After Chapter 5 data collection methods are related to marketing contexts as appropriate).

3.6 Probability or Purposive Sample?

A glossary of sampling terms is given in Figure 3. Whatever the type of design (for choices see Figure 1) the object is to draw (or select) individuals from the population in such a way that the sample represents the population being surveyed, whether this be one of consumers, retail outlets, industries or organisations.

> We want to ensure that the sample is large enough to pick up variations in behaviour and attitude which are relevant to our marketing plans, and to be reassured that these variations appear in much the same proportions in the sample as in the survey population.
>
> (The expression 'in much the same proportions' is used because the statistics derived from samples are estimates. One can be pretty sure that a properly designed and managed survey will yield *sample estimates* which reflect *population values* but one cannot be 100% sure.)

3.6.1 PROBABILITY (or RANDOM) SAMPLING

It is possible to calculate how close the sample estimates are likely to be to population values and the statistical procedure is described in Chapter 4. But, strictly speaking, this procedure should only be used if:

> every individual or item in the population has a known chance of being included in the sample;
> the draw for the sample is made using a random procedure so that human judgment does not enter into the selection or rejection of individuals or items.

To meet these requirements it is necessary to be able to locate every individual in the survey population on a list. For some populations this is an easy matter. For the student body of a university, polytechnic or other academic institution, for the membership of a professional body such as The Market Research Society or for the account or budget customers of a retail store, suitable *sampling frames* are readily available.

Each individual on the list is identified by means of a number and numbers are drawn at random until the sample has been filled. This is a *simple random sample*.

If the survey population is of any size, we may decide to adopt a systematic procedure.

Probability Sample. Each member of the population has a known (and non-zero) chance of being selected into the sample.

Purposive Sample. Selection of sample members is dependent on human judgment.

Stratification. The population is divided into homogeneous groups (strata) whose relative size is known. Strata must be mutually exclusive. A random sample is taken in each stratum.

Proportionate Sample. A Uniform Sampling Fraction is applied to all the strata, i.e. the proprtion of n (the number in the sample) to N (the number in the population) is the same for all strata.

Disproportionate Sample. Where there is a marked variation in the sizes of the strata in a population, it is more efficient to use a Variable Sampling Fraction. To calculate the sample estimates for the population as a whole, estimates derived from individual strata are weighted according to their relative size.

Quota Sample. A method of stratified sampling in which selection of sample members within strata is non-random.

Simple Random Sample. All the population members are listed and numbered and the sample is drawn in one stage.

Sampling Frame. A specification of the population which allows for the identification of individual items. The frame should be complete, up-to-date and without duplication of items.

Systematic Sample. The sampling interval is calculated (let $N/n = k$). The first member of the sample is drawn at random from a numbered list. k is added to the number of the randomly selected member. This identifies the second member and the procedure is repeated.

Multi-stage Sample. The sample is drawn in more than one stage, usually after stratification by region and type of district. Three stage drawing is quite common: first, constituencies; second, ward or polling districts; third, electors using the Register of Electors as a sampling frame.

PPS. With probability proportionate to size of population/electorate: used in multi-stage drawing and associated with the use of a systematic interval. A range of numbers, equivalent to its population, is attached to each item on the list (e.g. each constituency, each polling district) before the draw is made. A number between one and the total population, divided by the number of sampling points, is drawn at random (or generated by computer). This indicates the starting point; the list of items is then systematically sampled, the probability of selection being proportionate to the size of each item.

Figure 3. Glossary of Sampling Terms

Let us assume we need to draw 500 individuals from a survey population of 5,000: the sample members will amount to 1/10 of the survey population. We draw the first numbered individual at random, say this is the individual numbered 5. We then program a computer to generate the names of the individuals numbered 15, 25, 35 and so on until the sample is filled; i.e. to add 10 four hundred and ninety-nine times.

This is a *systematic sample* and this drawing technique is generally used in probability sampling. We have to be sure that the names are recorded on the sampling frame in a sufficiently random order, that there is no periodicity in the listing. Application of the fixed interval to a list recorded in a hierarchical way, say the Army List, could produce a biased sample.

For a national survey the Register of Electors is likely to be used as a sampling frame. (There is in fact a separate register for each polling district.) The Post Office's Postcode File may also be used. This is a frame of addresses. (When the Postcode File is being used in probability sampling, it is necessary to list individuals living at the randomly drawn addresses, to number them and then make the final draw, see Section 4.2.3.)

When the survey population is large and widely dispersed a probability sample will commonly be drawn in more than one stage — *multistage sampling*.

It would be possible to draw a sample of, say, 3,000 adults from the adult population of 42.6 million in Great Britain in one stage but:

- the sample members might well be found to live at addresses scattered throughout Great Britain without regard to region or population density;
- dispersal of calls would make it difficult to organise fieldwork and to supervise investigators;
- scattered calls would add to the time taken to complete fieldwork and so to the cost of the survey.

A more cost-effective procedure is to divide the population into geographic groupings (*geographic stratification*) which take account of region and population density and to draw the sample in more than one stage. We might for example, draw a sample of constituencies within regions at the first stage, of polling districts within this random sample of constituencies at the second stage, and of electors from the Registers for the selected polling districts at the third stage. A procedure for selecting non-electors at random is described in Chapter 4 where multistage drawing with probability proportionate to population size (PPS) is considered in more detail.

A sample is drawn in more than one stage *in order to cluster calls*. This improves administrative efficiency and reduces fieldwork costs, but if calls are unduly clustered we may end up with a sample which does not represent the variety in the population as a whole.

The decision as to how many constituencies to draw and then how many polling districts, is based on informed judgment. If we were using the postcode file as a sampling frame we would have to decide how many postcode areas, and sectors within areas, to draw.

Government statistics tell us a good deal about the varying life-styles of the population: about levels of unemployment, overcrowding, basic housing amenities, types of tenure, incidence of two-car households, proportion of immigrants and so on. Electronic data processing has made it possible to group these data so that types of environment are extracted from this wealth of statistics. In the original work on a *Classification of Residential Neighbourhoods* (ACORN),[4] every parish with a population of fifty or more was assigned to one of 32 environmental groups. It has been shown that an eleven-group classification, based on the original 32, is useful for marketing purposes for, when the population is assigned to one of the eleven groups, differences in buying behaviour are revealed.[5]

There are now available computer programs which ensure that, when sampling locations are drawn, variety in the economic and social circumstances of the population is duly represented.

It is common practice for research agencies to use a *master sample* of first stage units for all their survey work. The field force will be recruited and supervised in randomly drawn constituencies, administrative districts or postcode areas representative of the distribution and environmental circumstances of the population as a whole. Fieldwork might, for example, be concentrated in 200 out of 635 constituencies. Samples will be drawn in these constituencies as required.

A random procedure may be used up to and including the selection of respondents, or up to and including the selection of sampling points, as in Random Location sampling.

In Random Location sampling final selection of respondents is based on quotas. Quota samples are widely used in marketing research: cost-benefit analysis favours their use. In probability sampling, *the randomly drawn individual must be interviewed*. 100% response is difficult, if not impossible, to achieve but at least three calls must be

---

4. Webber, R.J. (November 1977), 'The National Classification of Residential Neighbourhoods: an Introduction to the Classification of Wards and Parishes', *PRAG Technical Papers*.
5. Baker, K., Bermingham, J. and McDonald, C. (1979), *The Utility to Market Research of the Classification of Residential Neighbourhoods*, MRS Conference 1979.

made at the address, and sometimes interviewers are instructed to make more than three. The cost of call-backs is added to the cost of drawing respondents from a sampling frame. The fieldwork for a national survey is likely to cost twice as much when probability methods are used throughout the drawing of the sample.

A probability sample design has two particular advantages:

Random drawing of the sample from the population makes it possible to establish a statistical relationship between the sample estimates and population values;

If names and addresses are drawn by a random process there is less danger of the composition of the sample being affected by the interviewer's likes and dislikes.

The reports published by the Office of Population Censuses and Surveys are based on probability samples. Government departments have to be prepared to answer politically loaded questions about sample estimates. It helps to be able to establish the statistical significance of the findings and to know that human judgment has not entered into the selection of respondents.

Psychologists and sociologists tend to use probability methods. They work in areas where motivations are often obscure and this makes it difficult to control the purposive selection of respondents.

Probability methods are also used to set up and maintain panels of consumers for the collection of trend data relating to buying behaviour or media habits. This is done on a shared-cost basis and the use of a

A   *(Higher managerial, administrative or professional)*
B   *(Intermediate managerial, administrative or professional)*
C_1 *(Supervisory, clerical, junior administrative or professional)*
C_2 *(Skilled manual workers)*
D   *(Semi-skilled and unskilled manual workers)*
E   *(State pensioners, widows, casual and lowest grade earners)*

This has always been one of the most dubious areas of market research investigation, but is also one of the most widely used classification systems. Along with age, it is generally used as a control in selection for quota sampling and therefore has to be assessed before the interview begins. A great deal of unsuccessful effort has been put into developing a classification system that is easy and simple for the inter-viewer to apply in the field with a reasonable degree of reliability and validity. The current convention is to use a socio-economic grouping, based exclusively on 'occupation of head of household'. This is described in great detail in a document published by the National Readership Survey.* (For JICNARS see also Section 9.4.)

* from: Wolfe, A., ed. (1973), *Standardised Questions, a Review for Market Research Executives*, London, The Market Research Society.

Figure 4. Social Class Classification

probability method to draw a pool of panel members encourages confidence in the findings. The panel is stratified to mirror the major demographic characteristics of the population as shown in official statistics and members are selected from the randomly drawn pool as required.

3.6.2 PURPOSIVE SAMPLING

In marketing research it is common practice to use quota samples. In developed countries a good deal is known about the structure of populations whether these be consumer, trade, industrial or organisational populations, and the records are regularly up-dated. Governments collect and publish statistics, as also do professional, industrial and trade associations (see Appendix 1, Secondary Sources). *A quota sample takes account of this wealth of statistical data.*

Let us assume that we are going to select a quota sample from the adult population of Great Britain.

We stratify the population by region. We may use the Government's ten Economic Planning Regions, or the Independent Broadcasting Authority's 13 television areas. These are often used in marketing surveys because of the importance of television as an advertising medium.

We stratify the population by social class group (see Figure 4) *and by age group.* These demographic characteristics are frequently used in the design and control of quota samples. At the present time the adult population of Great Britain breaks down as follows:

		By social class (%)		
AB	C1	C2	DE	Total
16	22	32	30	100

			By age (%)			
15–24	25–34	35–44	45–54	55–64	65+	Total
19	18	15	15	14	19	100

Source: National Readership Survey 1979 (2)

An interviewer's daily assignment of calls may be anything from 10 to 20 calls, depending on the nature of the survey. (Length of questionnaire is critical.) For the sake of simplicity let us assume that a quota has been set based on 100 calls for five days' work. The interviewer is instructed to contact 16 ABs, 22 C1s, 32 C2s and 30 DEs. Among these 100 interviews, 19 are to be with age group 15–24, 18 with age group 25–34 and so on. The social class and age controls are *independent* of each other. The interviewer might end up with a group of calls showing a distorted relationship between age and social class, so it is better practice to set the quota with *interrelated controls* but this adds to the cost of fieldwork. Using the same social class and age breakdowns, 100 calls might be distributed as follows:

Social Class	15—24	25—34	Age 35—44	45—54	55—64	65 & +	Total	Actual
AB	3	3	2	2	2	3	15	(16)
C1	4	4	3	3	3	4	21	(22)
C2	6	6	5	5	5	6	33	(32)
DE	6	5	4	4	4	6	29	(30)
Total	19	18	14	14	14	19	98	
Actual	(19)	(18)	(15)	(15)	(14)	(19)		(100)

The figures in brackets show how the adult population actually breaks down by age and by social class. Since people must be left whole it is often difficult to achieve an exact marriage when an inter-related quota is set.

It may be possible to combine groups so that the interviewer's task is simplified, saving time and cost. It may not, for example, be necessary to distinguish AB class (upper middle) from C1 class (lower middle) or the 25—34 age group from the 35—44 group. These decisions depend on the nature of the product field or service being surveyed and the extent to which exploratory research indicates that behaviour and attitudes vary by social class and age. For most fast-moving packaged goods, class is a weak discriminator and a breakdown of the sample by three social class groups — middle class, skilled worker and unskilled group — would be relevant for planning and control.

Quota samples are often controlled by social class and by age because other relevant data are classified in this way, an important example being the continuous surveys on which media planning is based (see Chapter 9). But other controls may be relevant, such as size of family, whether or not a housewife works outside the home. In a survey relating to convenience foods or to durables the interviewer is likely to be required to collect data from a laid-down proportion of 'gainfully occupied' housewives (19.6% of housewives work full-time, and 18.9% work part-time).

In other words, *the selection of respondents is purposive.* They are chosen to fit a quota designed to mirror relevant characteristics in the population. They are not drawn from the population by a random procedure. This is the essential difference between purposive and probability sampling.

A quota sample is as reliable as a probability sample, when, in practice though not in theory, the following requirements are met:

Up-to-date statistics relating to the structure of the population are available.

The quota is set in such a way that important population characteristics are interrelated, such as age and social class, age and size
of family or age and working outside the home.

Classification questions are carefully designed so that, for example,
the occupation of the head of the household is established with
some certainty (see note to Figure 4).

The interviewer's choice of location is restricted. This is not always
possible but where the decision as to which door to knock is taken
out of the interviewer's hands, the main criticism of quota sampling
is removed.

The selection of respondents features in the interviewer's training
programme.

It is difficult to control selection of individuals for interviewing if
contact is made away from the home, in the street or at work. In the
case of people at work, *an important control is the nature of the work*.
The numbers of men and women employed in the main categories of
job are readily available and the published statistics can be used to design
a suitable quota. If selection of respondents is not controlled in this
way the sample is likely to contain too many readily accessible workers,
such as men working on building sites and in public transport, at the
expense of those working on assembly lines or in offices.

3.7 Proportionate or Disproportionate Sample?

This is an important decision when making design choices. It is likely to
affect both the cost of a survey and the validity of the sample estimates
derived from it. In asking the question 'Proportionate or disproportionate
sample?' we are implying that the population can be divided into groups
(or strata) whose relative weight is known. We considered three
commonly used stratification factors when describing the selection of a
quota sample of adults from the British population: region, social class
and age.

In a proportionate sample each stratum has its population weight:

$$\frac{n \text{ (number in the sample)}}{N \text{ (number in the population)}} \text{ is } uniform \text{ for all strata.}$$

In a disproportionate sample we oversample small sized strata at
the expense of large sized strata but restore their due weights in the
population when we come to consider total results or proportions of
the total results:

$$\frac{n \text{ (number in the sample)}}{N \text{ (number in the population)}} \text{ } varies \text{ from one stratum to another.}$$

For the proportionate sample we use a *uniform sampling fraction* and for the disproportionate sample a *variable sampling fraction*. Exploratory research will have cleared our minds as to which strata in the population should be considered as separate and individual groups.

Let us assume we are going to survey the habits and attitudes of adult males with regard to shaving. We are interested in all males of shaving age but have a particular interest in the 15—19 age group because this group are developing their shaving habits and attitudes. But the group represents a small percentage of the male shaving population. If we use a *uniform sampling fraction* we either end up with too few interviews in this group and about the right number in other, larger groups; or we provide for a sufficient number in the 15—19 age group and conduct many more interviews than we need in the larger groups. Obviously, we would deploy the research budget to better effect if we used a *variable sampling fraction,* 'oversampled' the small group and restored their weight to the larger groups when the data relating to all men were processed by the computer.

Disproportionate samples are often the most cost-effective. (Questions of sample size and of confidence in sample estimates are dealt with in Chapter 4.)

In a stratified sample, whether a uniform or a variable sampling fraction is used, the risk of sampling error is reduced. If we drew the sample of adult males at random, without stratification, we might find ourselves with a 15—19 age group whose size did not equate with official statistics. By ensuring that each group is given its due population weight we remove a possible source of error.

There are more opportunities to use stratification in the design of purposive samples than in the design of probability samples. Any reliable statistical data about the structure of the population, relevant to the marketing objectives, can be used to stratify a purposive sample. For a probability sample it is necessary to be able to identify individuals within the strata in order to be able to make a random draw.

If we are going to use the Register of Electors as a sampling frame we can stratify geographically before making the draw because the registers tell us where people live: but social class and age of the respondent (to quote two commonly used ways of classifying respondents) are not known until *after* the interview. We can stratify after the interview and re-weight in accordance with official statistics.

3.8 The Judgment Sample

Figure 2 on 'Design Choices' shows two types of purposive sample, quota and judgment. We have seen that judgment enters into multi-stage probability sampling as well as into purposive designs. But the description 'judgment' is particularly applicable to industrial and trade research sampling.

In industrial and trade research we are concerned to sample output or sales turnover. *Our base for sample design is output or turnover and not the number of establishments or shops in a particular industry or trade.* 65% of grocery outlets in Great Britain can be described as small independents, but this category of shops only does 25% of the sales turnover of grocery outlets.

When we consult secondary data sources at the design stage (see Appendix 1) we soon realise that in many fields there are a few concerns so large that, if they were excluded from a sample in a probability draw, sample estimates would be unlikely to represent values in the real industrial or trade world. Any survey of the manufacturers of paints should include ICI Paints and any survey of the grocery trade should include Tesco. In this circumstance our sample design is:

Census of Dominating Firms + Sample of the Rest

Employees N		Establishments N	%	Gross Output £ 000	%
1–	10	1,862			
11–	24	1,498			
25–	99	1,172			
		4,532	79.2	1,382.0	13.3
100–	199	425	7.4	842.5	8.1
200–	499	459	8.0	1,820.6	17.7
500–	999	181	3.1	1,451.8	14.0
1,000–1,499		50	0.9	643.0	6.2
1,500&+		84	1.4	4,205.5	40.7
		5,731	100.0	10,345.4	100.0

In this case 4,532 establishments, each with less than 100 employees, account for 13% of gross output, while 84 establishments with 1,500 or more employees account for 41%.

Source: Census of Production

Figure 5. Stratification by Value of Output

If no one concern is so dominant that it must be included in the sample, we are likely to find that a comparatively small proportion of the industrial or trade population we are surveying (say 20%) does a substantial proportion of the business (say 80%); the '80:20' rule.

Stratification by volume/value is accordingly an important factor in the design of industrial or trade surveys. Figure 5 shows how the Government Statistical Office stratifies establishments in the 'Food, Drink and Tobacco' category.

This type of official information makes it possible to set quotas provided our market fits the official classifications. Informed judgment is needed in the design of a sample to represent the market for, say, a timing device used in a variety of industries, or one to represent the distribution of soft drinks, sold through a variety of outlets.

Given that the market has been stratified by volume/value there follows *the problem of identifying the enterprises in each stratum.* The official statistics provide information about the structure of industries and trades, but firms return this information on the understanding that names are not published. Fitting names to strata requires skilful judgment in the use of secondary sources.

Where it is possible to establish a complete list of firms within strata a probability design is theoretically possible (an example is given in Section 4.3), but purposive selection of firms within strata is the more general practice.

Survey design calls for the exercise of judgment, and research suppliers operating in this area are exceptionally well informed. They have on file detailed information about individual markets and every opportunity is taken to up-date this information.

Conclusion

In survey research cost-effective allocation of often scarce resources depends on:

— close collaboration between those who are commissioning the research and those responsible for its design and execution, both while the research proposal is being developed (Figure 1) and when the findings are interpreted;

— estimating what proportion of questionnaires (or other means of collecting data such as diaries) are likely to be satisfactorily completed before deciding whether to contact respondents in a personal interview, over the telephone or through the post (Section 3.5);

- using a disproportionate design when groups of interest in the population show marked variations in size (Section 3.7);
- using quota samples when the parameters of the survey population are well documented; provided sampling points are specified and the selection of respondents is controlled (Section 3.6), and there is proper provision for the training and supervision of the field force.

To use a probability sample where a quota sample would be suitable is to incur opportunity costs: the opportunity within the research budget to enlarge the sample or carry out further research.

CHAPTER 4

Describing Markets
-Focus on Sampling

Introduction

We have seen that there are two particular advantages to be gained from using a probability sample:

— human judgement does not enter into the selection or rejection of respondents;
— it is possible to measure the extent to which values in the population may vary from the estimates yielded by the sample.

In this chapter we focus on the second advantage and consider the application of probability theory to sampling in consumer and in non-consumer markets.

4.1 Basic Statistics

4.1.1 SAMPLE ESTIMATES AND POPULATION VALUES

In size most samples are small fractions of the population. It is not necessary to draw a large proportion of the population into the sample to achieve valid results. Samples of 3,000 are commonly used to represent the 42.6 million adults in Great Britain. Validity of the sample estimates depends on:

— the size of the sample in relation to the variability in the population where the subject of the survey is concerned (if habits and attitudes were uniform throughout the population, the responses of one individual would suffice);
— the care with which the sample has been drawn;
— there being an adequate number of respondents in any one group which is to be considered in isolation;
— avoidance of 'non-sampling errors' when the data are being

collected and analysed, errors such as 'interviewer bias' and use of ambiguous questions (Chapter 5).

There are, of course, very many possible samples of 3,000 in a population of 42.6 millions. Can we be confident that the sample we happen to have drawn is a representative one? We can't. But we can take individual sample estimates and establish what the relationship between sample estimate and population value is likely to be. Figure 6 summarises notation in common use and gives the formulae referred to in this section.

NOTATION*

	Population (values)	Sample (estimates)
Number of items	N	n
Mean	μ or $\bar{X}$	$\bar{x}$
Standard deviation	σ or S	s
Standard error of the mean	—	$s_{\bar{x}}$ or s.e. $(\bar{x})$
Proportion	π or P	p
Standard error of the proportion	—	s_p or s.e. (p)

SAMPLING FORMULAE

Standard deviation $\sqrt{\dfrac{1}{n}\,\Sigma(x-\bar{x})^2}$

See Section

Standard error of the mean $\dfrac{s}{\sqrt{n}}$ Applies *variables*   4.1.2

Standard error of the proportion   Applies *attributes*   4.1.3

$\sqrt{\dfrac{p(1-p)}{n}}$ or $\sqrt{\dfrac{p(100-p)}{n}}\%$ or $\sqrt{\dfrac{pq}{n}}$ 'q' is the proportion without the attribute

To estimate sample size: 4.1.4
Let Z stand for the number of standard errors required by the Confidence
Level (in market research it is usual to work at the 95% Confidence Level,   4.1.1
i.e. to set limits of ± 1.96 (or 2) standard errors around the sample estimate);   4.1.1
Let E represent the range of error around the sample estimate acceptable to
the decision maker; then the formula for estimating sample size is —   4.1.4

for *variables* using the standard error of the mean

$$n = \frac{s^2 \times Z^2}{E^2}$$

for *attributes* using the standard error of the proportion

$$n = \frac{pq \times Z^2}{E^2}$$

*   Moser and Kalton (1971), *Survey Methods in Social Investigation*, 2nd ed., London, Heinemann Educational Books.

Figure 6. Survey Research, Sampling: Basic Statistics

Let us consider a population value, say, the foot-size of adult women. Distribution of female foot-sizes is, of course, of moment to shoe manufacturers.

If we were to plot foot-sizes, one by one, on a piece of squared paper we would see a pattern emerge. *In due course* the plottings would be seen to be symmetrically distributed around their mean. If we outlined the shape of the distribution, as shown in Figure 7, we would see that the foot-sizes filled the area beneath a *normal curve*.

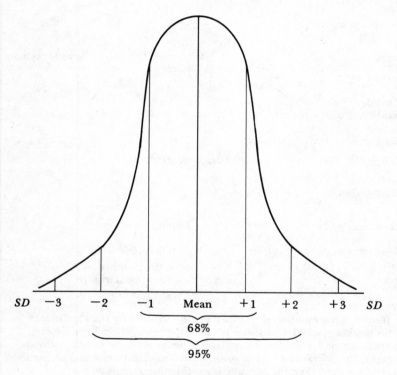

Figure 7. A Normal Distribution

Distance from the mean is measured by the *standard deviation* which takes account of the variability in a population. In a normal distribution:

68% of the area occupied by our plottings of shoe sizes would lie within − 1 and + 1 standard deviations from the mean;

95% would lie within − 2 and + 2 standard deviations (or, to be exact, ± 1.96)

99% would lie within − 3 and + 3 standard deviations (or ± 3.09).

Provided we are considering a sample of at least 30 people and the sample has been drawn using a probability procedure, we can use knowledge of the normal distribution to relate our sample estimates to values in the population as a whole.

It is possible to prove empirically that the means of all the possible samples in a population equal the population mean.

Draw the 10 possible samples of 2 from the five women with foot-sizes ranging 3, 4, 5, 6 and 7;
average the foot-size of each sample of 2;
take the mean of the ten averages.[1]
The answer is 5 which is the mean of 3 + 4 + 5 + 6 + 7.

If we were able to draw all the possible samples of women from a population and to plot the average shoe size of each sample, we would find that *the distribution of our plottings of means took the same symmetrical shape around the mean of all the average sizes as that shown in Figure 7.*

Mini exercises apart, we are not going to be able to draw all possible samples from the survey population, so how do we use this finding to calculate how much confidence we can have in an estimate given by our one sample?

4.1.2 THE STANDARD ERROR OF THE MEAN

We do not expect our sample estimate to be exactly the same as the population value. We are going to make an allowance for possible error and the size of the allowance will depend on:

- variability in the population — if all women had the same foot-size there would be no risk of error;
- the size of the sample;
- the confidence level we choose to work at.

Variability in the population is measured by the standard deviation. Without a census, we do not know how foot-sizes vary in the population as a whole, but we can consider the distribution of foot-sizes shown by our sample and calculate the standard deviation of these. We know the size of our sample, and we choose at what level of confidence we want to work.

---

1. *The 10 possible samples of two women take*   *Sample average*
   sizes: 3 and 4, 3 and 5, 3 and 6, 3 and 7   3½   4   4½   5
             4 and 5, 4 and 6, 4 and 7   4½   5   5½ $\frac{50}{10} = 5$
                   5 and 6, 5 and 7   5½   6
                         6 and 7   6½

Research data relate to amounts spent by samples of the population on a variety of items: items such as rent, rates, holidays, car insurance, petrol and, perhaps most frequently, food and other fast-moving necessities.

Let us assume that the average daily amount spent on food and necessities by a sample of 400 households is £6 and that the standard deviation from the mean shown by the 400 budget totals is £1.60 or 160p. Then the standard error of the mean is given by:

$$s_{\bar{x}} = \frac{s}{\sqrt{n}} = \frac{160p}{\sqrt{400}} = \frac{160p}{20} = 8p$$

If we choose to work at the *68% level of confidence* we allow for a possible sample error of ± 8p and conclude that the sample estimate of £6 represents a population value lying between £5.92 and £6.08.

But in choosing the 68% level of confidence we run a *one-in-three* risk of our sample mean being outside the range of all possible means covered by ± one standard deviation. If we allow for ± two standard errors of the mean, this risk is reduced to one in twenty.

At the *95% level of confidence* our sample estimate of £6 represents a population value lying between £5.84 and £6.16.

We have increased confidence at the cost of precision. To achieve a more precise estimate at the 95% level it would be necessary to increase the sample size. However, *to halve the allowance for error it would be necessary to multiply the sample size by four*. The 95% level is common practice in marketing research. The cost of working at a higher level of confidence is out of proportion to the benefit received. In any survey of human behaviour and attitudes there are possible sources of error other than those which can be statistically measured.

4.1.3 THE STANDARD ERROR OF A PROPORTION

In marketing research we are often considering *attributes* rather than *variables*. Attributes, such as being able to drive a motor car, are either present or not present. whereas variables, such as the amounts spent on petrol, have a range of values. Variables are reduced to means/averages; attributes to proportions/percentages.

The distribution of a population according to whether or not its members have a particular attribute is called *binomial distribution* from 'bi-nomen' meaning two names[2] : for example adults in Great Britain can be called 'drivers' or 'non-drivers' according to whether or not they hold a driving licence.

Let us assign the letter P to the drivers (using a capital letter because P relates to drivers in the population and not to drivers in a sample of the population). Then let us assign the letter Q to the non-drivers. $P + Q = N$ (the population). N is 1 if we are working in proportions or 100 if we are working in percentages: so Q is either 1 minus P or 100 minus P.

If we were to draw all possible samples from the population, the proportions shown to be drivers would vary, but distribution of the sample 'p's in relation to the population 'P' is known and so, as with the Standard Error of the Mean, it is possible to make allowance for sampling error. The Standard Error of a Proportion takes account of 'n', the number in the sample and 'p', the proportion with the attribute:

If 'p' is the percentage or proportion with the attribute and 'q' the percentage or proportion without: the standard error is calculated as follows:

$$s_p = \sqrt{\frac{pq}{n}} \text{ often written as } \sqrt{\frac{p(1-p)}{n}} \text{ or } \sqrt{\frac{p(100-p)}{n}}$$

Most market research data are presented in the form of percentages rather than proportions so we use percentages in the following example:

A survey shows that 40% of the women in a town drive cars. The estimate is based on a sample of 600. How precisely can this estimate be interpreted at the 95% level of confidence?

$$s_p = \sqrt{\frac{40 \times 60}{600}} = \sqrt{4} = \pm 2\%$$

At the 95% level of confidence, a likely range of error is ± twice 2%. The sample estimate of 40% indicates that the true proportion probably lies between 36% and 44%.

4.1.4 ESTIMATING SAMPLE SIZE

The formulae given in Figure 6 suggest that in order to estimate sample size we need to put figures to the following:

---

2. Ehrenberg, A.S.C. (1975), *Frequency Distributions*, New York, Wiley, Chap. 12.

- the standard deviation anticipated for individual variables (s);
- the proportion/percentage likely to hold each attribute (p);
- the number of standard errors required by the confidence level (Z);
- action standards set by the marketing department, the acceptable error (E).

The data needed to estimate (s) and (p) are an important product of exploratory research. If secondary sources do not give the necessary clues, an omnibus survey may be used (see Section 2.8).

When exploratory research has suggested that p is 40%, the range of acceptable error (E) is ± 2% and the confidence level requires allowance for $2s_p$, then:

$$n = \frac{pq \times Z^2}{E^2} = \frac{40 \times 60 \times 4}{4} = 2{,}400$$

Were we prepared to tolerate an error of ± 4% the required sample size would be 600

$$n = \frac{40 \times 60 \times 4}{16}$$

Doubling the allowance for error makes it possible to quarter the sample size. (Conversely, in order to halve the standard error, it is necessary to quadruple the sample size.)

Since surveys cover a variety of characteristics, and we are likely to want to consider these for a number of sub-groups within the total sample, the full statistical procedure is unduly laborious.

It is however, essential to have decided in advance how the results of a survey are going to be analysed and what measurements will be the most important. It is unfortunate if a particular estimate arouses marketing interest, and this estimate is found to be based on the habits or attitudes of so few individuals in the sample that a conclusion cannot be drawn. In determining sample size it is common practice to ensure that there are at least 50, and preferably 100, individuals in the smallest sub-group likely to be considered in isolation.

Sample size is, of course, often constrained by cost. We start with a budgetary allowance sufficient to buy a certain number of interviews. In the following example we can afford a total of 1,500 and we compare the efficiency of a design using proportionate stratification with one using disproportionate stratification (see Section 3.7).

A population of 50,000 persons is distributed over three areas: 10% live in area A, 40% in B and 50% in C. Exploratory research has stimulated marketing interest in an age group which accounts for 20% of the population in each area. We want to be able to consider the habits and attitudes of this age group in relation to the population as a whole. Given that we can afford 1,500 interviews, and that we are required to use a probability design, how should we proceed?

Design using a proportionate sample

Area	Population N	$N\%$	Sampling Fraction N/n	Sample n	Special Interest Group of 20% (n)
A	5,000	10	33.3	150	30
B	20,000	40	33.3	600	120
C	25,000	50	33.3	750	150
TOTAL	50,000	100	33.3	1,500	300

With a proportionate design we have an unduly small number of the age group in region A and a generous allocation to B and C.

Design using a disproportionate sample

Area	Population N	$N\%$	Sampling Fraction N/n	Sample n	Special Interest Group of 20% (n)
A	5,000	10	10	500	100
B	20,000	40	40	500	100
C	25,000	50	50	500	100
TOTAL	50,000	100	33.3	1,500	300

We make a judgment decision to allocate the 1,500 interviews we can afford, giving 500 to each region so using a variable instead of a uniform sampling faction. This gives us a satisfactory number of interviews in each of the three regions with the age group we are particularly interested in. We shall, of course, have to *restore their due weight to the three regional populations* when calculating total results for the three regions as a whole. (Had we not been committed to a probability design, we could have sampled disproportionately by age as well as by area, setting quotas to achieve the following allocation of calls:

Area	Population N	n	Special Interest Group of 20% (n)	Remaining 80%
A	5,000	500	250	250
B	20,000	500	250	250
C	25,000	500	250	250

The computer would be programmed to restore due weight to totals by area and by age, and a more cost-effective design would be achieved.)

4.1.5 EFFECT OF DESIGN ON SAMPLING ERROR

The basic formulae given in Figure 6 relate to simple random samples. In a simple random sample all the individuals in the population go into the draw and the sample is drawn in one stage.

— *If we stratify the population and draw a simple random sample from each stratum, we reduce the sampling error.* If we sampled a population of polytechnic students without prior stratification we might, by chance, draw too many engineers and too few business studies students, or too many full-time students and too few part-time ones. In a survey relating to courses we might need to be sure that engineering and business studies were duly represented, while for a survey about amenities we might want to ensure that the attitudes and behaviour of part-time students carried due weight.

There is here a clear case for stratification whether we are considering courses or amenities and we can use a probability design because the student records enable us to assign students to strata.

— *If we draw in more than one stage, with probability proportionate to size of population, we increase the sampling error.* The multistage procedure has the effect of clustering the members of the population included in the sample. The effect of this has been investigated using estimates derived from simple random sampling as the criterion. The standard errors arrived at using the formulae given in Figure 6 are corrected for design effect by multiplying them by a *design factor* of between 1.0 and 2.5. Even the National Readership Survey (Section 9.4) 'recognised as having a particularly good sample design'[3] has been estimated to have a design factor of 1.4. The size of the design factor depends on the closeness with which calls are clustered when the sample is drawn. Clustering has a stronger effect on sampling error than stratifying.

— *If the sample embraces 10% or more of the population* (as might occur in a survey among students), *we apply a correction factor, known as the finite multiplier,* $\sqrt{(N-n/N-1)}$. This has the effect of reducing the standard error: but surveys are usually based on smaller sampling fractions.

4.2 Drawing Procedures

4.2.1 DRAWING WITH PROBABILITY PROPORTIONATE TO SIZE (PPS)

The PPS procedure is associated with multi-stage sampling. Let us assume that the first-stage sampling unit is the constituency. The 623

Parliamentary constituencies in Great Britain are first stratified by region using either the Government's ten Economic Planning Regions or the Independent Broadcasting Authority's thirteen.

The order in which the constituencies are listed within regions is important because we are going to draw the first constituency at random and then take a systematic interval (see Section 3.6.1).

Every individual in the population must have had a chance of being included in the sample when we get to the end of the drawing process: but first of all we want to ensure that the regional distribution of constituencies, together with their varying population densities, are duly represented in the sample.

Having stratified by region, we may take account of population density by sorting each region's constituencies into four groups: conurbation (those lying entirely within a conurbation), 'other 100% urban', 'mixed urban and rural' (constituencies in which 50% or more of the population live in urban administrative districts), and 'rural' (less than 50% live in urban administrative districts).

Thus far the ordering of the list of 623 constituencies is as follows:

Region 1
Conurbation[4] constituencies
Other 100% urban constituencies
Mixed urban and rural constituencies
Rural constituencies
Region 2
Conurbation constituencies
Other 100% urban constituencies
Mixed urban and rural constituencies
Rural constituencies

And so on until all the regions have been covered.

We have four strata relating to population density within each of ten regions (assuming we are using the Standard Regions). Within each of these strata (or cells) it is quite usual to list the constituencies in descending order according to the ratio of Conservative to Labour (or Labour to Conservative) votes cast at the most recent General Election. This is done because voting tends to correlate with social economic class. The final list is therefore stratified by an approximation to social economic class as well as by population density and regional distribution. This is *implicit stratification*, i.e. stratification is 'implied' in the way in which the first stage sampling units (in this case constituencies) are listed.

---

3. Collins, M. (1978), 'Sampling', Chap. 4 in Worcester, R.M., and Downham, J., eds., *Consumer Market Research Handbook*, 2nd ed., Wokingham, Van Nostrand Reinhold.
4. A 'conurbation' is an aggregation of urban districts, e.g. Greater London.

In order to draw with PPS it is necessary to accumulate the electoral populations of the constituencies, so that *each constituency is represented by a range of numbers equal to the size of its electorate* (Figure 8). Let us assume that we have decided to draw a Master Sample of 200 constituencies and that the total number of electors on the Registers is 40,000,000.

> $N/n = 40$ million over $200 = 200,000$
> Draw a number at random between 1 and 200,000, say 85,000
> The constituency with this number in its range is the first drawn.
> Add the sampling interval of 200,000 to 85,000 = 285,000.
> The constituency with this number in its range is the second drawn, and so on.
> The sampling interval of 200,000 is added on 199 times.

The procedure used to draw first stage sampling units with PPS is illustrated in Figure 8. The twelve Birmingham constituencies are listed according to the ratio of Conservative to Labour votes cast at the last election in each constituency: then electorates are recorded and accumulated. If we were drawing from the complete list of 623 constituencies in Great Britain,[5] Birmingham's twelve would be well down the list in Region 7, and a substantial number of electors would have accumulated before Hall Green was recorded. However, for the purpose of this example we start with Hall Green and this constituency is represented by the range $1 - 67,683$.

Constituency*	Electorate	Electorates accumulated		
Hall Green	67,683	67,683		
Selly Oak	64,631	132,314		
Yardley	57,574	189,888	. . .	175,000 drawn at random
Northfield	78,873	268,761		
Perry Barr	51,794	320,555		Add N/n
Erdington	64,341	384,896		228,725
Stechford	61,115	446,011	. . .	403,725
Edgbaston	68,645	514,656		
Handsworth	45,018	559,674		Add N/n
Sparkbrook	45,910	605,584		228,725
Ladywood	33,989	639,573	. . .	632,450
Small Heath	46,602	686,175		
N	686,175			
N/n	228,725			

The three constituencies selected with probability proportionate to their electoral populations are Yardley, Stechford and Ladywood.

* Ordered according to the ratio of Conservative to Labour votes cast at the last General Election.

Figure 8. Twelve Birmingham Constituencies Listed for Drawing of Three with PPS

---

5. The UK total is 635. There are 12 constituencies in N. Ireland.

The decision as to how many constituencies to carry out fieldwork in is based on informed judgment. There are available statistical data to show how the population varies. Webber's work on the Classification of Residential Neighbourhoods (Section 3.6.1) is based on these data. Savings in cost and improved supervision have to be weighed against undue clustering of sampling locations. There is less risk of undue clustering if respondents are selected at the second stage, i.e. after the constituencies have been drawn, but this would still produce rather a widely dispersed sample.

At the second stage wards or polling districts may be listed, their electorates accumulated and a second draw made using PPS.

Let us assume that we are drawing a sample of 3,000 people using a master sample of 200 constituencies. The varying sizes of the constituencies has been allowed for in the PPS procedure so we have to make 15 calls in each constituency. The extent to which we cluster the calls will depend on the subject of the survey and the extent to which habits and attitudes vary where this subject is concerned. We could, for example, draw five names from each of three polling registers or three names from each of five registers to get our 15 per constituency; for here again variation in the size of polling districts will have been taken account of in the PPS drawing procedure.

4.2.2 DRAWING FROM THE REGISTER OF ELECTORS

The names and addresses of all British subjects aged 18 and over who are entitled to vote and have registered are listed in the Register of Electors. The returns are made in October and the Register is published in February of the following year. From the marketing point of view the main weakness of the Register as a sampling frame is the fact that it excludes young adults and immigrants. There are procedures for including 'non-electors' in the sample but let us first draw the electors.

Let us assume that we are making five calls in each of three polling districts drawn with PPS. In one of these three polling districts there are 845 electors listed on the register and numbered 1 to 845 ($N/n = 845/5 = 169$). We draw a number at random between 1 and 169. Let us say this is 109. By adding the sampling interval onto the random start we draw the following respondents:

109 Marks, Ann M., 10 Bran End Road
278 Low, James W., Brambles, The Spinney
447 Fellows, Jean B., 40 Garden Fields
616 Crisp, Elizabeth M., Mill Cottage, Rosemary Lane
785 Humphreys, Christopher A., 12 High Street.

We stop at this point if the intention is to interview electors, but our interest is more likely to be in all adults, *'non-electors' as well as 'electors'*. The following procedure makes it possible to extend the draw to non-electors while giving every adult a known (and non-zero) chance of being included in the sample:

— a name and address are drawn from the Register using the method described above;
— the interviewer works to a sample issue sheet: all the electors at the same address as the selected elector are listed in the order of the Register on the sample issue sheet;
— the selected elector is starred;
— *the total number of electors at the address is the sampling interval*;
— the interviewer is instructed to list all non-electors aged, say, 16 and over in the household in descending order of age;
— the sample issue sheet is lined and, starting with the starred elector, the sampling interval is indicated on the sheet by means of further stars so that the investigator is shown whom to interview among the non-electors.

The procedure takes account of the fact that *the probability of selection for non-electors* is:

the number of 'non-electors' at the drawn elector's address
the number of 'electors' at that address.

4.2.3 THE POSTCODE ADDRESS FILE AS A FRAME

The procedure of drawing a sample in more than one stage with PPS is being applied to the postcode units in the same way as to parliamentary or local government units. As compared with constituencies or administrative districts, wards and polling districts, the postcode units are:

	'These different units are best explained by taking a typical postcode, RM3 6HS:
RM	This is the postcode AREA denoted by the letters at the beginning of the postcode. There are 120 AREAS in the UK.
RM3	The postcode DISTRICT denoted by the first half of the postcode. There are nearly 2690 DISTRICTS in the UK.
RM3 6	The postcode SECTOR of which there are 8880 in the UK.
RM3 6SH	The complete postcode. The 21¾ million addresses in the UK are covered by 1½ million postcodes.

> Each postcode defines a group of, on average, 15 houses. However, large users of the post, that is any address receiving over 20 pieces of mail a day, have their own unique postcode.
> Every address in the UK, except those in the Isle of Man and the Channel Islands, is postcoded.'[6]

It will be readily appreciated that, with the Postcode File as a sampling frame, it is possible to draw a national sample in more than one stage, stratifying by postcode area, treating districts and sectors as first and second stage units, and arriving at a sample of postcodes (i.e. groups of on average 15 homes) at the third stage; the draw at the first and second stages being made with probability proportionate to the number of addresses in each district or sector.

The Postcode File is used by Audits of Great Britain as a frame for their syndicated Home Audit of consumer durables, based on a large sample of *households*, 35,000 audited quarterly. (The sample has to be large because durables are infrequently bought.) AGB draw in two stages having stratified by Postcode Area, drawing sectors at the first stage and postcodes at the second. Their interest is in households. To use the postcode as a frame for adults it would be necessary to list all the individuals at selected postcodes and then draw the required number of respondents; or to interview every adult at each of the 15 addresses covered on average by each selected postcode. A more efficient method would be to select postcodes at random and then select respondents to fit a quota relevant to the subject of the survey, i.e. to use a Random Location design.

4.2.4 USE OF A CLASSIFICATION OF RESIDENTIAL NEIGHBOURHOODS (ACORN) IN SAMPLE DESIGN

In Chapter 3, à propos multi-stage drawing and the clustering of calls, we recognised the importance of ensuring that the sample represented the population's variety of habit and attitude where the subject of the survey was concerned. As we saw in Section 3.6.1 under multi-stage sampling Webber arrived at 36 clusterings of variables such as level of employment, incidence of two-car families, level of basic housing amenities, type of tenure, and assigned each parish of fifty or more inhabitants to one of these 36 environmental groups. Webber's work on the Classification of Residential Neighbourhoods has generated programs that are being used in the design and drawing of samples.

The British Market Research Bureau's 'Eleven Family Solution' is based on Webber's 36 clusters. Data published by the British Market Research Bureau[7] show differences in buying behaviour of marketing

---

6. *Postal Coding*, The Post Office.
7. Bermingham, K., McDonald, J. and Baker, C. (1979), *The Utility to Market Research of the Classification of Residential Neighbourhoods*, MRS Conference 1979.

Family	Clusters	Description	Proportion of Population
1A	1 — 4	*Areas of recent growth — skilled working class areas (e.g. Basildon)*	12%
1B	5 — 7	*Areas of recent growth — modern middle status housing (e.g. Chesham)*	8%
2A	8 — 10	*Victorian/Edwardian terraced housing — low unemployment/stress (e.g. Birkenhead)*	15%
2B	11 — 12	*Poor quality housing in areas of economic decline (e.g. Accrington)*	6%
3	13 — 15	*Rural areas (e.g. East Anglia)*	6%
4	16 — 22	*Areas of Urban Local Authority Housing (e.g. Bethnal Green)*	18%
5	23 — 24	*Areas in Scotland suffering from acute social disadvantage (e.g. Glasgow)*	3%
6A	25 — 27	*Central city areas of high immigrancy (e.g. Brixton)*	6%
6B	28 — 29	*High status inner city areas of multi-occupancy (e.g. Richmond)*	5%
7A	30 — 34	*Traditional high status suburban areas (e.g. Esher)*	18%
7B	35 — 36	*Seaside and retirement resorts (e.g. Worthing)*	4%

BMRB's Eleven Family Solution

significance between the inhabitants of these disparate environments.

Since Webber's work is based on Government statistical data, and the administrative classifications used by the Government, it is possible to use environmental groups based on his work to stratify, for example, enumeration districts. There are 125,000 enumeration districts and each embraces an average of 150 households.

The computer programs vary but, *taking enumeration districts as the first stage unit*, the listing for the draw might be as follows:

Standard Region 1
Classified Residential Neighbourhood groups listed in order of, say, affluence.
Enumeration districts listed within their CRN group.
Standard Region 2
As above.
And so on until all ten regions and 125,000 enumeration districts are covered.

The populations of the enumeration districts are accumulated and districts are drawn for the sample with PPS following the standard procedure, random draw and systematic interval.
At the second stage:

Electors or their addresses may be drawn using the Registers covering the selected enumeration districts:

or streets may be drawn from within the selected enumeration districts with probability proportionate to the number of addresses in them, and *quotas set relevant to the subject of the survey*.

In the second case we have a *Random Location Sample*.

* * *

We have been considering the procedures used to sample consumer markets. Most consumer markets embrace a large number of households, or individuals, and these are distributed over such a wide area that it is necessary to cluster calls while ensuring that the geographical distribution of the population is represented in the sample. When drawing a probability sample it is, at the same time, necessary to ensure that every household/individual in the population has a known chance of being included in the sample.

In non-domestic markets the situation is different. Here a limited number of manufacturers or traders may account for a substantial proportion of output or turnover (see Section 3.8) and it is necessary to recognise their importance in the market when designing a sample. Opportunity to apply probability methods is limited while, working with often imperfect information, construction of purposive samples requires judgmental skill.

* * *

4.3 Sampling 'Non-Domestic' Populations

The description 'non-domestic'[8, 9] is useful because it reminds us that practical considerations affecting the sampling of manufacturing industries also apply to the distributive trades, government departments, local authorities and the service industries: compare Kotler's 'producer, reseller and government markets'[10].

In Section 3.8 we stressed the need to exercise informed judgment when designing 'non-domestic' samples and said:

> Where it is possible to establish a complete list of firms within strata a probability design is theoretically possible. . . . But purposive selection of firms within strata is the more general practice.

8. McIntosh, A.R. and Davies, R.J. (October 1970), 'The Sampling of Non-domestic Populations', *Journal of the Market Research Society*.
9. McIntosh, A.R. (October 1975), 'Improving the Efficiency of Sample Surveys', *Journal of the Market Research Society*.
10. Kotler, P. (1980), *Marketing Management, Analysis, Planning and Control*, 4th ed., Englewood Cliffs, N.J., Prentice-Hall.

In this section we look more closely at stratification of 'non-domestic' markets by volume/value of output or turnover, at the problem of establishing a complete list of establishments and consider the relevance of probability methods.

4.3.1 STRATIFICATION BY VOLUME/VALUE

In consumer markets with rare exceptions, the individual purchase has little effect on total sales. In non-domestic markets, where one or two firms may dominate, these dominating firms must be included in the sample if sampling estimates are to reflect the behaviour and attitudes of the industry as a whole (see Section 3.8).

There are some markets which can be described as 'mass industrial markets'[8], markets for such items as photocopiers, automatic type-writers, and 'industrial wiping cloths'[9]. Here buying behaviour of the individual customer is less crucial.

But in any non-domestic market there is going to be sufficient variation in the demand of different sized establishments for it to be desirable to design a sample which attaches due weight to variations in size.

Figure 5 (page 43) illustrates a situation in which 79.2% of establishments account for only 13.3% of gross output while 1.4% account for 40.7%. The 84 establishments which constitute the 1.4% make a contribution to gross output out of all proportion to their numbers. Let us assume that we decide to draw a sample in which the 84 are self-selecting and all size categories are represented *in proportion to their contribution to gross output*, the constitution of the sample would be as follows

Employees N	Establishments N	%	Gross Output %	Sample n	%
1 — 99	4,532	79.2	13.3	27	13
100 — 199	425	7.4	8.1	16	8
200 — 499	459	8.0	17.7	37	18
500 — 999	181	3.1	14.0	29	14
1,000 —1,499	50	0.9	6.2	13	6
1,500 & +	84	1.4	40.7	84	41
	5,731	100.0	100.0	206	100

There is a wealth of statistical information available about the structure of manufacturing, distributive and service industries. The 27 *Standard Industrial Classifications* used by the Government Statistical Service are broad (the above table is based on order III) but the 27 SIC orders are sub-divided into 181 *Minimum List Headings* (MLH) and some of these are further divided into 'optional sub-divisions'. The

closeness with which the SIC/MLH definitions fit marketing requirements varies. The mass industrial market will embrace a number of
classifications. But the official statistics usually make it possible to
define a non-domestic population in terms such as those used in this
example.

The official statistics enable us to set quotas, and the chances are
that we will decide to proceed on a purposive basis, using names
of establishments derived from internal records, directories and
business associates to fill the quotas.

*To draw a probability sample we would need to acquire a complete
list of establishments: a sampling frame.* It is clearly desirable that we
should be able to assign firms to strata before we draw: to stratify after
drawing is likely to be wasteful of effort, time and money.

4.3.2 SAMPLING FRAME SHORT-COMINGS

In order to draw a sample at random we need a list which is complete,
up-to-date and without repetition of items. None of the generally used
non-domestic frames quite meet these requirements. They are useful
sources of names for a quota sample (see Appendix 1) but are likely to
be inadequate for a probability sample.

The financial directories, e.g. the *Stock Exchange Yearbook* and
Dunn and Bradstreet, define the overall worth of an enterprise but
may not record separately that part of the enterprise in which we
are interested. They give 'no indication of the geographical location,
size or activity of individual plants'.[8]
Kompass Register relates enterprises to Standard Industrial Classifications but subsidiaries may be omitted and information relating
to financial standing and to size may be inadequate for the purpose
of stratification.
Trade directories vary in their effectiveness. Omissions within and
duplications between directories occur.
Trade associations: Important enterprises do not necessarily support
their trade association.
The classified yellow pages computer file is invaluable when it
comes to making contact with establishments selected for the
sample, but it does not include information about the size of
establishments. To use the yellow pages file as a sampling frame
necessitates telephone screening.
Records built up over time from representatives' reports, the
financial press, industry and trade association sources together
with previous research are valuable sources of marketing information. But they are unlikely to be sufficiently complete for a
probability sample.

Knowing the size structure of a market, and being able to relate establishments to the size structure, are crucial to sound estimates of market size.

It is possible to project from sample estimates to the real world with confidence in the results if:

— the market in question fits the SIC/MLH classification system;
— there is a complete, up-to-date and unduplicated listing of establishments available;
— the source of information has been located within establishments; and
— unambiguous answers have been given to survey questions.

There are usually a good many 'ifs' and 'buts' attached to the projections: so much so that, particularly in a market extending over several industrial classifications (e.g. heating and ventilating equipment) there may well be a case for the *sequential approach*:

(a) Decide what return (e.g. in terms of return on investment or contribution to profit) is required to make the venture viable.
(b) Translate this into minimum demand for the product or service.
(c) Estimate its potential popularity in terms of market share, taking account of variable marketing expenditures.
(d) Sample the market until sufficient potential has been located.

4.3.3 A PROBABILITY PROCEDURE

In large scale consumer surveys cost-effectiveness is achieved by drawing the sample in more than one stage with PPS so that calls are clustered (see Section 4.2.1). It is possible to apply a similar procedure to non-consumer markets when these are of a 'mass industrial' nature. McIntosh and Davies have appraised the Valuation Lists as a sampling frame.[8] Rating authorities, after regional stratification, would be the first-stage units. They can be drawn for the sample according to their total rateable value, or according to the nature of the rated premises which are classified as 'industrial', 'shop', 'office', 'other commercial' and 'domestic'.

The official statistics, 'Rates and rateable values' in England and Wales, and in Scotland, are published annually. The rating authority's records are regularly updated (as might be expected) and the valuation lists are 'with very few exceptions'[8] available for inspection and copying at local authority offices.

The rating statistics make it possible:

— to list rating authorities within Economic Planning Regions, accumulate rateable values and attach to each authority a range

of numbers representing its rateable value (instead of electorate, see Section 4.2.1),
— to draw sufficient rating authorities to allow for regional variations (more marked in non-domestic markets than in consumer markets) using the PPS procedure;
— to use the Valuation Lists as a sampling frame for this first-stage sample of rating authorities (which may serve as a Master Sample).

The valuation lists give the names of the ratepayers, types of premises and rateable values. The rateable value is based on an assessment of the rental value of the premises. It is 'a good indicator of the physical size of an establishment'.[7]

In order to construct a list of firms from the valuation lists as a frame it would probably be necessary to make some telephone calls, or to refer to the 'yellow pages' computer file. Drawing in more than one stage makes this a practical proposition. Screening calls are a big item in non-domestic research costs.

Also by concentrating research in certain carefully drawn rating authorities, data accumulate as surveys are carried out. Accumulation and filing of data make a significant contribution to non-domestic research.

The assumption is, of course, being made that rateable value indicates a firm's substance in the market concerned. The correlation must depend on the nature of the market: it would be close for floor coverings and strip lighting.

To complete the probability draw, it will be necessary to stratify firms according to their rateable value and to draw from the strata at random, probably using variable sampling fractions. Purposive selection of firms within strata would probably be more cost effective.

Conclusion

Use of a probability procedure to draw a sample of individuals, households, firms or other 'unit of enquiry'

— makes it possible to measure sampling error when translating sample estimates into population values;
— ensures that human likes and dislikes do not influence the selection or rejection of units for the sample.

It is possible to cluster calls while still ensuring that every item in the population has a known (and non-zero) chance of inclusion in the sample. Drawing in more than one stage with PPS reduces fieldwork costs and makes for improved supervision: but this procedure, as we have seen, is quite a complicated and lengthy one.

The procedure when it is used to draw a Master Sample is likely to be cost effective in consumer markets and there are certain non-consumer markets of a 'mass' nature offering opportunities for the use of a Master Sample drawn in more than one stage with PPS.

Drawing in more than one stage makes it possible to concentrate the sampling frame for the final draw e.g. to draw from a comparatively small number of Registers. This concentration is particularly valuable where non-consumer surveys are concerned, because sampling frames do not come ready-made in non-consumer markets. It is usually necessary to construct them.

The advantages to be derived from probability sampling are dearly bought. In non-consumer surveys it is usually necessary to compromise and in consumer survey work there is a cost-effective case for drawing sampling locations at random and then setting quotas relevant to the nature of the enquiry.

CHAPTER 5
Describing Markets
– Collecting Data
by Means of Questions

Introduction

As we have seen in Section 3.4 there are two broad ways of collecting descriptive data about consumer behaviour, observing and questioning. We return to observational methods when comparing the data yield of consumer panels and retail audits (encountered earlier in Sections 2.4.3 and 3.4) in Chapter 10 (see also Figure 28); and when considering the development of pack designs (Section 7.5), the pre-testing of advertisements (Section 8.4) and the measurement of TV viewing (Section 9.3).

This chapter focuses on 'question-and-answer' as a means of finding out about the habits, awareness and attitudes of consumers vis-à-vis the products and services available to them and the needs these products and services are designed to meet. The chapter proceeds from a general discussion of types of questionnaire and kinds of question to a detailed examination of the stages in the development of a questionnaire and consideration of the questions themselves, 'the art of asking questions'.[1]

Attitude questions are given a separate section at the end of the chapter. There are certain techniques in common use for measuring attitudes and these are best considered in isolation; but, in a descriptive survey, attitude questions are likely to be introduced into the questionnaire as and where relevant to questions of behaviour and awareness.

5.1 Why Describe?

The descriptive function is far-reaching. It embraces:

— description of consumer behaviour — what is bought, where it is bought and how it is used;

---

1. Payne, S.L. (1951), *The Art of Asking Questions,* Princeton, Princeton University Press. The classic text on this subject. Excerpts are quoted in Seibert, J. and Wills, G., eds. (1970), *Marketing Research,* Harmondsworth, **Penguin.**

— description of consumer awareness — awareness of available products, services, brands; their characteristics and the claims made for them;
— description of consumer attitudes — towards the relevant activity (motoring, clothes washing, shaving) and the products, services, brands available for pursuing the activity.

However, description is not an end in itself. We describe markets in order to locate opportunities (see Chapter 6 on Market Segmentation) and, more frequently, in order to keep track of 'our' performance in relation to the performances of competitors (see Chapter 11 on Evaluating Performance and Predicting). In the last analysis the questions about behaviour, awareness and attitude are asked so that future behaviour may be anticipated.

So why do we not just ask consumers what they are going to do? Now questions about intentions, such as intentions to buy (or to invest capital) can usefully be asked if sufficient data have been collected over time to establish relationships between intentions as expressed and actions as actually taken.

Many research enquiries are 'one-off', designed to aid the making of a particular and immediate decision ('ad hoc'). Lacking trend data we arrive at hypotheses regarding future behaviour as follows:

— by first asking questions about present experience of the product or service — about what is being bought, used, owned or done now;
— we then ask questions about past experience in order to determine whether present behaviour is habitual;
— lastly, answers to awareness and attitude questions, taken together with answers to the behavioural ones, help us to decide what the respondent's future behaviour is likely to be.

An *attitude* is 'a learned pre-disposition to respond in a consistently favourable or unfavourable manner with respect to a given object'.

An *opinion* is the expression of an underlying attitude. An individual might hold the attitude that smoking is anti-social and express the opinion that people who smoke in non-smoking carriages should be put out at the next station.

The distinction is a fine one and the terms are often treated as interchangeable.

Attitudes are the product of experience (what has happened to the respondent), awareness (what has been noticed and learnt) and volition (what is wanted or willed). Attitudes are recorded to help explain behaviour so that informed assumptions may be made about future behaviour. (For techniques used to elicit and measure attitudes, see Section 5.5.)

5.2 Kinds of Question and Types of Questionnaire

The 'shorthand' used when discussing questionnaire design is summarised below:

Closed questions: The respondent chooses between possible answers to a question. If there are only two possible answers (apart from 'don't know' or 'no preference') the question is *dichotomous* (either/or):

'Is you mower a rotary mower	(Code no.)[2]
or a cylinder mower	(Code no.)
DK	(Code no.)

(The mower has to be one or the other.)

If there are more than two possible answers, apart from DK, the question is *multi-choice*:

'Is your mower driven by petrol	(Code no.)
mains electricity	(Code no.)
battery	(Code no.)
human effort, unaided	(Code no.)

Open-ended questions: The respondent is left free to answer in his or her own words, and the interviewer is required to write down the answer as given:

'Would you tell me why you chose a rotary mower?'

Direct questions: The respondent is asked about his/her own behaviour without equivocation, as in the questions given above.

Indirect questions: The respondent's own behaviour or attitude is inferred from answers to questions about the behaviour or attitude of other people:

'Why do you think people have pets?' or

'Why, would you say, do people go to church?'

(Respondent reluctance to give true answers can also be overcome by using a projective technique such as 'sentence completion' or 'word association': see Section 5.4.3 on Projective Techniques).

Most survey research data are collected by means of structured questionnaires using direct questions:

Structured questionnaire: The order in which questions are asked together with their wording are laid down. The interviewer must not alter or explain questions. Many questions are closed and the possible answers to most questions are precoded so that all the interviewer has to do is to ring a code number. (For coding see Section 5.3.5.)

Unstructured questionnaire: Most of the questions are open-ended. The interviewer is free to change the order of asking questions and to

---

2. See Section 5.3.5 and Figure 10.

explain them. The questionnaire may take the form of a check-list for discussion. The unstructured questionnaire is used in 'depth' interviews, group discussions and in non-domestic surveys.

Electronic data processing puts a premium on questionnaire 'structuring' and this may be counter-productive, impeding instead of facilitating data collection:

> Both the interviewer and the respondent have suffered from the computer revolution. The practice of recording answers on grids and scales, which are lovely and easy to analyse, causes boredom and frustration in the interview situation, unless the subject is absolutely rivetting.[3]

By making the processing of data so fast and effortless EDP removes or weakens two obstacles to the lengthy questionnaire, sometimes leading to

> an increasingly turgid and irrelevant questionnaire, more and more sections of which had their genesis in that terrible phrase 'we might as well add it'.[4]

With these caveats in mind let us now consider the structured questionnaire focusing on the stages of its design.

5.3 Design of a Structured Questionnaire

We are going to consider the stages in the development of a structured questionnaire from the formulation of hypotheses during exploratory research (Chapter 2) to the pilot test in which the proposed questionnaire is tried out on members of the survey population. (The proposed sampling method may be tried out at the same time.) These stages are illustrated in flow-chart form in Figure 9.

By the time that we come to design the questionnaire we should know what topics are relevant to the decision-making task, and from what population the sample is to be drawn. We ought to have arrived at tentative ideas (hypotheses) about behaviour and attitudes in the market; and we should be clear as to the conclusions we are going to need to be able to draw, depending on whether our hypotheses are accepted or rejected.

In order to do this we have to decide:

---

3. Farbridge, V. (December 1980), 'Introduction (a review and a few thoughts)', in 'Fieldwork and Data Processing', supplement no. 177 to the *MRS Newsletter*, London, The Market Research Society.
4. England, L. (December 1980), 'The Dangerous Dialogue', in 'Fieldwork and Data Processing', supplement to the *MRS Newsletter*.

(a) in what detail we need to ask questions about the survey topics — the level of generality (see Section 5.3.2);

(b) how we are going to relate answers to respondents — the plan of tabulations (see Section 5.3.3).

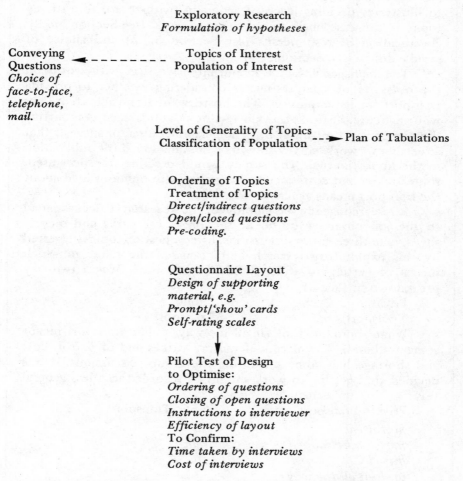

Figure 9. Stages in the Development of a Questionnaire

5.3.1 FORMULATION OF HYPOTHESES

Considering what conclusions we may want to draw does not mean that we are prejudging the answers: we are just making sure that, when the time comes to draw conclusions, the data are available, and available in sufficient detail, for us to be able to accept, or reject, our conjectures about the market we are describing (see Section 2.9).

Possible Demand for Works Transport: extracts from a case history to illustrate: deciding levels of generality with regard to a survey topic, in this case 'means used to get to work' (see Section 5.3.2); classification of respondents (see Section 5.3.3) and choice of sample design (see Section 3.7).

The management of a labour-intensive firm with works on the outskirts of a large town is considering whether to provide transport for its employees. The board want to be able to predict who might use the firm's transport without, at this stage, committing the company to setting it up. The personnel director suggests that a 'getting to work' survey should be commissioned for publication in the house journal. The survey would describe transport used, routes taken and costs incurred together with opinions held about the transport means available.

A research agency was employed. The Research Officer assigned to the job observed traffic at the firm's car parks and bicycle sheds, held three group discussions, listed question topics suggested by this exploratory research and discussed the detail in which means of getting to work should be recorded. Was a two-way breakdown sufficient?

| Private | Public |
| Transport | Transport |

What about on foot (if all the way, public transport meant some walking)? The effects of railway strikes and of petrol cost and shortage had come up during the group discussions. It was decided that getting to work should be recorded in a less general way:

Private Transport	Public Transport
motor car	*bus*
motor bike/moped	*train*
bicycle	
on foot all the way	

Suppose *more than one means of transport were used*: car to station, then train, or train then bus. . . . And what about variations in habit? It was decided to *stratify calls by day of the working week* and to ask a question about getting to work *today*: then to find out if today's journey had been different in route taken and transport used from other journeys to work in the rest of the previous week. Use of 'generally', 'regularly', 'usually' could then be avoided (see Section 5.4).

Observation of traffic into the car parks at the exploratory stage had revealed that lifts were given, car owners taking it in turn to act as chauffeur. The effect of petrol shortage and increased costs had, the group discussions suggested, developed *the habit of sharing transport*. Company cars and car allowances also came up. It was hypothesised that sharing costs and company funding might affect reactions to attitude statements on the questionnaire.

It was finally agreed that data about the topic 'means used to get to work' should be collected in the following detail:

Motor Car, Driver	Bus
No passenger	
With passenger(s)	Train
Company car/allowance	
Motor Car, Passenger	
Motor Bike/Moped, Driver	
Motor Bike/Moped, Passenger	
Bicycle	
On Foot All the Way	

There were, of course, other topics on the list. We move onto *classification of the survey population*. Company cars apart, was there likely to be a relationship between means of transport used and job done? Would a simple dichotomy be sufficient:

Staff	Shop Floor

Or would it help management to decide whether to introduce a transport service if employees were classified in more detail, so that the habits and attitudes towards getting to work of smaller groups could be compared? The following classification of respondents was considered:

Staff	Shop Floor
Management	*Supervisory*
Sales	*Wage-earners*
Clerical	*Piece-workers*

But it was soon agreed that the following classification would be more *relevant to the survey objectives*:

Staff	Shop Floor
Itinerant, i.e.	By 'Shop'/Department,
sales representatives,	*e.g. paintshop,*
service engineers	*despatch*
On the Spot	

The decision to distinguish the 'itinerant' group from the 'on the spot' group was taken because it was hypothesised that those who had to get to the office every day would have different attitudes from those who came in and out at irregular intervals, while the irregular habits of the latter would confuse the overall 'staff' behaviour data.[5] *The decision to relate 'means of getting to work' to shops or departments* in the works was determined by the management's desire to know where bus or train strikes or a petrol shortage would be most damaging, should there be marked variation in habit from one department to another. (Since all employees and their jobs were recorded on a computer file, it was possible to draw a *stratified probability sample, using a variable sampling fraction* (see Section 3.7). Shop floor employees far out-numbered staff and some shops were very much larger than others. A disproportionate design therefore made more efficient use of the research allocation than a proportionate one.)

5.3.2 LEVELS OF GENERALITY

Oppenheim has described the survey design process as 'an arduous intellectual exercise'.[6] We have to make decisions not only about the topics to be included in the questionnaire but also about the detail in which they should be covered. We must be careful not to leave some critical aspect out, but the questionnaire which provides for every possibility puts off respondents, demoralises interviewers, wastes time and therefore money, and antagonises decision-makers. *The data must be actionable* (see Section 2.1).

In designing the questionnaire it is also necessary to take into account how we are going to break down the survey population. When it comes to making decisions, *what groups are going to be critical?* The sample should be designed to yield enough individuals in each critical group for us to be confident that they represent this group in the population. On the other hand, each interview costs money. The group's behaviour and attitudes must be relevant to the decisions we anticipate having to make. The best way of deciding what classifications are relevant is to take each survey topic in turn and consider the importance of each group in the survey population in relation to it. (The relationship between topics and population is developed in Section 5.3.3.) A detailed picture of the kind of decisions that have to be made by the research planner at this stage is given in the case described on page 72.

5.3.3 PLAN OF TABULATIONS

The topics have been listed in the required detail and the population has been classified into relevant groups (see Figure 9). This is a good

---

5. It was recognised that all the 'itinerant' group would have company cars, but so, of course, would some of those who worked 'on the spot'; while the reasons for isolating the 'itinerant' group still held good.
6. Oppenheim, A.N. (1970), *Questionnaire Design and Attitude Measurement*, London, Heinemann Educational Books.

point at which to plan the tabulations, bearing in mind that too much detail is as counter-productive as too little detail. We need to take each topic in turn and to decide which groups in the survey population warrant individual attention when it comes to discussing *this* topic.

The agreed classification of respondents may usefully be applied to every answer, but this is not invariably the case: and we are likely to want to consider other groupings, such as of those whose answers to the questionnaire show them to be alike in their behaviour.

Taking an example from the 'Works Transport' case, it goes without saying that we are going to put questions about a particular mode of travel, say its advantages and disadvantages, to those who use it. But in planning tabulations we may still have to make a number of decisions. Take those who come to work by car:

> Do we put these attitude questions to all of them, passengers as well as drivers;
>
> to those who come all the way as well as those who come part of the way?
>
> Or do we focus on drivers who have used no other mode of travel to work during the period covered by the survey?

Tabulations need to be decided upon before the questionnaire is written because the wording of the questionnaire must make it crystal clear whose answer is required to each question. This applies when an interviewer is putting the questions in a personal or telephone interview, and when the questionnaire has been mailed to a respondent for 'self-completion'.

Decisions about the tabulations also affect sample size. Particularly crucial for the calculation of sample size is the decision whether or not to break down the behavioural groupings by a demographic classification. Where 'getting to work' is concerned we might hypothesise that the 'shop floor' attitude towards driving to work is sufficiently different from that of the 'staff' to warrant this further breakdown of the motor car drivers. The further breakdown would necessitate a larger sample and the additional cost might not be justified. (For further reference to sample size see Section 4.1.4.)

It may be helpful, when considering tabulations, to set up a matrix with topics in detail down the side and standard demographic and other groupings across the top. The plan of tabulations can then be seen at a glance: and we will have ensured that nothing of importance is left out.

5.3.4 ORDERING OF TOPICS

It is good common practice:

> — to open with one or two general, bland questions which the respondent is expected to find easy to answer; then

— to explore present behaviour in the market before delving into the past, i.e. to focus on what is being done, used, bought, eaten *now* before asking about earlier experience;

— to record behaviour before putting attitude questions. (Answering behaviour questions concentrates the respondent's mind on the topic in question so that he/she is ready to express an opinion about it, or to take up a position on a self-rating scale (see Section 5.5 on attitude measurement);

— to take topics in a logical order so that the respondent is not confused;

— to withhold topics that might be embarassing until the personal or telephone interview is under way or, in the case of a mailed questionnaire, until the respondent's interest may have been aroused by the earlier questions;

— to be prepared to try more than one place in the questionnaire for the 'difficult' topic, at the pilot stage;

— to try to avoid boring sequences in the questionnaire, e.g. a run of multi-choice questions or too many rating scales one after the other;

— in a personal or telephone interview, to make sure that the topics are ordered in such a way that ideas, influencing answers to later questions, are not put into the respondent's head. The mailed questionnaire is likely, if filled in, to have been read right through first.

Classification questions are often embarrassing or difficult, but they can be left until the end in the case of a probability sample, for the respondent drawn at random must be interviewed. In the case of a quota sample, some classification questions need to be asked at the outset, because it is necessary to establish that the respondent fits into the quota set (see Section 3.6.2).

In a postal survey classification questions are reached at the end of the questionnaire. They are unlikely to be as disturbing as they would be in an interview because the respondent is not always asked to fill in his or her name and address.

'Show cards' are often used to take the embarrassment out of age and income questions, the respondent being asked to point at the slot they fit into. An example for age might be, depending on the requirements of the survey:

'Would you show me on this card your age last birthday?'
16—24
25—44
45—64
65 +

One hesitates to give an example for income because it is necessary first to define income and then to distinguish between weekly, monthly and annual income. Also, the figures soon get out of date.

In the case of a mailed questionnaire the respondent ticks in the appropriate box, while in a telephone interview age and income brackets, if used, must be kept few and broad.

> *It is clearly desirable that questions designed to classify respondents should as far as possible be standardised* so that the results of surveys can be compared. The Market Research Society set up a Working Party in 1971 'to consider whether the use of standard questions in survey research should be encouraged, and if so to put forward recommendations'. The recommendations, based on research agency practice, are summarised in a booklet published by the Market Research Society.[7]

5.3.5 THE TREATMENT OF TOPICS

We are going to consider the actual wording of questions in Section 5.4, but, before writing the questionnaire, we need to decide whether we should treat the topics in an 'open' or 'closed' way, and in a 'direct' or 'indirect' way.

In survey research there is a practical case for pre-coding, and also for closing as many questions as possible. The respondent is given a choice of answers plus 'don't know'. The interviewer has merely to ring the code number alongside the respondent's choice of answer. Too many closed questions may bore the respondent but interviews and data processing take less time than they would if the question were open and the answers had to be put into coding categories *after* the interview. Also the closed pre-coded question is more likely to yield valid data: there are fewer opportunities for lapses of memory on the part of the respondent and for the incorrect recording of answers by the interviewer.

> *Open*: 'What extras and/or accessories were already fitted when you bought your car?'
> (The respondent tries to remember. Perhaps goes out to look at the car. The interviewer writes down items as they occur to the respondent.)
> *Closed*: 'Which of these extras and/or accessories were already fitted when you bought your car?' [SHOW CARD]

---

7. Wolfe, A.R., ed. (1973), *Standardised Questions, a Review for Market Research Executives*, London, The Market Research Society.

	Col. 9
Wing mirrors	1
Seat belts	2
Radio/tape recorder	3
Heater	4
Head rests	5
Fog lamps	6
Reversing lights	7

These data would appear on a punched card as shown in Figure 10.

The punch-card is still widely used. Each respondent is respresented by a unique card or by a unique set of cards. One card is often sufficient: it accommodates 12 responses (the rows 0—9 plus two extras, here shown as V and X) to each of 80 questions (the columns). If there are more than 12 coded answers, the question will need more than one column. The questions include classification questions.

In the following example, the punched holes indicate:

A woman in C_1 class aged 25—44 owning a convertible with all the extras and/or accessories quoted in the multi-choice question above except head rests and reversing lights.

Col. 1		*Col. 2*		*Col. 9*
Male	0	Saloon	1	(See multi-choice
Female	1	Estate	2	closed question
AB	2	Coupé	3	above)
C_1	3	Convertible	4	
C_2	4			
DE	5			
15—24	6			
25—44	7			
45—64	8			
65+	9			

Codes are also punched on *paper tape* (only eight rows but as many columns as required), and direct on to *magnetic tape*. The 80 column punch-card does not depend on computer processing.

Figure 10. From Coding to Punching

We need to distinguish between questions which are pre-coded and closed (as in the car accessories example) and questions which are *pre-coded but put to the respondent as if open.* In both cases the respondent answers and the interviewer rings the relevant code number but in the first case all possible answers are put to the respondent and memory is stimulated.

In order to pre-code questions it is necessary to anticipate the possible answers. For standard classification questions (such as age, class, sex) and when providing for such regular items as 'DK' 'No pref.' 'Anything else'/'Any other', pre-coding is a straightforward matter. But in order to pre-code answers to most survey questions, prior knowledge of the range of possible answers is needed. Exploratory research will have suggested what answers are to be expected and the pilot test will confirm the completeness of the list, provided an 'anything else?' is included and respondents are given time to think whether or not there is 'anything else'.

A questionnaire consisting entirely of 'closed' questions is boring for both respondent and interviewer. Open questions break the monotony. But when designing a survey to describe a market as many questions as possible should be precoded and open questions necessitating handwritten answers kept to a minimum.

If a closed question means choosing between more than three possible answers, it is best to list the choices on a show-card. This assumes a personal interview. On a mailed questionnaire they would be set out alongside the printed question.

If a topic proves to be 'difficult' or 'embarrassing' at the exploratory stage, we may decide to approach it indirectly when it comes to formulating survey questions. In survey research we need the comfort of numbers so our treatment of the subject must be a *quantifiable* one. We might ask a 'third person' question such as 'Why do you think people . . . ?' (It gets increasingly difficult to think of a 'difficult' or embarrassing topic!) We return to this subject in Section 5.4.

5.3.6 QUESTIONNAIRE LAYOUT

We have to provide for the following:

- identification of the job by means of a reference number;
- identification of each individual questionnaire by means of a reference number;
- identification of the interviewer in the case of a personal interview;
- introductory remarks;
- classification of respondents, plus, in some personal interviews, the respondent's name and address;

apart from the questions relating to the survey topics.

The job may be one of many being handled by a research agency. In addition, it may be necessary to identify a batch of punched cards long after the job is finished. In the case of a personal or telephone interview it is good practice to check a proportion of calls. Alternatively, quality may be controlled by comparing the answers recorded by one interviewer with those recorded overall.[8]

In a personal interview, the card (complete with the interviewer's photograph) introduces the interviewer (provided the research supplier is a member of the scheme), but it is still important to explain to the respondent why his/her privacy is being invaded. This applies whether the data are being collected face to face, over the telephone or by mail.

In a structured survey the words used will be standard so that each respondent is introduced to the subject of the survey in the same way. These introductory remarks often appear at the beginning of the questionnaire, but if the questionnaire is mailed the introductory remarks are more likely to be the subject of a covering letter.

Good morning/afternoon/evening.
SHOW INTERVIEWER CARD[9]
I am from Researchplan. We are conducting a survey on do-it-yourself activity and the sort of jobs people do around the home and would be grateful for your help.

We discussed the placing of the classification questions and the ordering of topics in Section 5.3.4. Here we are concerned with the effect of the layout of the questionnaire on the respondent in the case of a mailed questionnaire and on the interviewer in the case of face-to-face and telephone enquiries.

The questionnaire layout must clearly distinguish questions from instructions.

It is good practice to use upper and lower case letters for questions and capitals for instructions, as in the example shown above.

There must be no doubt as to who is to answer the question, e.g.:
ASK THOSE WHO WENT BY AIR

---

8. During the past two years particular attention has been paid to field-work standards. The *MRS Interviewer Card Scheme* now has a membership of over thirty companies supplying research.
    'These companies all operate above, or at least to, the standards laid down by the Scheme. All have been visited by Interviewer Card Scheme inspectors, who have required access to all their documentation relating to training supervision, quality control and the office procedures and records that are kept by each company. At the end of the inspection companies have compiled a short summary describing their field-work operation.'
    The Market Research Society Yearbook 1981, London, The Market Research Society.
9. We assume 'Researchplan' is a member of the Interviewer Card Scheme.

'Did you get there on time?'
or, for a mailed questionnaire:
'IF YOU WENT BY AIR . . .'.

This extract from a questionnaire illustrates the following 'ground rules':

— questions are best clearly separated from answers in the layout of the questionnaire;
— the route through the questionnaire should be immediately clear (see Q.1 'SKIP to Q.3');
— the interviewer must be told whether to read out the pre-coded answers (compare Q.2 and Q.4);
— and when to show a card (the instruction at Q.4 might have been SHOW CARD instead of READ OUT).

In this example we assume that the first four columns on the punch card are allocated to classification data.

Col. 5

Q.1 Do you own an electric drill?

    Yes 1
    No   2 SKIP TO Q.3

Col. 6

Q.2 What brand or make of drill
    do you own at the moment? Black & Decker 1
    Wolf (and so on, 2
    down to)
    Other   8

Col. 7

Q.3 Do you use a drill in your
    day-to-day work?

    Yes 1
    No   2

IF NOT A DRILL OWNER, NOR A
USER AT WORK CLOSE INTERVIEW

Col. 8

Q.4 About how often do you use some
    sort of power drill? READ OUT
    Less than once
    a week   1
    At least once
    a week   2
    At least every
    two weeks   3
    About once a
    month   4
    Less than once
    a month   5

The interviewer must be left in no doubt as to whether or not to read out coded answers. By reading out the answers as coded the interviewer stimulates the respondent's memory. If some memories are stimulated and others not, bias is introduced.

Finally, in an open-ended, uncoded question ample space must be left for taking down the respondent's answer in the respondent's own words.

5.4 The Art of Asking Questions

This is the title of a classic work on the subject. Here we would overload the text if we attempted to do more than set out some generally accepted principles, together with examples. What follows is for those who have to accept or reject questionnaires, and for those who have to answer examination questions about questionnaire design. If you are engaged in writing questionnaires professionally, the sources quoted at the foot of this page will give you further guidance.[10]

The content of the questionnaire is, of course, determined by the research objectives as laid down in the research proposal (see Section 3.2). The way in which the questions are put will be influenced by:

— the nature of the survey population, and
— the method chosen to convey the questions to the survey population (see Section 3.5).

There is, of course, interaction between these three factors. If our research objective were to predict demand for private motor cars, we might well decide to focus our enquiry on the behaviour and attitudes of new car buyers and to send questionnaires through the post because the subject is of particular interest to this survey population. (We would, of course, need to define 'new' and to take account of new cars, other than outright 'company' cars, whose funding is aided by employers. It would also be desirable to repeat a survey of this kind at regular intervals to establish trends!)

We have determined the topics to be covered and in what detail individual topics should be investigated. Now, as we formulate each question, we need to ask ourselves:

Has the respondent *got* the information?
Will the respondent understand the question?
Is the respondent likely to give a true answer?

10. Payne, S.L. (1951), *The Art of Asking Questions,* Princeton, Princeton University Press; Oppenheim, A.N. (1970), *Questionnaire Design and Attitude Measurement,* London, Heinemann Educational Books; and Wolfe, A.R., ed. (1973), *Standardised Questions, a Review for Market Research Executives,* London, The Market Research Society.

5.4.1 HAS THE RESPONDENT GOT THE INFORMATION?

It is easy to assume that the respondent has had the experience necessary to give a valid answer to your question. You ask a respondent 'Which do you prefer for cooking, gas or electricity?' and she may well answer 'gas', having had no experience of electricity. She may, of course, use solid fuel: or she may not cook at all.

Or the respondent may give you an opinion about packaged tours without having been on one. On the whole, respondents feel they *ought* to have an opinion. They also, on the whole, aim to please the interviewer by having an opinion to give in return for the question.[6]

The respondent may not have the information because he/she is not the right person to ask. The housewife may not know how the house is insured. The professional buyer, or purchasing officer, may not know why this particular piece of laboratory equipment is being used.

> *It is good practice to find out about a respondent's actual experience of a product or service before putting questions about how it is used or regarded.*

5.4.2 WILL THE RESPONDENT UNDERSTAND THE QUESTION?

At the pilot stage we may find that a commonly used word is variously interpreted. Everyday words like 'lunch', 'dinner' and 'tea' can be ambiguous. 'Tea' may be confused with 'supper', 'dinner' may be a mid-day meal or an evening one, and 'lunch' may be a 'bite' or a sit-down meal. If you want to find out how and when bacon is used, it is safer to pin the questions to 'mid-day meal', 'evening meal' and 'main meal'.

Words like 'generally', 'regularly' and 'usually' are a common source of ambiguity. Faced with a question about what they generally/regularly/usually do, respondents either describe their recent behaviour or answer in terms of the way in which they like to think of themselves behaving, and perhaps do, *sometimes.*

It is better to be flatfooted and ask in the first instance about the current or most recent happening ('How did you get to work this morning?').

An unfamiliar word in a question either leads to misunderstanding or puts the interviewer into the undesirable position of having to interpret the question. Words like 'faculty', 'facility', 'amenity', 'coverage' are not helpful in an 'everyday' context, though they would be appropriate if the respondents were academics, insurance brokers, hoteliers or media planners. The following enjoyable example was given on an MRS course:[11]

'Are there facilities for your cat to urinate indoors?'.

---

11. Read, G.J. (1977), *Asking Questions about Behaviour*, MRS Course.

The recommended wording was:

'Is there a dirt tray for your cat indoors?'.

It is easy, but of course wrong, to ask *two questions in one*:

'Do you think Tide gets clothes clean without injuring the fabric?'

and *to ramble on,* so that the thread of the question is lost:

'Do you buy your dog any dog treats — by dog treats I mean any item that is outside the dog's normal diet, is consumable at one occasion (i.e. excluding rubber toys) and is not fresh food, e.g. human biscuits or fresh bones?'

Instead of trying to define 'dog treat' in the question it would be better, as recommended, to list all the items regarded as 'dog treats' on a card and SHOW CARD.

5.4.3 IS THE RESPONDENT LIKELY TO GIVE A TRUE ANSWER?

Given that the respondent has the information and understands the question, what are the chances of the question eliciting a true answer? There are three outstanding hazards:

— the respondent may find it difficult to verbalise;
— the respondent's memory may be defective;
— the respondent may be reluctant, or unwilling, to answer the question.

The respondent may find it difficult to verbalise. The respondent has an answer to give but cannot find the words to put it into; or the respondent is so slow that the interviewer records 'don't know' and moves on to the next question. This hazard is avoided when questions are closed and the respondent has merely to choose between possible answers. If the question is open but pre-coded, the interviewer may be tempted to read out the code answer categories to hurry the interview along. This is not desirable!

The respondent's memory may be defective. Memory varies from one individual to another, and with the importance of the event. Questions about the new car are more likely to get true answers than questions about the brand of motor spirit last bought. Three practical measures help to ensure true answers when the answer depends, as many do, on remembering are:

— recall can be aided by means of a check list;
— the respondent may be asked to keep a diary; or
— a recording mechanism may be installed, for example the 'set meter' used in TV monitoring.

The diary and the mechanical device properly belong to observation as a means of collecting data (see Section 3.4). The check list is a questionnaire component. We have met it in the form of the closed question.

By showing a card or reading out a list we are stimulating memory and we have to be sure that this is what we want to do. Ask a housewife what electrical appliances there are in the house and you will probably get an incomplete answer. (She may, for example, overlook the power drill in the garage.) Show her a list of appliances and, provided the list is complete, the answer stands a good chance of being true. If we need to know what comes to mind unprompted, we can always ask the open question first (unaided recall) and then SHOW CARD.

The respondent may be reluctant, or unwilling, to answer the question. We all have ideas as to what is expected of us by other people. We all have a self-image which we aim to preserve. We do not want to give ourselves away or show ourselves in a poor light.

Oppenheim[6] quotes five barriers to true answers:

(a) the barrier of awareness, 'People are frequently unaware of their own motives and attitudes . . .';

(b) the barrier of irrationality, 'Our society places a high premium on sensible, rational and logical behaviour . . .';

(c) the barrier of inadmissibility; and

(d) the barrier of self-incrimination.

(c) and (d) are two aspects of the same problem, the problem of reconciling our every-day behaviour and attitudes with those we consider desirable (c) and those we consider acceptable (d). (We may fancy ourselves as being able to carry our liquor but be wary of revealing our actual consumption of alcohol.)

(e) The barrier of politeness. 'People often prefer not to say negative, unpleasant or critical things'. (The respondent may be motivated by kindness, the interviewer 'is only doing her job', by a desire to get the interview over as quickly as possible, or by fear of repercussion.)

Oppenheim's barriers are, perhaps, more critical in social than in marketing research, but research at the exploratory stage may alert us to a sensitive area in our survey.

Association of the consumption of animal fat with coronary risk means that today spreading margarine on bread, buns, scones, etc., is not only socially acceptable but even an indication of a prestigious, because stressful, life.

Not so long ago to spread margarine was regarded as an indication of lower class poverty. It was difficult to get housewives to admit that they spread margarine instead of butter. One questionnaire adopted the following approach: 'Housewives have been telling us

> that they use butter and margarine for different spreading purposes for their family'. Having suggested to her that some housewives admitted to using margarine as a spread, the housewife was then taken through 'spreading purposes' (toast, sandwiches, etc.), the use of 'butter or margarine' featuring in each question.

A disarming approach of this kind can be effective when it is necessary to ask questions which imply standards of behaviour such as how often teeth are cleaned, or hair is washed. Another way of softening the challenge is to ask the respondent when he/she last *happened* to go to the pub, to take the dog for a walk . . . .

Projective techniques have been developed by clinical psychologists to enable their patients to express motivations which come up against Oppenheim's 'barriers'. Projective techniques are sometimes used in marketing research to uncover motivations behind the opinions expressed about products or services and the communications designed to advertise them. The more commonly used techniques are:

> *Sentence completion*: The respondent is asked to complete a series of sentences without 'stopping to think'.
> *Word association*: Here the stimulus is a word and the respondent is asked to give the first word that comes into his/her head. It *might* be 'cholesterol' in response to 'butter'.
> *Thematic Apperception Test (TAT)*: The respondent is shown illustrations of critical situations and is asked to describe what is going on.
> *Cartoon test*: Similar to the TAT except that the characters have balloons coming out of their mouths, or heads, and one balloon is waiting for the respondent to fill it in.

In each case the respondent is being given an ambiguous stimulus. The stimulus is meaningful to the psychologist but not to the respondent who is being given opportunities to express his own behaviour and attitudes without self-censorship. Interpretation of the data collected can also be ambiguous. This also applies to the responses to 'third person' questions. The respondent, on being asked 'why do you think people . . .', may well give what he/she believes to be the behaviour or views of 'people', and fail to project his own.

5.5 Asking Questions about Attitudes

In Section 5.1 we defined *attitude* as:

> a learned predisposition to respond in a consistently favourable or unfavourable manner with respect to a given object

and *opinion* as:

> the expression of an underlying attitude.

We said that the distinction between 'attitude' and 'opinion' was a fine one. In this section we do not attempt to draw the distinction, using 'attitude' throughout, as is common practice.

Respondents hold attitudes about general subjects (or 'attitude objects') such as motoring, and about specific objects, such as a Range Rover. Where specific objects are concerned attitudes can be held about physical or functional properties, like acceleration and petrol consumption, or about subjective and emotional ones such as the kind of life style suggested by Range Rover ownership.

Attitudes are the product of the respondent's experience to date: what he has become aware of, and what he has come to want. They are, of course, influenced by the respondent's view of what society regards as desirable and this influence depends on the extent to which he is inclined to conform.

We ask respondents about the attitudes they hold to help us predict their future behaviour in the market. In making predictions we are careful to relate the attitudes expressed to the respondent's present and past behaviour (see Section 5.1).

5.5.1 ESTABLISHING THE 'UNIVERSE OF CONTENT'

When we ask an attitude question we sample a 'universe of content',[6] the body of ideas held by the relevant population about the 'attitude object', say motoring or running a car. 'Depth' interviews or group discussions during exploratory research will have generated a variety of statements about products or services in the market we are investigating and the contexts in which they are used. We can be reasonably sure that we have spanned the dimensions of the attitude when we no longer meet fresh ideas about the attitude-object, but we cannot, of course, be entirely sure.

In order to quantify the results of this qualitative work we need to arrive at a list of statements representing *the universe of content*. If exploratory research has been adequately thorough we have in the transcribed recordings of 'depth' interviews and/or group discussions:

- the ideas held about the attitude-object by the population we are going to survey;
- the expressions used by the population when talking about these ideas.

The same basic idea may be expressed in different ways by different respondents and the compilation of an *attitude battery* requires considerable skill. Decisions have to be made about the order in which ideas (or topics) are put, and the number and variety of attitude statements associated with each topic.

When constructing the battery, and when analysing the responses, it is important to recognise that, among the statements listed, some are likely to be more important to the respondent than others. A respondent might agree strongly with both of the following statements:

> convenience foods are a necessity to the modern housewife;
> convenience foods make it possible to give more time to the family;

but the second statement might count for more than the first with the respondent concerned.

It is also important to bear in mind the fact that, in agreeing with a statement such as 'convenience foods are a necessity to the modern housewife' the respondent may be either expressing a belief ('I accept this as a true statement') or making an evaluation ('I identify with this point of view').[7]

5.5.2 CHOOSING THE TYPE OF SCALE

We have now to decide in what form to administer the attitude statements to the respondent. At the simplest we put the statement, in words or in writing, and ask the respondent whether he/she 'agrees', 'disagrees' or neither with it:

Convenience foods are a necessity to the modern housewife	Agree	1
	Disagree	2
	Neither agree nor disagree	3
	Don't know	4

This is a *nominal scale*. We sum the responses by adding up the number in each of the four categories and, for each statement, comparing the 'Agree', 'Disagree', 'Neither' and DK numbers. We could, of course, compare the individual statement scores with the scores for the battery as a whole.

To establish the relative importance in rank order of the attitude statements we might construct an *ordinal scale*. If we were investigating attitudes towards biological detergents we might, for example, ask respondents to rank statements such as 'removes stains', 'saves time', 'no need to soak', 'gets clothes cleaner', 'the modern way' in order of importance. To summarise the responses we would allocate a number to each rank. Given five items to be ranked, the first/top position scores five, the second scores four and so on down to the fifth which scores one.

The ordinal scale lacks sensitivity. The rank order gives no indication of the intensity with which attributes are viewed. The attribute ranked first may, for example, be far and away first for the respondent who may not find much to choose between the rest. This limitation also applies to the nominal scale. We have no indication of how strongly those who reply 'Agree' do agree, nor how strongly those who reply 'Disagree' do so.

In order to get an indication of the strength or weakness with which an attitude is held, we need to construct *rating scales*. We are going to consider two commonly used types of rating scale:

Likert summated rating scales;
Osgood semantic differential scales.

5.5.3 LIKERT SCALES

A statement is put to the respondent and the respondent is asked 'Please tell me how much you agree or disagree with . . .' It is common practice to give the respondent the choice of five positions on the scale ranging from 'strongly agree' to 'strongly disagree'.

The scale may be put to the respondent in the form of words printed on a card, or on the questionnaire in the case of a postal survey; or it may take the form of a diagram. For the *verbal rating scale* the Market Research Society's working party[7] suggested the following approach

'I am going to read out some of the things that people have said to us about. . . . Please tell me how much you agree or disagree with each one SHOW CARD; pick your answer from this card.'

Agree strongly
Agree slightly
Neither agree nor disagree
Disagree slightly
Disagree strongly

For a postal survey the approach would, of course, need to be modified ('Here are some of the things . . .'). Whether in a personal interview or through the mail respondents rate themselves. These are *self-rating scales*.

The *diagrammatic rating scale* based on the Likert approach is as follows:

Strongly agree	Slightly agree	Neither agree nor disagree	Slightly disagree	Strongly disagree
0	0	0	0	0

The statement is read out by the interviewer, or written on the question-naire in the postal survey. The respondent is invited to point at the position that expresses her feeling in response to the statement, or to tick in the appropriate position in the case of a postal survey.

In a personal interview the interviewer has the scale with her to show to the respondent. It is a form of SHOW CARD.

The words used to denote varying strength or weakness of attitude are not immutably those quoted so far. A Likert type scale might range from 'very true' to 'very untrue' or from 'a very important reason for . . . ' to 'an unimportant reason for . . . '.

The responses are analysed by allocating weights to scale positions. Given five scale positions we might allocate 5 to 'strongly agree', 3 for the mid position, 1 for 'strongly disagree', or vice versa: it does not matter provided we are consistent. If the scale battery includes both positive and negative attitude statements, as most do, we have to make sure that 'strongly agree' for a negative statement rates 1 and not 5.

We are going to want to be able to compare the sample's total response to individual statements with its response to the battery as a whole, remembering that the statements have been chosen to span the dimensions of this attitude-object, i.e. to represent 'the universe of content'. We are also going to want to be able to compare the summed scores of individual statements, to see how responses to statements correlate. We return to this subject in Chapter 6 when, under market segmentation, we discuss psychographic groups.

5.5.4 SEMANTIC DIFFERENTIAL SCALES

Likert type scales are commonly used to investigate general subjects such as motoring, do-it-yourself, clothes washing. They are also used to rate agreement/disagreement with the specific attributes of individual models of motor car, makes of power drill, or brands of detergent. But in prac-tice scales of the semantic differential type are found to be easier to administer and more meaningful to respondents when it comes to *rating responses to statements about the specific attributes of named products and services.*

A product or service is designed to have certain desirable attributes. We want to find out whether or not, and how strongly, these desirable attributes are associated with our product, as compared with the compe-tition. Let us assume that our product is a motor car and that we want to investigate attitudes towards power, styling, driver's image, petrol consumption and reliability in relation to our make/model and others in the market. Following Osgood and his colleagues we might construct the following double-ended scales:

good acceleration	0 0 0 0 0 0 0	poor acceleration
up-to-date styling	0 0 0 0 0 0 0	out-of-date styling
thrusting driver	0 0 0 0 0 0 0	sluggish driver
extravagant consumption	0 0 0 0 0 0 0	economical consumption
reliable	0 0 0 0 0 0 0	unreliable.

The respondent is asked to rate each model in turn on these attitude dimensions. It is important that the order in which the cars are named, whether by the interviewer or on a postal questionnaire, is rotated so that, for example, the Allegro is not always considered first.

Semantic scales can be either *monopolar* (sweet . . . not sweet) or *bi-polar* (sweet . . . sour). With bi-polar scales it is important that the two poles should be perceived as opposites by the survey population.

5.5.5 KELLY'S 'PERSONAL CONSTRUCTS'

'Depth' interviews and group discussions centred on general subjects, such as clothes washing, tend to be more fruitful of attitude statements than those centred on the attributes of specific products or brands. (The car market is probably an exception. Discussion of individual motor cars can generate as much interest as discussion about motoring in general.)

A structured 'depth' interview procedure, based on Kelly's theory of personal constructs, helps respondents to express their views about individual brands, products, models:

- The product (or service) field is represented by names on cards, photographs of models or of packs, or by the packs themselves, depending on what stimulus is most appropriate. (We will assume a pack of cards.)
- The respondent is handed the pack of cards and is asked to discard any brand, name, model that is unfamiliar.
- The retained cards are shuffled by the interviewer who deals three to the respondent.
- The respondent is asked to say *one way in which two* of the brands or models named on the cards *are the same and yet different from the third*.

The answer is the respondent's personal construct and it can be used to form a semantic scale: for example, faced with cards showing three shampoos, a respondent might reply:

these two are scented, that one isn't (mono-polar semantic scale)

or

these two are for greasy hair, that one's for dry hair (bi-polar scale).

The shuffling and dealing of triads goes on until 'the respondent can no longer think of any reason why two items are different from the third'[12] The procedure is fully described in Green and Tull[13] and by Peter Sampson in the Consumer Market Research Handbook.[12]

5.5.6 SOME FURTHER CONSIDERATIONS

It has been found that too many scale positions confuse respondents and demand too much of their capacity to discriminate. However we need at least five because there is a tendency to avoid the extreme scale positions, especially the negative one.

Giving the respondent an even number of scale positions to choose from forces choice; there is no middle position to accommodate uncertainty. Opinions vary as to whether this is a desirable practice or not. When choice is forced a more clear cut verdict 'for' or 'against' is delivered but this may, of course, be dangerously misleading.

If a product or service is liked, the respondent may automatically rate it high on all attributes (the halo effect): and, in the course of scoring his/her own attitude on a large number of attitude scales the respondent may get into the habit of going for the same position on the scale.

This going for the same position on the scale is less likely to happen if favourable (positive) and unfavourable (negative) statements are interspersed.

When attaching weights to responses to attitude statements it is important to discriminate between favourable and unfavourable statements and to maintain a consistent direction. This requirement is well illustrated by Green and Tull:[13]

> *Consumer attitudes towards the advertising industry.*
> Item 1: Advertising contributes very importantly to America's industrial prosperity.
> Item 2: Advertising merely inflates the prices I must pay for products without giving me any information.
> Item 3: Advertising does inform the public and is worth the cost.
> Item 4: The American public would be better off with no advertising at all.
> Item 5: Advertising old products is a waste of the consumers' dollar.
> Item 6: I wouldn't mind if all advertising were stopped.
> Item 7: I wish there were more advertising than exists now.

12. Sampson, P. (1978), 'Qualitative Research and Motivation Research', Chap. 2 in Worcester, R.M. and Downham, J., eds. (1978), *Consumer Market Research Handbook*, 2nd ed., Wokingham, Van Nostrand Reinhold.
13. Green, P.E. and Tull, D.S. (1978), *Research for Marketing Decisions*, 4th ed., Englewood Cliffs, N.J., Prentice-Hall.

Three of these scale items (or attitude statements) are favourable towards the advertising industry (1, 3 and 7), and four are unfavourable (2, 4, 5 and 6).

A Likert type scale is used:

Strongly Approve	Approve	Undecided	Disapprove	Strongly Disapprove

and each subject (or respondent) underscores 'the description that most suits his feeling' toward each statement.

Green and Tull use the following weights:[14]

+ 2	+ 1	0	−1	−2

For items classified as favourable these weights are used without modification. For items classified as unfavourable, the order of the weights is reversed 'so as to maintain a consistent direction'.

Application of the weights is illustrated in the following example based on the responses of one subject to the seven items.

Item	Response	Weight
1	Strongly approve	+ 2
2	Disapprove	+ 1
3	Approve	+ 1
4	Strongly disapprove	+ 2
5	Disapprove	+ 1
6	Strongly disapprove	+ 2
7	Strongly approve	+ 2
	Total score	11

(As a matter of interest, it is assumed by Green and Tull that these seven items are taken from a scale battery of 100 items.)

The data derived from weighted responses to rating scales are used as the basis of sophisticated statistical analyses (see Chapter 6, where the application of multivariate techniques to market segmentation is discussed). It is important to remember that:

— the scale positions and the weights attached to them are arbitrarily fixed;
— with the scales in common use in marketing research, distance between positions appears equal but for the respondent this is not necessarily the case: e.g. the distance in strength of feeling between 'approve' and 'strongly approve' may well be different from the distance between 'disapprove' and 'strongly disapprove', but responses are weighted as if the distances were equal.

The rating scales in common use give us useful assessments of the

---

14. The procedure is the same if weights running from 5 for 'strongly approve' down to 1 for 'strongly disapprove' are used.

way in which consumers respond to attitude statements about products and services and the needs these are designed to meet. The statistical data derived from rating scales enable us to make comparisons and draw useful conclusions: but they are not, strictly speaking, *measurements*.

Conclusion

The questioning techniques discussed in this chapter may be applied to a wide range of descriptive surveys, from a simple recording of products, services and brands in current use to the collection of data about how these were acquired, how they are used, why they were chosen and how far they go to meet felt needs.

Asking questions remains the most fruitful way of collecting statistical data about consumer behaviour. From an examination of the relationships between habits, awareness, attitudes and needs revealed in answers to questions it is possible to arrive at a sufficiently robust understanding of consumer behaviour to formulate hypotheses as to 'what might happen next', or 'what might happen if'.

The marketing decisions arrived at have ultimately to be put to the test (see Chapters 7–10): but the extent to which thoroughly explored questioning can reduce uncertainty about the requirements of the market is considered in the next chapter.

CHAPTER 6

Market Segmentation

Introduction

To 'segment' is to 'divide into parts' (*OED*). In the marketing context these parts may be groups of consumers with like requirements or groups of products/services with like attributes.

A *marketing company* may adopt a segmentation strategy for two main reasons:

- to locate a new opportunity, a 'gap' or unfulfilled (or only partly filled) need in a market;
- to position its brand (or brands) vis-à-vis competitive brands so that the company brand is favourably placed within the product field.

A *market researcher* is likely to approach design of a segmentation study from one of two angles:

- collection and analysis of data relating to the habits, attitudes and needs of consumers with a view to sorting consumers into homogeneous groups differentiated by their life styles and buyer behaviour (*consumer typology*);
- collection and analysis of data relating to the products/services/ brands available in the market, focusing on how these are perceived by consumers, with a view to sorting the brands into groups of those with like attributes in consumer eyes (*product differentiation*).

The 'gap' or new opportunity sought by the marketing company may be located (if it exists) using either of these research approaches. Product positioning is more closely associated with the second approach: but, since in both cases the data are derived from description of consumer

95

habits, attitudes and perceptions, the distinction between the two is by
no means 'hard and fast'. Given the structure of this book, segmentation
is of particular interest as a means of locating new opportunities (see
Section 1.4); but marketing companies necessarily devote most of their
attention to the reinforcement of existing branded lines and many
segmentation studies are designed to help a company improve the
competitiveness of an existing product.

In this chapter we first consider why marketing companies adopt
segmentation strategies, then focus on the research methods used.

6.1 Why Segment?

On the face of it, to segment a market flies in the face of economic
theory. What about economies of scale, the long production run for a
mass market?

The segmentation approach to market planning developed in the
UK in the late fifties and became fashionable in the sixties. The development was associated with the final end of rationing and the revival of
competition as a marketing force. Acceleration of technological progress
following the end of the war, together with increased social mobility
and growth in the variety of wants felt by consumers, encouraged
competitive marketing activity.

Marketing interest in the changes taking place in the habits and
attitudes of consumers was further stimulated by the need to counter
the growing power of retail enterprises. The producer's strength at the
point of sale was eroded by the abolition of Resale Price Maintenance
in 1976, removing the producer's right to specify the price at which the
product should be sold to consumers. A more critical factor was the
development of 'own label' branding by retailers.

Manufacturing for the retail trade is now 'big business' and many
important manufacturing companies create competition for their
branded lines by supplying the retail trade with 'own label' brands which
usually compete with the manufacturer's brand on price.

> Market segmentation makes it possible for the manufacturer (or
> marketing company) to sidestep competition from 'own label',
> while preserving and developing his brand identity at the point of
> sale.

By meeting the requirements of those whose wants are not being
satisfied, by concentrating marketing effort on a market segment, the
manufacturer can expect to create a loyalty sufficiently strong to
counteract the more general appeal of low priced brands, and in particular the retailer's 'own label'. In addition, by consistently focusing

effort on a target segment, a satisfactory relationship between marketing costs and sales revenue can be achieved. But

The mere fact that a market segment is not being served, or is being served poorly, is not sufficient. Three additional conditions must be considered.[1]

Kotler's three 'conditions' are:

Measurability. we must, of course, be able to establish the size of the segment characteristics;

Accessibility: it must be possible to distribute to the segment and to communicate with it through the media;

Substantiality: the segment must be sufficiently large and demanding to generate an adequate contribution to profit.

Having located this measurable, accessible and sufficiently substantial area of want, it is, of course, necessary to develop a product or service to which both consumers and distributors respond. Research funds are laid out with maximum cost-effect when the target segment and its wants have been established; for it is then possible to work to an unequivocal brief specifying:

— the kind of people to be asked to discuss ideas about product and communication (concept testing); and to take part in experiments to help determine final choices; together with

— the grounds for choice, i.e. the criteria to be used in the design of concept tests and experiments, and in the interpretation of results.

6.2 Segmentation Variables

In the search for a target segment we consider the ways in which those in the market vary. These variables are summarised in Figure 11. They fall into two broad categories:

— variables which are descriptive: the geographic, cultural, demographic and 'behaviour in the product field' groups; and

— variables which are explanatory: the social-psychological group.

Most segmentation studies use a mixture of the two, demographic and product use variables together with the social-psychological group variables derived from research into attitudes.

---

1. Kotler, P. (1980) *Marketing Management, Analysis, Planning and Control,* 4th ed., Englewood Cliffs, N.J., Prentice-Hall.

6.2.1 GEOGRAPHIC AND CULTURAL

In Great Britain these two groups of variables 'hang together'. Among the native population television has minimised regional differences in habit and attitude, while the motor car has blurred distinctions between town and country dwellers. Wants tend to be 'like' but geographic concentration of vulnerable industries (e.g. steel, textiles, cars and trucks) creates areas of economic hazard and so constrains buying behaviour.

Immigrant populations are geographically concentrated and culturally distinct and these populations represent significant segments in the markets for food, toiletries, cosmetics, air travel and packaged holidays.[2]

In Northern Ireland there is acute cultural segmentation, and for a company planning for overseas markets as near home as Belgium and Italy, geographic and cultural variables are critical.

Geographic
Cultural
Demographic
     Social Economic Group
     Income
     Age
     Terminal Education Age (TEA)
     Family Life Cycle

Behaviour in the Product Field
     Heavy, medium, light purchasers
     Brand loyalists, switchers

Social—Psychological
     Innovators . . . Late adopters
     Reference groups   } Academic Origin
     Personality, standardised inventories

     Principal Benefit sought
     Psychographic groups   } Marketing Origin
          Consumer Typology/Lifestyle
          Product Differentiation

(Variables used in Non-domestic Markets:
     Geographic, cultural
     Application, e.g. SIC
     Organisational buying behaviour
     see Section 4.3)

Figure 11. Segmentation Variables

---

2. Hodgson, P. (April 1975), 'Sampling Racial Minority Groups', *Journal of the Market Research Society*.

6.2.2 DEMOGRAPHIC

Social class is now a weak discriminator in many product fields, particularly for fast-moving consumer goods. This is especially so among younger age groups. *But we have to remember that media research data are classified by social class (and by age group).*

Income is difficult to establish: not only because of reluctance to give the information (this can be reduced by asking the respondent to point to an income range on a card). The main difficulty is establishing what income is, as the standard question shows:

> Which of these comes nearest to your (his/her) total take-home income from all sources, that is after deducting income tax, national insurance, pension schemes and so on? SHOW CARD[3]

In many surveys the data relate to buying for a family by the housewife. Here definition of income is further complicated by the fact that family income often derives from more than one wage packet.

Age still discriminates in many markets but perhaps less powerfully than it used to. From the advertising creative point of view the 'Family Life Cycle' is a more helpful variable.

Family Life Cycle. With or without marriage, the family remains a basic social unit in Great Britain. Demand for many products and services is related to the stage reached in the family life cycle. These stages are commonly defined as:

Young single	Young couple, no children	Young couple, youngest child under six	Young couple, youngest child six or +	Older couple, with children 18+ at home	Older couple, no children at home	Older single

Terminal Education Age. TEA was developed as a classification variable to provide the discriminatory power lacking in social class. The standard question is: 'How old were you when you finished your *full-time* education?'[3] With the development of silicon chip technology, and the effect of this on consumer habits and attitudes, TEA is likely to become increasingly relevant to segmentation studies.

6.3 Behaviour in the Product Field

Price is a segmentation variable familiar to economists and price is, of course, an important determinant of consumer choice. In many markets,

---

3. Wolfe, A.R., ed. (1973), *Standardised Questions, a Review for Market Research Executives*, London, The Market Research Society.

from motor cars to pet foods, products are tailored to fit into specific price segments. But, from the marketing point of view, price is one element in the marketing mix, and interest is focused on the inter-relationships between variables affecting ultimate choice, and extent of use, such as the relationship between size of family, social grade, housewife gainfully, or not gainfully, employed and the extent to which variously priced brands are bought and used. (Price as a product attribute is considered in Section 7.6).

Given adequate data users of products/services can be divided into *'heavy', medium' and 'light' user categories* according to amount bought and frequency of buying. This kind of analysis is best based on trend data derived from consumer panels, whether the data are recorded in diaries or by means of regular audits. We need to remember that those who buy the product are not always those who use it, and to distinguish between data based on household panels (e.g. the Attwood Consumer Panel and the Television Consumer Audit) and data based on panels of individuals (e.g. the Motorist's Diary Panel and AGB's Personal Purchases Index).

Apart from 'heavy', 'medium' and 'light' buying it is also possible to sort the individuals on panels into *'loyalists'* and *'switchers'* according to how their buying moves between brands. All these 'buying behaviour' groups can be described in geographic and demographic terms.

Moving away from fast-moving consumer goods, for washing machines, refrigerators, electric fires and other durables, trend data is less essential, though once-a-quarter auditing (as in the AGB Home Audit) establishes first acquisition and subsequent replacement of durables more conclusively than an ad hoc survey can.

(For a durable product geography may be important, e.g. truly rural areas do not have piped gas, while hardness or softness of water can also influence marketing decisions. Family Life Cycle and whether or not the housewife works outside the home count in segmentation studies relating to durables).

6.4 Search for Explanatory Variables

The segmentation variables considered so far are important for 'measurability' and 'accessibility'. They help to define the size of segments and how best to reach them through the media. All these variables are, however, descriptive: they do not explain behaviour. We can observe associations between the demographic variables and those relating to behaviour in the product field and we can infer reasons for the behaviour, but the observed associations tend to be rather obvious ones, such as that large families are heavy users of breakfast cereals.

It was for a time anticipated that procedures developed and tested by anthropologists, sociologists and, more particularly, psychologists might be applied to the segmentation of consumer markets, for example:

- division of the population into innovators (2.5%), early adopters (13.5%), early majority (34%), late majority (34%) and late adopters (16%) following the *'diffusion of innovations'* theory; or
- establishing the kind of individuals with whom consumers sought to identify themselves following the *'reference group'* theory; while
- the psychologists' *standardised personality inventories* looked particularly promising as a source of segmentation variables, since these standard lists of attitude and behaviour questions were designed to sort individuals into homogeneous personality groups.

The personality inventories developed by Eysenck in the UK and Cattell in the US, to quote two outstanding examples, have been extensively tested for validity and reliability. (Do answers to this list of questions indicate an individual's membership of a distinct personality group? Does this list of personality questions stand up to use over time with different individuals?) Given that there were available personality inventories which had been tested for validity and reliability, was it not wasteful, indeed frivolous, to start again from scratch when seeking to group consumers for marketing purposes?

Attempts to apply academic theories to marketing added to the understanding of consumer behaviour but they were not sufficiently focused on the marketing context to provide usable techniques. As an example of the kind of problem encountered, Russell Haley[4] quotes application of the Edwards Personal Preference Schedule to the consumer market for toilet tissue.

The Edwards scales are designed to reveal personality traits such as 'autonomy', 'dominance', 'order', 'endurance'. In the toilet tissue case it was found that purchases of single and double ply tissue correlated with consumer responses to the Edwards inventory. Knowing about the personality traits of single and double ply toilet tissue users might well inspire the creative group in an advertising agency but questions relating to the 'measurability', 'assessibility' and 'substantiality' of the segments remain to be answered.

It was *generally* found that responses to standardised inventories did not correlate well with consumer behaviour, while the 'rather abstract relationships'[4] established were of only marginal help when it came to making marketing decisions. *The fit was not good enough.*

4. Haley, R.E. (July 1968), 'Benefit Segmentation; a Decision-oriented Research Tool', *Journal of Marketing*, pp. 30–35.

6.5 Benefit Segmentation

The 'benefit' approach to segmentation focuses on product or brand use but introduces psychological variables into the segmentation study. Consumers are grouped according to the principal benefit they seek when they make buying decisions. Figure 12 reproduces Russell Haley's benefit segmentation of the toothpaste market. Haley pioneered the 'principal benefit' idea and this is now a classic example.

Segment Name	The Sensory Segment	The Sociables	The Worriers	The Independent Segment
Principal Benefit Sought:	*Flavour, product appearance*	*Brightness of teeth*	*Decay prevention*	*Price*
Demographic Strengths:	*Children*	*Teens, young people*	*Large families*	*Men*
Special Behavioural Characteristics	*Users of spearmint flavoured toothpaste*	*Smokers*	*Heavy users*	*Heavy users*
Brands Disproportionately Favoured	*Colgate, Stripe*	*Macleans Plus White Ultra Brite*	*Crest*	*Brands on sale**
Personality Characteristics	*High self-involvement*	*High sociability*	*High hypo-chondriasis*	*High-autonomy*
Life-style Charactistics	*Hedonistic*	*Active*	*Conservative*	*Value-oriented*

* i.e. on offer.

Source: Haley, R.I. (July 1968), 'Benefit Segmentation; a Decision-oriented Research Tool', *Journal of Marketing*, pp. 30–35.

Figure 12. Russell Haley's Benefit Segmentation of the Toothpaste Market

The 'benefit' approach to segmentation is particularly relevant to market planning for existing brands. It effectively describes, and begins to explain, the branded product field as it is. Haley's analysis takes note of segmentation variables other than benefit sought, as Figure 12 shows: but the *criterion* for segmentation is *principal benefit sought*. As Haley points out 'the benefits which people are seeking in consuming a given product are the basic reasons for the existence of true market segments': but consumers do not always find it easy to define the benefits they seek or to give true answers (as we saw when discussing Oppenheim's 'barriers', see Section 5.4).

6.6 Psychographics

The answer was to develop personality inventories based on *attitudes expressed by consumers* when discussing

> *the relevant activity*, i.e. motoring, leisure, feeding the family, housekeeping, shaving, insuring against risks; and/or
> *the products, brands, services available* for carrying out the activity. Which did consumers know about and how well did these meet the demands of the activity?

In a segmentation study the attitude statements forming the inventory (or battery) of scales are elicited from group discussions, depth interviews or Kelly 'personal construct' interviews as described in Section 5.5. As a general rule the statements are put to consumers in the form of either Likert type, or Semantic Differential scales, depending on whether the segmentation study is designed to type consumers or to group products according to the ways in which consumers perceive them.

A segmentation study will necessarily include questions of a demographic and product use nature as well as the attitude battery. The range of questions will depend on how far it is intended to explore the *life-style* of those in the market. Do we intend to collect data about consumers' needs, values, activities and interests outside the product field and the context in which products (or services) are used? The answer depends on whether preliminary research suggests that the more far ranging data will be relevant, interpretable and actionable.

The main stages in a psychographic segmentation are commonly as follows:

Exploratory or Preliminary Research ⟶

a list of attitude statements. (Qualitative research.)

Questionnaire Piloted ⟶

reduction of attitude statements to a critical short-list.
(Quantitative research + factor analysis.)

Main Survey ⟶

clustering of consumers or of products/brands as perceived by them.
(Quantitative research + cluster analysis.)

Exploratory or preliminary research. A company embarking on a segmentation study is likely to have a good deal of descriptive data on file and to know what kind of consumers to invite to group discussions or depth interviews. (Section 2.7 covers this question of 'whom to invite' in greater detail.) Qualitative work goes on until we are satisfied that we have collected a good (if not exhaustive) pool of consumer ideas relevant to the market.

Taped recordings are transcribed, consumer statements sorted into groups according to topic, and attitude scales constructed. There may be 60 to 100 attitude statements on the original questionnaire.

Piloting the questionnaire. The battery of attitude statements is likely to be long and repetitive, especially if we are seeking to type consumers. The same attitudes can be expressed in more than one way; and some statements count for more than others when it comes to accounting for consumer variability.

With a limited number of attitude statements it would be possible to establish associations between consumer responses by drawing up a correlation matrix:[5] but it would clearly be difficult to 'read' a 60 × 60 correlation matrix (in segmentation studies scale batteries can run to more than sixty items). We therefore need the means to deal with the inter-relationships of many variables quickly.

Statistical techniques which simultaneously examine the relationships between many variables are known as multivariate statistical procedures.[5]

Provided it is done on an adequate scale (say 200 calls) the pilot test gives us the opportunity to use the multi-variate technique called *factor analysis* to reduce the battery of attitude statements to a small number of factors each made up of a group of highly correlated scales representing a particular dimension of the overall attitude. In the following example four factors were found to account for most of the variability shown in the answers of respondents to questions about saving.[6]

Exploratory stage: Depth interviews generated a list of some 25 attitude statements.

Pilot stage: These statements were put to 130 members of the public in the form of scales and weights were attached to their responses (see Section 5.5).

---

5. From Holmes, C. (1978), 'Multivariate Analysis of Market Research Data', Chap. 13 in Worcester, R.M. and Downham, J., eds., *Consumer Market Research Handbook*, 2nd ed., Wokingham, Van Nostrand Reinhold. This is a helpful review of multivariate techniques in common use. Green, P.E. and Tull, D.S. (1978), *Research for Marketing Decisions*, 4th ed., Englewood Cliffs, N.J., Prentice-Hall, is recommended to those seeking a statistically more rigorous treatment of segmentation procedures than is given here.
6. Morton-Williams, J. (1971), 'Research on the Market for National Savings', Case Study No 3 in Adler, M.K., ed., *Leading Case Histories in Market Research*, London, Business Books Ltd. Quoted in the *Consumer Market Research Handbook*, 2nd ed., Chap. 5.

Factor analysis: Multivariate analysis of the scores derived from the responses of the sample to individual statements yielded four factors. Each of these factors represents a different dimension of the overall attitude towards saving:

Factor 1. Temperamental difficulty in saving
(e.g. 'I have never been able to save');

Factor 2. Sense of solidity
(e.g. 'If you've got a bit of money saved you are not so likely to be pushed around');

Factor 3. Concern with independence
(e.g. 'I hate to feel I might have to ask someone for financial help');

Factor 4. Feeling of financial security
(e.g. 'I feel it's unlikely I shall have any financial emergencies in the near future').

Let us consider Factor 1 more closely. It is associated with five attitude statements compared with four for Factors 2 and 3 and three for Factor 4.

Factor 1. I have never been able to save.

Unless you have some specific reason to save, it's better to spend and enjoy it.

I believe in enjoying my money now and letting the future take care of itself.

I don't feel it's necessary to save just now.

I can't help spending all I earn.

The Survey. The object is to locate homogeneous clusters of consumers, or of products as perceived by consumers. The clusters must:

(a) fulfill the three conditions for market segments of 'measurability', 'accessibility' and 'substantiality';
(b) be sufficiently distinct one from another to offer choices of marketing strategy.

We now use a large sample, say 2,000, and a multivariate procedure called *cluster analysis*.

Factor analysis examines correlations between variables across respondents;
Cluster analysis looks for correlations between respondents across the segmentation variables.

The cluster characteristics will depend on the nature and range of the questions put to respondents. As with all survey work it is necessary to develop hypotheses before going into the field.

As an example, let us assume that we are clustering drinkers according to their use of, and attitudes towards, alcoholic drinks. Qualitative work at the exploratory stage may have suggested that there are at least four types of drinker — social, compulsive, restorative and self-compensating. Unless our questionnaire includes items which make it possible for respondents to reveal these proclivities, cluster analysis will neither prove, nor disprove, this hypothesis.

It would be helpful if the statistical procedure were to show a definitive association between the level of response to one particular attitude statement and membership of a particular cluster. In practice, it requires the responses recorded in answer to something like twelve statements to establish the membership of one of four or five psychographic clusters.

This adds to the space on the questionnaire needed for *'classification-of-respondent' questions*, for any marketing company undertaking a segmentation study is likely to want to be able to use the segmentation criteria routinely in subsequent surveys, just as questions are routinely asked about occupation, age, etc.

If the psychographic questions produce psychographic types who show consistent results over time in terms of buying behaviour, or response to advertising campaigns, the reliability of the procedure used to type consumers is confirmed.

Consumer panellists are classed according to their psychographic type and behaviour in the product field is analysed by psychographic as well as by demographic criteria. An early segmentation study was made by Attwood Statistics. This sorted housewives on the Attwood Consumer Panel into types showing the following characteristics:

Conscientiousness related to housework;
Economy consciousness;
Conservatism in brand choice;
Traditionalism in housework;
Willingness to experiment in shopping.

Knowing that a majority of the purchases of their brand was regularly made by housewives in the 'traditional' group would suggest to a company marketing household cleaners that plans for changing the product and its communication should be viewed with doubt: but that there would probably be a case for introducing a second product designed for the more experimental.[7]

---

7. These conjectures are based on a case included in Lunn, A., 'Segmenting and Constructing Markets', Chap. 14 in Worcester, R.M. and Downham, J., eds., (1978), *Consumer Market Research Handbook*, 2nd ed., Van Nostrand Reinhold.

6.7 A Motorists' Typology

Here is a brief summary of a comprehensive and carefully planned survey of motorists' behaviour and attitudes carried out by England, Grosse and Associates for Esso Petroleum. The survey was first made in 1969 using a quota sample of 2,000 motorists. It was repeated three times and, as will be seen, the research design produced a stable typology.

1. The Uninvolved
Very low interest or involvement with car or with motoring. This group seldom tinkers with the car and does very few repairs; does a low mileage, has little technical ability, and gets little satisfaction from maintaining the car.

Likely to be older white collar; this group includes most women motorists. This group relies heavily on the garage and will follow the dealer's advice in the choice of motor oil.

2. The Enthusiast
A high degree of interest and involvement with the car and with driving and working on it. This is almost the reverse of the Uninvolved group. These people do many repairs, have high technical ability and obtain much satisfaction from maintenance. They have many accessories on their cars, enjoy talking about cars, and are interested in Motor Sport. Nearly all are male and an above average proportion, about half, are working class. They have a high level of driving experience, and are likely to own an older, second-hand car.

Nearly all change and top up the oil themselves and have strong opinions about brands. Have a strong tendency to buy from non-garage outlets, especially motorist accessory shops.

3. The Professionals
These are highly involved with driving and with the car, but only as a necessary part of the working life. Mainly use the car for business, do high mileage, but do little of the servicing or repairs themselves.

Likely to be male and white collar, driving relatively new car — often a company car.

Mainly concerned with keeping the car on the road, they leave servicing to the garage, and tend to buy petrol company brands of oil.

4. The Tinkerer
Through a combination of economic necessity and enthusiasm, are more involved in working on the car than in driving it. Much the reverse of the Professional group, they get much satisfaction from maintenance work and tinkering, but although they do many repairs they have low mileage.

Tend to be male and working class, very often skilled. Car likely to be old, second-hand, used mainly for pleasure and driving to work.

They do most of the minor work on the car but may leave bigger jobs to the garage. Tend to top up and change oil themselves, but are brand-conscious.

5. The Collector
An enthusiasm for collecting trading stamps is the distinguishing characteristic of this group, which tends to be normal in most other respects. They tend to be young and inexperienced.

Source: England, Grosse and Associates (1969)

Figure 13. The Five Types of Motorist

Preliminary Work

'Considerable preliminary work, both qualitative and quantitative, ... enabled the input variables to be selected with reference to a broad preliminary idea of the kind of typology we expected to find.'[8]

Main Survey

Cluster analysis of answers to 14 input variables yielded five motorist types

Size of Cluster Groups, Percentage of Total Sample

	1969	1971	1972	1975
1. Uninvolved	27	19	22	23
2. Enthusiast	20	19	20	20
3. Professional	15	27	23	25
4. Tinkerer	24	22	20	24
5. Trading stamp Collector	14	13	15	8

The five segments are described in Figure 13 on the previous page. ('Company cars' and the effect of Incomes Policy on this benefit are shown in the Type 3 estimates; decline in the popularity of trading stamps in the Type 5 estimates).

Variables Used in the Cluster Analysis

Significant in the solution

Number of accessories on car
Mileage driven per week
Self-assessment of driving ability
Frequency of 'tinkering' with car
Extent to which servicing work is done personally
Self-assessment of technical ability
Satisfaction from working on the car
Trading stamps as criterion of garage choice

Insignificant in the solution

Use of car for work or pleasure
Liking of driving
Loyalty to petrol brand versus loyalty to garage
Frequency of polishing car
Petrol brand as criterion of garage choice
Quick service as criterion of garage choice

---

8. Lowe-Watson, D. (February 1976) 'Segmentation: Applications in Motoring', MRS Course.

The Kind of Questions Asked

The following are examples of the questions asked to collect data about the variables listed above:

Number of Accessories on Car: SHOW CARD A. 'Which of these extras and/or accessories were already fitted when you bought your car and which ones have you fitted since you bought the car? (Multi-choice, closed question.)

Self-assessment of technical ability: 'How would you rate your technical ability and knowledge of motor cars? Would you say it was well above average, above average, average, below average or well below average?' (Five-point verbal scale of the Likert type.)

Trading stamps as criterion of garage choice: 'Suppose you moved your home to a new district and had to find a garage. What would you look for in choosing a garage?' (Open-ended question.)

All the questions are focused on the car and the motorist's relationship with it.

The Motorist Typology is an excellent case of a segmentation study designed to sort consumers into homogeneous groups. The value of the segmentation approach is particularly well put:[8]

1. By maximising the differential between segments we create a powerful tool for discriminating in terms of attitudes, buying behaviour, media exposure and so on.

2. By maximising the homogeneity within segments we can create a typology. For each segment we can describe a stereotype in considerable detail. We, and the marketing people, can study these stereotypes in the round and try to understand them. This can be a considerable help to marketing planning in helping us to predict reactions to marketing activities or to changes in the market environment.

6.8 Product Segmentation or Brand Mapping

Had the objective been to cluster products rather than consumers, product differentiation rather than consumer differentiation, the segmentation procedure would commonly follow the three stages described in Section 6.6:

exploratory or preliminary research;
piloting the survey;
survey;

but the focus would be on consumer use and perception of types of product or service and, more especially, brands.

At the exploratory stage groups and individuals would be stimulated to talk about specific brands, their advantages and disadvantages according to purpose (e.g. spreading and cooking in the case of margarine). Depending on the point of view of the researcher, the ideal product would be talked about. (Some consider this adds richness to the data, others doubt the validity of statements about the ideal). Kelly constructs might be used to help elicit scale items (see Section 5.5).

At the pilot stage: attitude statements are more commonly put to respondents in the form of semantic differentials than as Likert type scales.

As in consumer typing, results of the pilot are likely to be factor analysed in order to extract the most influential attitude dimensions and to reduce the criterion variables to a manageable number.

At the survey stage: the main difference comes in the way in which the results are presented. In place of descriptions of consumer types our attention is focused on brand maps.

Brand mapping. It is easy to visualise brand positioning based on consumer responses to one semantic differential scale. Let us assume a soft drinks market containing seven brands, A–G. Consumers have been asked to rate these brands on a seven-point scale running from:

refreshing . . . . cloying.

A mean score is computed for each brand and the positions are plotted on the continuum refreshing to cloying. If no two brands scored equally on this dimension we might get a result like this:

refreshing   A F   E G D   B C   cloying.

If we had asked consumers to rate their Ideal brand on the same dimen- sion, the result might have been

refreshing   I   A F   EGD   BC   cloying.

the scores for the seven named brands representing their *distance* from the ideal.[9]

   It is also a simple matter to plot responses to two semantic dif- ferentials: let us assume 'economical to use' to 'extravagant to use' for the second dimension.

   Let us assume that *F* and *E* are two brands marketed by the same company, and that strategic planning decisions are being based on responses to these two semantic differential scales.

---

9. When questions related to specific attributes are asked about the Ideal brand as well as about available brands, the respondent's answers are more meaningful than when a general question is asked about 'your ideal soft drink'.

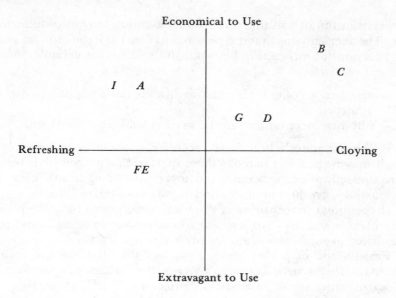

Figure 14. Brand Positioning

There is a clear case for re-positioning one of these two brands which consumers perceive as much the same. The re-positioning might be achieved by making one brand more economical than the other, say by moving *F* more closely to *I*, the Ideal. A more 'value for money' image could be attached to the brand by modifying the formulation, changing the type of container used, or altering the advertising campaign (a re-launch if all three measures were taken).

Figure 14 shows that Brand *A* is in a strong position because of its closeness to the Ideal as perceived by consumers. *B* scores on 'economical in use' but is seen to be 'cloying'.

In some product fields 'extravagance' can be a plus quality but perhaps not for soft drinks. Theoretically, there is a gap in this market for a cloying rather than refreshing a product which tends to be extravagent in use: but it will be a long way from the Ideal. The gap is a 'non-starter' and in some circumstances this may in itself be a significant finding.

In evaluating responses to attitude statements, it is of course necessary to take account of the fact that some attributes will count for more with the respondent than others. The respondent may rate two product qualities favourably on two attitude scales, but one favourable response will be more important than the other (see Section 5.5.1).

We have been considering the relationship between two attitude dimensions. It is more difficult to conceive of a 'map' showing the inter-relationship of a number of product attributes in multi-dimensional space. The fact remains that it is possible to chart the position of brands, taking account of interaction between all the criterion variables, and for the map to show:

— whether a company's existing brands are competing with each other;
— whether there is a gap in the market waiting to be filled.

If the company's brands are seen by consumers to be much the same, it may be possible to move them apart so that perceived differences are maximised; price, packaging and advertising being brought into play with, possibly, product modification and a complete re-launch.

If consumer perceptions of the Ideal carry conviction, the position of the ideal brand may suggest ways in which an existing brand might be modified in formulation and/or presentation.

Finally, the map may show a gap but the observed gap may not make marketing sense. There is a gap in the automobile market for a high performance car at an economic price.

When collecting data about consumers' perceptions of products, services or brands it is, of course, essential to establish the consumer's demographic characteristics and product experience. This is because:

— the perceptual map of ABC_1 consumers may differ from that of $C_2 DE$ consumers; while
— the perceptions of 'loyal' users of a brand may well differ from those of 'switchers';
— demographic and user groups may vary significantly in their perceptions of the Ideal; while
— knowledge of the demographic characteristics of target consumers is essential for media planning.

Conclusion

A segmentation study carries application of the marketing concept an important step forward: the outcome of the segmentation study is a strategic plan focused on the declared needs of a target in the market which has been carefully defined. This applies whether the study is made with the object of initiating a new product or of improving the positioning of one or more brands already in the product field: and both research approaches ('consumer typology' and 'product differentiation') yield the required data about consumers, their needs and perceptions.

The segmentation study provides the blueprint for the development, or improvement, of a brand; the product as perceived by consumers being an integrated mixture of formulation, packaging, price and communication, i.e. it is a *brand*.

CHAPTER 7
Experimentation

Introduction

In Section 6.1 the point was made that, having located a measurable, accessible and sufficiently substantial area of want it was now necessary to develop a product or service which appealed to the target segment. In due course Chapter 7 focuses on the use of experiments to optimise brand characteristics before the brand is exposed on the open market. This stage is commonly called 'pre-testing' and the brand characteristics emphasised in this chapter are formulation, packaging and price — the product as perceived by consumers. But perception of the product is, of course, modified by the way in which it is advertised. The effect of advertising on the brand image is taken into account in Chapter 7 but the pre-testing of advertising communications is considered in more detail in Chapter 8.

Chapter 7 opens with a review of the theoretical aspects of experimental design. This section of Chapter 7 (Sections 7.1 to 7.3) equally applies to Chapter 10 on Experiments in the Field. Before a product or service reaches the stage where it is ready to be made public, a number of Go/No Go decisions have to be made. These decisions are arrived at in Chapters 7, 8 and 9.

When a target segment and its wants have been defined, it is possible to work to a clear brief regarding the kind of people who should be recruited for experiments, and the criteria for judging the acceptability or otherwise of brand characteristics. But a segmentation study is by no means the only source of ideas for new products, or for ways of improving existing ones. Greenhalgh suggests the following sources of ideas for new product development apart from segmentation studies:[1]

---

1. Greenhalgh, C. (1978), 'Research for New Product Development', Chap. 15 in Worcester, R.M. and Downham, J., *The Consumer Market Research Handbook*, 2nd edition, Wokingham, Van Nostrand Reinhold.

Creative flair. R and D breakthroughs. Deliberate search procedures (such as regular scrutiny of the register of patent applications). Deliberate invention.

'Deliberate invention' embraces a variety of techniques for stimulating (a) consumers and (b) non-consumers or experts to give birth to new product ideas.[1] Where consumers are concerned 'deliberate invention' uses qualitative approaches such as the group discussions employed at the exploratory stage of a segmentation study (see Section 6.6).

Many marketing experiments are designed to improve the acceptability of a 'going' brand by manipulating one or more components of the marketing mix. Most of the theory and procedures considered in this chapter apply whether we are dealing with a new product introduction or modification to an existing brand. Differences arise when the research process moves into the open market and these are considered where relevant in Chapter 10.

EXPERIMENTAL DESIGN

7.1 From Description to Experimentation

An experiment has been defined as:

> A way of organising the collection of evidence so that an hypothesis may be tested. (Jahoda.)

To arrive at an hypothesis which is both meaningful and relevant it is necessary to have to hand data about the consumers and products in the market. The data will often have been collected by descriptive studies and, if a segmentation approach has been used, the company is well placed to design experiments: for detailed knowledge of the market makes for more pertinent and so effective

- choice of hypothesis to be tested;
- decisions regarding the criteria to be used when measuring and analysing results of the experiment;
- control of environmental factors;
- selection of the subjects to take part in the experiment.

For an on-going brand, or for a new brand in a familiar market, 'detailed knowledge of the market' is likely to be derived from previous product research and from monitoring of own and competitors' achievements in the product field (see Chapter 11). Kotler's diagram showing 'the experiment as a system' is a useful introduction to the forces at work in an experiment:

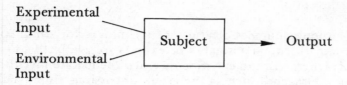

In many texts, the Experimental Input is called the Independent Variable and the Output is called the Dependent Variable. The Environmental Input is made up of extraneous variables, some of which can be foreseen, others not; i.e. some of which are controllable variables and others uncontrollable variables. The Experimental Input is the treatment applied to subjects whether this is one variable, e.g. sweetness, or a combination, e.g. sweetness plus colour in a soft drink.

7.2 Focus on Theory

An understanding of the theory associated with experimental design will help us to explain and evaluate the procedures commonly practised when products are being developed for the market.

7.2.1 THREATS TO VALIDITY

'History', 'Maturation', 'Instrument Effect' and 'Testing' or 'Learning' effect are considered at greater length in Moser and Kalton[2] and Green and Tull.[3]

History: Outside events may affect the dependent variable during the course of the experiment.

> Let us assume that we have designed an experiment to test the effect on sales of Brand X paint of a home decorating campaign. If there were a prolonged strike in the test area during the course of the experiment, and if this strike affected a substantial number of workers, results of the experiment might be deceptively encouraging, enforced 'leisure' having stimulated home decorating. In this situation, increased sales would not be attributable to the campaign: and the experimental results would be spurious.

2. Moser, C.A. and Kalton, G. (1971), *Survey Methods in Social Investigation*, London, Heinemann Educational Books.
3. Green, P.E. and Tull, D.S. (1978), *Research for Marketing Decisions*, 4th ed., Englewood Cliffs, N.J., Prentice-Hall.

Clearly, the longer an experiment goes on the greater the risk of history contaminating results.

Maturation: This effect relates to changes in the test subjects in the course of the experiment. They may, for example, get tired.

> If we were comparing the effects of two sales training programmes we might find that test subjects 'played back' what they had learnt better at the beginning of the day than at the end. If we were aiming to compare two training methods, and failed to arrange that both groups contained comparable proportions of 'fresh' and 'stale' subjects, the results might then be spurious.

Instrument effect: As might be expected, this relates to inconsistent or faulty instruments and in experimentation the instrument is often a questionnaire administered by an interviewer. Mechanical instruments are also used: tachistoscopes, psychogalvanometers and projectors feature in experiments described in this chapter, and in Chapter 8.

Continuing with the sales training example, we might expect the training officer to suffer fatigue too, so that the questionnaire is administered less effectively towards the end of the day.

Testing or Learning effect: This is particularly relevant to company image, public relations and advertising research.

> Let us assume that we have been commissioned to create a campaign to improve the image of a company in its employee catchment area. We decide to do a 'before and after test': to ask a sample of local people what they know about the kind of work the company offers, the amenities it provides and so forth; then to run the campaign, going back at a later date to see what effect the campaign has had on the experimental group's view of the company.
>
> We cannot attribute greater awareness and changed opinions to the campaign because the respondents' attention will have been drawn to the company and its activities by the first call. What they learn at the first call may stimulate the sample to pay more attention to the campaign than they would otherwise have done, and to pick up information about the company which might otherwise have passed over their heads.

For this reason we either use an 'after-only' with control design when testing communications (see Section 7.2.2); or we take the 'before' measurement on one group and the 'after' on a group matched to the first (i.e., we use matched samples).

Selection of test subjects: This is not just a matter of ensuring that those who receive the experimental treatment represent the target for whom the product is designed. We also have to ensure that experimental and control groups are matched. (For the role of the control group see Section 7.2.2).

Before designing an experiment it is necessary to know what demographic and product use characteristics are critical. Experience in the product field often acts as an initial filter: for example, if we were developing a medicated bubble bath we would need to know whether the target consumers were bubble bath users, users of medicated bath products or both. Age and class might be critical demographic variables when it came to setting quotas for the experimental and control groups. To attempt to match the groups by age within class (or vice versa) as in an inter-related quota (Section 3.6.2) adds to the time needed to recruit and to the cost of the experiment. It is common practice to sort the test subjects into age and into class strata; then to use a random process when assigning members from within these age and class strata to either the experimental or to the control group. If combinations of age and class are found to differ from the experimental to the control group, or from one experimental group to another, it is possible to standardise results by weighting, as in a disproportionate sample.

Depending on the context, there are other effects to be taken into account, and an extended list will be found in Moser & Kalton,[2] pp. 216—220.

7.2.2 CONTROL: EXPERIMENTAL GROUPS

A control group is used in an experimental design to make it possible to discount the effect of unforeseen extraneous variables. The control group is matched to the experimental group. It is questioned, or observed, at the same time as the experimental group; but the control group does not receive the treatment, nor, of course, is it asked those questions which relate to the experimental treatment.

Control groups are not always used in marketing experiments. Decision may be based on the responses of two or more matched experimental groups to alternative product formulations, pack designs or advertisements.

In comparative tests, especially in tests to decide product formulation, control may be exercised by setting a standard against which alternatives are assessed: for example, one group may be given the existing product and another the formulation which is thought to be an improvement on it, both products being wrapped and presented in the same way. In this case the control group receives a treatment but it is one against which the experimental treatment is judged. But when two possible advertising treatments are shown to two matched groups we have a design based on two experimental groups.

However well-designed an experiment may be, there is always a risk that an observed difference may be due to sampling error, and not to the effect of the treatment. The statistical procedures used to establish the significance of the differences observed are summarised in Appendix 2, at the end of this book. Unless subjects have been assigned to groups at random, or groups to treatments, these calculations should, strictly speaking, not be made.

7.3 Experimental Designs in Common Use

The designs set out in Figure 15 are the basis of most of those in common use. The notation developed by Campbell and Stanley (1963)[3] is a useful shorthand which helps to concentrate ideas about experimental procedures. The following comments relate to Figure 15.

After-only without a control group. This is not a true experiment but it is not uncommon for an increase of sales over target to be attributed to some marketing tactic, like a sales promotion or increased advertising, when other factors have contributed. In other words, the collection of evidence has not been organised 'so that an hypothesis may be tested'. (But it is sometimes possible to guard against spurious results by asking questions: claimed awareness of an advertisement can be validated in this way.)

After-only with Control. Given that the experimental and control groups are well matched, that observations are made at the same time and that the environmental input is the same for both, we can use the control group to discount factors other than the treatment as contributing to the result shown by the experimental group.

Before-after. By observing the experimental group at a suitable interval before and then after it receives the treatment we get a less ambiguous measurement than with an after-only design, but where there is danger of the respondent learning from the pre-test an after-only design is to be preferred; but

Before-after with control makes it possible for us to allow for any contamination of the experimental result (as in the case of after-only with control).

Time Series is an extended 'before-after' and it may be used with or without a control group (or area). In 'real-life' market tests it is common practice to take a number of observations before and after introduction of the new product, pack, price or advertising. The interval

Notation: X exposure to the experimental treatment
            O measurement or observation taken
            Sequence of events from left to right

Design				Measurement*
After-only		X	O	O
After-only		X	O_1	$O_1 - O_2$
with control			O_2	
Before-after	O_1	X	O_2	$O_2 - O_1$
Before-after	O_1	X	O_2	$O_2 - O_4$
with control	O_3		O_4	$(O_2 - O_1) - (O_4 - O_3)$

Time series†

$O_1 O_2 O_3 O_4$ X $O_5 O_6 O_7 O_8$ Mean of 4 post-treatment observations —
                                            mean of 4 pre-treatment observations

Time series with Control

$O_1 O_2 O_3 O_4$ X $O_5 O_6 O_7 O_8$ $\left(\begin{matrix}\text{Mean of } O_5 \ldots O_6 \\ \text{minus} \\ \text{Mean of } O_5' \ldots O_6'\end{matrix}\right) - \left(\begin{matrix}\text{Mean of } O_1 \ldots O_4 \\ \text{minus} \\ \text{Mean of } O_1' \ldots O_4'\end{matrix}\right)$

$O_1' O_2' O_3' O_4'$ $O_5' O_6' O_7' O_8'$

Cross-sectional   Matches groups
                  X_1 O_1 $O_1 \ldots O_n$ compared.
                  X_2 O_2 (see Section 7.3)
                    .   .
                    .   .
                    .   .
                  X_n O_n

Randomised block
Latin Square   See Section 7.3
Factorial

* We assume a positive result throughout.
† The number of observations taken pre- and post-treatment will not necessarily, of course, be four as here.
  The mean of the observations are taken when the effect of a particular treatment, e.g. of a sales training programme, is being measured.
  When the data are being used to forecast, e.g. sales, the time series will be extrapolated (see Section 11.3.1).

Figure 15. Experimental Designs in Common Use

between observations is related to the rate at which the product is purchased by consumers, and the data are often derived from consumer panels. The repeat buying rate is an important factor in brand share prediction. (See Chapter 10.)

With 'going' brands it is common practice to predict what would happen, if the experimental treatment were not introduced, on the basis of the trend data collected 'before'. The effect of the experimental treatment, say a pack change, is then measured by comparing the actual 'after' observations with the 'after' predictions. Beecham's AMTES model is designed to measure what would happen if a change in the marketing mix were not made (see Section 10.5.2).

Cross-sectional. Different levels of treatment such as different prices, levels of advertising and incentives to sales representatives are applied to a number of matched groups at the same time. The main problem is matching the groups.

Randomised Block. So far we have assumed that the only difference between groups is the kind of treatment they receive: in other words that, having matched groups on critical characteristics, the environmental effects will be the same for all groups. It may well be that previous research has alerted us to differences, for example of region or location, which may influence results.

Blocking is stratification applied to experiments. Use of stratification to reduce sampling error in surveys was discussed in Section 4.1.6.

Let us assume that we need to measure the effect on sales of three pack designs.[4] A supermarket chain has agreed to have the experiment staged in some of their branches. Previous research has suggested that there may be regional differences in consumer reaction to the three packs. We accordingly:
— stratify by region, say North, South and Midlands;
— arrange for the test to be made in, say, three branches in each region;
— use a random process to assign pack design to branch in each region as follows (*T* stands for treatment).

Region	Three branches in each region		
North	T1	T2	T3
Midlands	T1	T2	T3
South	T1	T2	T3

The product is on sale in all three pack designs in each region. We are assuming that the supermarket branches do not have distinct regional characteristics. The statistical figure work (Analysis of Variance) is shown in Appendix 2. Briefly, the design makes it possible for us to isolate the *between regions* source of error so that we are left with a smaller residual error to take account of when considering the *between treatments* results: i.e. the design is cost-effective because we can use a smaller sample than would be the case if we had not 'blocked' (or stratified).

---

4. The following example is based on one quoted by Cox, K.K. and Enis, B.M. (1973), *Experimentation for Marketing Decisions*, Glasgow, Intertext.

Latin Square. The randomised block design illustrated above controls one extraneous variable. If the product were one which sold through more than one type of retail outlet, we might have decided to use a Latin Square design. The Latin Square is a cost-effective design which makes it possible to allow for two extraneous sources of variation, in our case region and type of retail outlet.

In the Latin square design it is conventional to think of the two extraneous sources of variation as forming the rows and columns of a table. Treatment effects are then assigned to cells in the table randomly, subject to the restriction that each treatment appears once only in each row and each column of the table. Consequently the number of rows, columns and treatments must be equal, a restriction not necessary in randomised block designs.[4]

The finished design might look as follows:

Three Regions, Three Types of Retail Outlet (A,B,C)
Three Treatments (T1, T2, T3)

Region	Type of Retail Outlet		
	A	B	C
North	T2	T3	T1
Midlands	T1	T2	T3
South	T3	T1	T2

The Latin Square is an economical design for the measurement of main effects, in this case variation due to region and to type of retail outlet. Each treatment (in the case we have been considering, a pack design) is tested in each type of retail outlet and in each region. We can estimate error due to these two sources of variation using Analysis of Variance (see Appendix 2): but *we are assuming that the treatment effects will not be contaminated by interaction between them.* We allow for the effects individually but not as the one, here region, influences the other, retail outlet.

Factorial design. If it is necessary to take account of the interaction of variables, as opposed to measuring main effects, a factorial design is used. Anticipating product testing, let us assume we are developing a soft drink. We may expect that, in a taste test, there is likely to be interaction between the colour of the drink and the amount of sweetener in it: that the more acid the yellow of a lemon drink, the sourer the response to taste.

Say we are experimenting with three variations of colour and three degrees of sweetness, then the factorial design would be as follows:

Sweetness		Colour	
	a	b	c
A	Aa	Ab	Ac
B	Ba	Bb	Bc
C	Ca	Cb	Cc

Every possible combination of colour and sweetness is allowed for in the design, which requires nine matched groups of testers.

This can be an expensive design and we may find that we have not used a sufficiently large sample when it comes to considering the significance of results. If there is any doubt on this score the test should be replicated, or repeated, so that there are sufficient testers' judgments to warrant the drawing of firm conclusions. Replication may avoid the waste incurred when an unnecessarily large sample is drawn in the first instance: but it extends the time taken up by the test and there is always the possibility, of course, that time itself may affect results.

So far Chapter 7 has served as a general introduction to experimental design. As the examples given show, the theory covered applies both to experiments of a 'laboratory' type and to those carried out in the open market and the subject of Chapter 10.

From now on Chapter 7 focuses on the use of experiments to optimise brand characteristics before exposure on the open market. This pre-testing stage concludes in Chapter 8, where advertising is more closely considered.

It is assumed that research resources may now be devoted to the development of a product, or service, concept and that this concept (or idea) fits company resources and aspirations. Many companies have a laid-down procedure for screening suggestions at the outset, well before company funds and staff time have been invested in them: see, for example, Kotler's 'Product-idea-rating device'.[5]

PRE-TESTING PRODUCTS

7.4 The Whole and its Parts

Market description may suggest introduction of a new product or modification of an existing one. Analysis of data about consumer

---

5. Kotler, P. (1980), *Marketing Management, Analysis, Planning and Control*, 4th ed., Englewood Cliffs, N.J., Prentice-Hall.

behaviour and attitudes may yield tentative ideas, or hypotheses, about the kind of product required, the way in which the product should be packaged and priced, and how it should be brought to the attention of potential consumers.

Before considering ways of testing hypotheses about these individual components we have to recognise that, once the product is out on the market, consumer perception will be influenced by the interaction of all four: as well as by environmental factors such as the actions of competitors and distributors, not to mention the state of the world at the time.

Product formulation, packaging, pricing and communications are likely to be the subject of separate experiments on the way to 'real-life' testing in the market of the complete offering: firstly, on grounds of cost, and secondly, to help assess the contribution made by constituent parts to the overall performance.

With regard to cost: even a small scale test in the market makes notable demands on resources. The product must be available in sufficient quantity to meet demand and it has to be associated with properly finished packaging and advertising.

> *A product development programme will, therefore, include experiments specifically designed to aid decisions about formulation, packaging, price and communication: but it is likely also to include attempts to assess the interaction of these components.*

The product concept may be introduced to the experimental group in the form of a rough advertisement before the product is tried and responses to the product both before and after actual trial are compared. Pack designs may be presented to testers along with designs for advertisements, while questions about selling price are likely to be asked at every stage. The fact that the whole may well be different from the sum of its parts is taken account of in this chapter and in Chapter 8.

7.4.1 'LAB.' V. 'FIELD'

A carefully controlled experiment, conducted in 'lab.-like' conditions, yields results which are unambiguous. The experiment has *internal validity*. But the conditions in which the test is carried out are not those in which the product would normally be chosen or used and the lab.-like experiment lacks *external validity*.

The field or market test, on the other hand, is conducted in a real-life context. The findings have external validity but they may well have been distorted by market influences or local happenings so that they are ambiguous and difficult to interpret.

The more that is known about the forces at work in the market from descriptive work, the easier it is to control them or to allow for them when drawing conclusions.

The following comparison of laboratory and field product testing procedures is based on an analysis which draws on Unilever experience.[6]

	Lab.-type (internal validity)	Field (external validity)
Place	*Testing centre/hall/mobile van*	*Where product normally used, kitchen, bathroom, garage, etc.*
Treatment	*Atomistic (usually)*	*Holistic (usually)*
Length of Trial	*On the spot assessment*	*Normal use*
Subjects	*Expert panel* *Ad hoc sample(s)* *Test panel, both normally drawn from the Target Group*	*Ad hoc sample(s)* *Test panel, both normally drawn from the Target Group*
Design	*Comparative or monadic*	*Monadic*

Figure 16. Lab.-type Compared with Field Conditions

7.4.2 MONADIC V. COMPARATIVE TESTS

In a monadic design the respondent experiences only one test product. In a comparative test the respondent is given more than one product to try: the products may be given to the respondent simultaneously, or they may be given in sequence.

Comparison sharpens perception and so comparative tests are more sensitive than monadic tests: but the comparative procedure is further removed from real life than the monadic procedure. In real life products are usually judged in the light of current or recent experience of a similar product. In a *monadic test* responses to the test product are similarly based on current or recent experience in the same product field: with the critical difference that the test product is likely to be in a plain package without benefit of pack design and advertising support.

In Section 7.4.7 we describe how General Foods, who have followed a programme of monadic testing, aim to get closer to real life by simulating pack design and advertising support before asking respondents to try products. Meantime, one would expect respondents to favour known and properly 'dressed' products over anonymous 'blind' ones but this is not necessarily the case (see Section 7.4.4).

If the test programme is based on a series of *paired comparison*

---

6. Penny, J.C., Hunt, I.M. and Twyman, W.A. (January 1972), 'Product Testing Methodology in Relation to Marketing Problems', *Journal of the Market Research Society*.

experiments, one test product can stand as a control throughout. The control product may be the market leader or the leader in a particular market segment. If a brand is being re-positioned, the control can be a product it is desired to move closer to in terms of consumer perception. If a product is being re-launched, the existing product is the control product.

Since, at the outset, all products are likely to be tested 'blind', the difference in dress and communication between the test product and a product actually on the market is obviated. If the same individuals make all the tests, sampling error is reduced (but we must of course ensure that learning from test experience does not contaminate results).

It may be that there is no obvious control product and a number of possible product formulations are to be compared. This situation might arise if a range of prepared foods was being developed, say. In this situation a *Round Robin* would be an efficient design to choose. Given four different fillings *A, B, C* and *D* the procedure would be to test:

A v. *B* *B* v. *C* *C* v. *D* *A* v. *C* *A* v. *D* and *B* v. *D*.

If the tests were made by six matched groups of 50 from a sample of 300, each filling would be tried by 150 respondents.

7.4.3 USE OF TESTING PANELS

Companies continuously engaged in product testing, such as Heinz, Spillers and Unilever, place products with panels of consumers. Demographic and product use characteristics of panel members are recorded and the computer is programmed to retrieve experimental and control groups suitable for the test concerned. Test products are distributed by hand, or through the post, to panel members and the proportion returning the test questionnaire through the post is usually substantial (over 70%).

There is a risk that panel members may learn from their testing experience and cease to be typical. A methodological experiment carried out by the Unilever research company, Research Bureau Limited,[5] suggests that this risk has been exaggerated. But Unilever markets a wide range of products, and the panel is a large one, so that it is easy to ensure that individual members (while being kept interested) are not over-exposed to a particular type of product. If members receive products too infrequently, they are liable to lose interest, so that the questionnaire response rate drops.

7.4.4 THE 'FRIENDLINESS EFFECT'

There is some evidence that respondents are biased in favour of the test product: that faced with a 'blind' product to test against their 'usual' product they will tend to choose the test product. In a test for Proctor and Gamble, housewives were asked to compare a test detergent with the detergent they were using. The 'blind' test product was in fact identical with the product in use, but 59% favoured the test product.[7]

At the ESOMAR conference in 1969, Dr. Johan J.M. van Tulder reported on a series of tests using Biotex designed to establish 'the level of the friendliness effect'. Testers were given cues as to which product was the test product: the stronger the cue the greater the degree of preference shown.

The friendliness effect is particularly relevant to monadic testing. In an interesting article on 'The Monadic Testing of New Products' this propensity is attributed to 'gratitude' and 'novelty appeal': the respondent has been singled out to try something new.[8] (This article also describes methods used by General Foods to add realism to monadic testing, see Section 7.4.7).

7.4.5 ORDER EFFECTS

In comparison tests care is taken to ensure that the trial order is rotated. This is easy to control in a test centre or if products are placed one after the other. If two products are distributed at the same time, the tester is told which one to try first, half the sample being told to try one first, and half the other.

It is hoped that the instruction will be followed because there is evidence that preference is biased in favour of the product tried first. Some of this evidence is summarised in Figure 17. In all these tests the order of testing had been rotated.

It has been suggested that 'the first product pre-empts the favourable response', that it achieves 'the level of sensible enthusiasm' the respondent is prepared to reach. As Oppenheim points out, 'Our society puts a premium on sensible behaviour'.

'Testing' or 'Learning' effect (Section 7.2.1) may also be at work:[9]

> When testing razors we found that the first razor used in a paired comparison test was generally much preferred, and we thought at the time that this might be due to the respondents having learned, by the time they were testing the second razor, what a new razor

7. Clarke, A.A. (July 1967), 'Propensity for the Participant to React Over-favourably to the Test Product', *Journal of the Market Research Society*.
8. Brown, G., Copeland, A. and Milward, M. (April 1973), 'The Monadic Testing of New Products', *Journal of the Market Research Society*.
9. Davis, E.J. (1970), *Experimental Marketing*, London, Nelson.

could do for them. In this context the second razor did virtually nothing compared with the first, while the first had done a great deal compared with their old razor.

Six taste tests with cakes and breakfast cereals, items systematically rotated, summary of results:*

Preferred first tried	66%†
Preferred second tried	31%†
No preference	3%

$n = 472$

A typical example from among 50 canned soup tests, controlled temperature, identical utensils, order rotated; variety the same in each test, i.e. tomato v. tomato, oxtail v. oxtail.**

	Tried A first %	Tried B first %	Total %
Prefer A	51	28	40
Prefer B	47	67	57
No preference	1 '100'	5 100	3 100
n	152	152	304

* from: Berdy, D. (October 1969), 'Order Effects in Taste Tests', *Journal of the Market Research Society*.
† difference significant at the 99% level.
** from: Daniels, P. and Lawford, J. (April 1974), 'Effects of Order in the Presentation of Samples in Paired Comparison Tests', *Journal of the Market Research Society*.

Figure 17. Order Effects in Taste Tests

7.4.6 PREFERENCE AND DISCRIMINATION

The consumer's propensity to prefer the test product in monadic tests and the first tried in comparative tests arouses doubt in the stability of responses. If money and time were no object there would be a strong case for repeating product tests, as in the Pillsbury Mills case reported by Boyd and Westfall.[10]

Two cake mixes were tested 'blind' on the same sample. The code numbers on the packs were altered and the sampler was asked to try another two mixes, the two pairs of test products being identical.

50% preferred the same cake mix in both tests: 50% switched their preference. It could be argued that this was just a case of 'heads I win', but among the stable preferrers there was a 3:1 vote in favour of one of the two mixes.

10. Boyd and Westfall (1972), *Marketing Research, Text and Cases*, Itaska, Illinois, Irwin.

In most product tests a definite preference is being sought. It is hoped that new '*A*' will be preferred to old '*B*': or that there will be a significant difference between the preference score of new '*A*' (1) and that of new '*A*' (2). *But occasions arise when it is hoped that respondents will not notice any difference.* This occurs when a product is established on the market and either substitution of another ingredient reduces production costs and so contributes to profit; or a source of supply is interrupted and an alternative source has to be found.

The substitute ingredient will not be used unless those concerned with the marketing of the product are satisfied that users will not notice the difference. Testers are reluctant to show lack of discrimination: many are going to guess and *there are two types of error to be avoided.* If there *is* an observable difference, but the experiment does not reveal this, the position of an established brand may be undermined. If there is *not* an observable difference, and the results of the experiment suggest that there *is* (a more likely happening), we pass up the opportunity to make a cost saving or to ensure supplies.

The *triangular discrimination test*, developed in the brewing industry, is one way of approaching this problem. There are two test products, new '*A*' and existing '*B*'. The sample is split in half. Each half is given three products to test: one gets triad AAB, the other ABB. The products are presented 'blind' with ambiguous code numbers (A and B would certainly not be used).

The respondent is told that one product is different from the other two and is asked to find the different one. It is assumed that a third of the respondents will guess right and that the measure of discrimination is the percentage correctly picking the modified product less 33.3%. If 40% picked correctly, the measure of discrimination would be $[(40 - 33)/0.67]\%$, i.e. of the order of 10% instead of 7% because we have assumed that one third of the testers will guess right.

Discrimination tests are not always triangular. Respondents may, for example, be told that, out of a group of five products, two are of one type and three of the other. This is a more severe, but perhaps rather intimidating, test of discrimination.

7.4.7 PERCEPTUAL WHOLES ARE MORE THAN THE SUM OF THEIR PARTS

This is the atomistic v. holistic dilemma referred to earlier on. The problem is illustrated in a methodological test carried out by J. Walter Thompson:

> Two matched samples were asked a straight question as to which they preferred of two products: one sample was given two products out on the market and the other the same two products in plain

packs with only a code to differentiate them. The results were as follows:

	'Blind'	'In normal packs'
Preferred brand A	27%	39%
Preferred brand B	47%	40%
No preference/DK	26%	21%

'What can pre-testing do?', Stephen King, ADMAP 1968.

In the 'blind' test the products were being judged on taste or performance (we do not know the product field). In the 'normal pack' test previous experience (which could of course be taken into account), packaging, price and advertising message all come into play.

Now in a monadic test respondents deliver verdicts on a 'blind' product in the light of their experience and knowledge of the product field. They are often asked what brand they use and are then encouraged to compare the test product with this brand. The test product has the advantage of being new and different, and the possible disadvantages of not being supported by pack design and advertising message.

General Foods and their research agency have expressed the view[8] that:

Whatever the difficulties of interpretation, research is only relevant if it attempts to simulate the situation in the market place.

Comparative tests are further removed from 'the situation in the market place' than monadic tests. Is it possible to bring monadic tests closer to the market place? This is the objective of the procedure followed by General Foods for convenience desserts:[8]

(a) Housewives are recruited for a hall or mobile caravan test according to product use and demographic criteria.

(b) The testers are shown a videotape film, or story board, illustrating the product concept. They are also shown a pack design.

(c) The testers are questioned about their reactions to these communications about the product, which they have not as yet tried.

(d) The test product is taken home and tried.

(e) In an interview a week later the housewife is asked the same questions as after the concept test, so that it is possible to compare response to the product after use with response to the idea of the product conveyed by advertising message and pack design.

(f) Responses are measured as follows:
  - on a general evaluation scale ranging from excellent to poor;
  - in a purchase intention question, at a quoted price, on a scale ranging from 'I would definitely buy it' to 'I would definitely not buy it';
  - likes, dislikes and perceived similarity to other desserts are recorded;
  - the test product (and sometimes the respondent's 'ideal' product) is rated on a number of attributes.

This type of procedure goes some way to reflect the circumstances in which new products are actually encountered by introducing advertising message and pack design, together with an idea of price, before the product is tried.

It follows that, as in real life, response to the product will be influenced by the way in which it is introduced. It is, of course, possible to try out more than one message and more than one pack design, not to mention price, together with a particular product formulation. The programme of tests could be rather expensive because testing or learning effects make it necessary to test each combination of elements on a separate sample, while results may be affected by the degree of finish of advertisements and packs. We return to the subject of concept testing in Chapter 8 where we focus on the procedures used to pre-test advertising messages.

The decision whether to test the components of the perceived product individually, or in combination, is a vexed one. A company such as General Foods draws on a considerable experience of product tests. By consistently following standard procedures a company accumulates normative data: it is able to compare pre-launch test results with post-launch performance.

PRE-TESTING PACKS

7.5 Function, Impact and Image

Packaging, both 'inner' and 'outer', is a significant item in the costing of a product; and packaging research is a wide-ranging subject involving studies carried out by R and D, Production, Distribution and the suppliers of packaging materials, as well as those commissioned by Marketing among distributors and consumers.

We need to distinguish between tests to assess the functional efficiency of a pack, its visual impact at the point of sale and the image of the product conveyed by the packaging.

7.5.1 FUNCTIONAL TESTING

To give a product the best possible chance of success its pack must function well:

— on the production line;
— as bulked quantities travel along the distributive channel to the point of sale;
— at the point of sale after bulk has been broken;
— when being used by the consumer.

The pack has to protect the product from deterioration and from pilfering. It must stand up to handling and the shape should lend itself to efficient stacking, wrapping and palletisation. At the point of sale how the pack behaves compared with the competition is important. Does it 'hog' shelf space, or fall over? When it reaches the consumer, ease of opening, of closing (if not used up at once), of dispensing the contents, together with being steady on its feet, are critical variables to be considered in experimental design.

The suitability of the materials used and of the method of construction are tested by R&D, Production and by the suppliers of containers. Suppliers such as Metal Box, who make plastic as well as metal containers, are so close to the consumer market that it serves their purpose to carry out research among consumers as well as among manufacturers and distributors.

The supplier has to satisfy the manufacturer that his product will not deteriorate and that it will reach the point of sale in good order. Suppliers of packaging materials are particularly interested in consumer responses when introducing an innovation, such as the aerosol and the ring-top opener for cans. The innovation is likely to involve a considerable investment: the research findings help to persuade manufacturers to adopt the innovation, as well as improving it.

Distributors' complaints and the reports of sales representatives are the usual sources of information regarding the behaviour of the pack before it makes contact with the consumer at the point of sale. *Here our concern is with the product as it presents itself to the consumer.*

If the product is used up in one go, as with a can of beer, and the critical factor is ease of opening and dispensing, the experiment can be staged in a hall, mobile van or research centre; and the data are best collected by means of observation.

Some consumers get fussed when faced with an unfamiliar method of opening or dispensing and it is necessary to create a relaxed atmosphere. This is difficult to achieve if the tester's efforts are being closely watched and recorded by an observer, and a method used by Metal Box has much to commend it.

> When the ring-top can-opening device was introduced as an alternative to the tear off tag, consumers were invited into a mobile van to try one against the other. A hidden camera filmed the way in which the consumers approached and handled the cans.

The camera can also be used to record whether or not consumers read instructions, and whether one form of instruction appears to be easier to follow than another. (See p. 31 re. use of hidden cameras.)

Individuals vary in their dexterity and with tests of functional efficiency there is a case for using a comparative design, with each respondent trying both types of opening, assuming there are two to be tried. It is probably sounder to allow for the learning effect by rotating the order in which packs are tried, than to rely on samples being matched not only on product use and demographic criteria but also on handiness: but this is a matter of opinion.

If the product is used, closed and then re-used, the experiment needs to be carried out where this goes on — kitchen, bathroom, garage, etc. — and data are likely to be collected by means of a questionnaire. In this context, variations in dexterity are less critical though still material. They are less critical because results will be based on how easy/difficult the respondent finds the opening, closing and dispensing: on consumer perception rather than observed behaviour.

To isolate the effect of function it is, of course, necessary to use plain packs as in a 'blind' product test. If the opportunity is taken to test 'visuals' at the same time, response to visual effects may contaminate response to functional efficiency. On the other hand, we have to remember that when the product reaches the market, consumer response will be conditioned by the visuals. We are back to the atomistic/holistic dilemma.

7.5.2 VISUAL IMPACT

As we all know, products have to speak for themselves at the point of sale. There is usually no one around to make the introduction.

The term 'impact' is used here to mean 'stand out' value. Tests of 'stand out' value are usually based on observation by means of the tachistoscope or, as in William Schlackman's 'find time' procedure[11] with a slide projector.

---

11. Schlackman, W. and Chittenden, D. (1978), 'Packaging Research and Name Testing' in Worcester, R.M. and Downham, J., *Consumer Market Research Handbook*, 2nd ed., Wokingham, Van Nostrand Reinhold.

The tachistoscope enables an image to be exposed for controlled lengths of time. Lengths of exposure likely to be used in a pack test are from 1/200 of a second up to 1/10. The respondent is either looking into a box-like instrument or at a screen. After each exposure the respondent is asked what, if anything, was seen.

This simple procedure is useful for comparing the visual impact of elements in a pack design such as colour, brand name or message: but it does not simulate the context in which the respondent is going to meet the pack. A closer approach is made to reality when:

— the respondent is shown the test pack along with two or three control packs, care being taken to simulate the size of the packs as they might 'loom up' on the shelf at the point of sale;
— after each timed exposure the respondent is asked to pick the three or four packs out from a display which reproduces the company in which the pack is likely to find itself on the self-service shelf.

In a test of this kind results are likely to be contaminated by learning and it is advisable to use matched samples. If responses to the control products are of the same order for both samples, we are reassured that the samples are *matched for acuity* (i.e., speed of perception and response), as well as on the more obvious criteria.

When designing experiments to measure visual impact it is necessary to take into account variations in sharpness of eyesight and the speed with which individuals respond to the image. They may, for example, be required to press a button as in the 'find time' design described below.[11] Organisations specialising in pack testing use standard acuity tests.

When recruiting for an experiment it would be time-consuming to take acuity into account as well as product use and demographic characteristics. It may be necessary to weight results when the acuity of matched samples is found to differ: but acuity is affected by age and familiarity with the product field so matching on these variables may obviate the problem.

In the *'find time' procedure* pioneered by William Schlackman[11] matched samples are used and the respondents are allowed to familiarise themselves with a test pack. They are told that this may, or may not, be present in the displays which will be projected onto a screen.

— Some nine displays, typical of the product field at the point of sale, are photographed and the photographs are prepared for slide projection.
— In about six out of the nine slides the test pack is among its competitors, in six different positions. It is absent from the other three slides.

— The slide remains on the screen until the respondent presses a button to signal that the test item has been found, or has not, as the case may be.
— The measure of 'stand-out' value is the time taken to find the test pack when it is present. This is automatically recorded when the button is pressed.

Test items: two versions of a new pack design for a confectionery product ($V1$ and $V2$) plus the current pack (P).
Design: Monadic using three matched samples of 50.
Procedure: Each sample is shown nine slides of which six contained $V1$, $V2$ or P.

Pack	Mean reaction time in sec.	t-test* value	Significance level
$V2$	1.77 ⎫		
P	1.59 ⎭	1.99	not
$V1$	1.98 ⎫		
P	1.59 ⎭	3.71	0.001
$V2$	1.77 ⎫		
$V1$	1.98 ⎭	2.05	0.05

In this table results are compared for the three possible pairs. Clearly, neither new version is an improvement on the current pack design.

* For statistical tests, see Appendix 2.

Figure 18. A 'Find Time' Experiment

7.5.3 IMAGE OF THE PRODUCT IN THE PACK

The product has been designed to meet the requirements of a target group in the market. If a segmentation study has been made, the characteristics of the group, and the benefits wanted by it, are certainly known. The pack has to tell these consumers that it contains a product with the desired qualities.

In a programme of image tests respondents are asked for their perceptions of the product in the pack *before they have tried it*. The following test was carried out on members of a test panel in a test centre:

At the test centre panel members were asked what products they usually used for their main wash and for their light hand-wash.
If they used a washing powder they were introduced to the experiment as follows:

'I am going to show you two different packets of a washing powder called Coral. The manufacturer is considering two different versions of the product, and would like to know what housewives think about them'.

(The interviewer was instructed to SHOW FIRST PACK. ALTERNATE AT EACH INTERVIEW).

'I would like you to tell me what you think about the product in this packet by indicating where you think it would come on this scale. If you point to the largest box you strongly agree with the statement. If you point to the smallest box you think the statement applies very slightly to the product'. (There were seven sizes of box.)

The respondent then rated each pack in turn on the following criteria *without having tried the product*:

Suitable for all modern fabrics
Gets white nylon really white
Suitable for machine and handwash
Washes thoroughly but gently
Cares for delicate fabrics
Up to date
I would buy

Test items: 'A mild beverage', two labels: *L* and *M*.
Design: Simultaneous comparison test (i.e. two bottles were 'placed' at the same time). Four days' trial.
Procedure: Respondents asked to use one bottle first, then, on completion, the second. Order rotated. Consumers told the interviewer would be returning to ask them about their experience.

	L	M	DK	Total
Product found most acceptable	20	75	5	100
Product which was mild	25	65	10	100
Product most bitter	70	28	2	100

$n = 200$

Conclusion: '*M* moves the product more effectively in the direction of the marketing intention than does *L* '

Source: Brown, Copeland and Milward (April 1973), 'Monadic Testing of New Products', *Journal of the Market Research Society*.

Figure 19. The Pseudo Product Test

When a consumer meets a new product at the point of sale, the decision whether or not to try it is influenced by ideas about the product conveyed by its pack.

Having carried out this concept test, the marketing company concerned might well have put the same questions to the test panel after actual trial. Comparison of the responses would show whether or not the product came up to expectation: if it exceeded expectation, the pack design might need modification.

The pseudo product test is designed to measure what William Schlackman describes[11] as 'symbolic transference'.

Influence of the labels on taste perceptions is further evidence of the importance of testing the whole as well as its parts.

7.5.4 THE BRAND NAME

Marketing companies may apply the company name to all their products, as in the case of 'Heinz'; or give each branded line a distinctive name, the practice pursued by the Unilever marketing companies and by Beecham.

Ideally, the brand name should convey or support the product concept. If the product has a 'unique selling proposition' the brand name should, if possible, reiterate this: for example, 'Head and Shoulders' for an anti-dandruff shampoo. If the packaging and promotion are being designed to convey an emotional benefit in the context of a 'brand image', the name will be chosen to support the image, as in 'Close-up' for a toothpaste. (For 'USP' and 'Brand Image' see Section 8.3.3).

Before brand names are tested for their power to communicate the nature of the brand, it is necessary to establish that:

— the name is available for registration in the countries in which the brand is going to be marketed;
— the name has no dubious or unhelpful associations in these countries;
— the name is easy to pronounce, read and remember.

Ease in pronouncing the name may be tested by asking consumers to read over a short list of names, taking note of hesitations and of any variations in emphasis. A tape recorder makes it possible to play back responses.

The 'stand out' value of the name is likely to be tested as a component of the pack design, after the 'runners' have been reduced to a few, perhaps in a tachistoscopic test or in a 'find time' test (see Section 7.5.2).

The communicative power of the name is tested by establishing its associations in the mind of consumers:

- in the first instance by means of 'free association', consumers being asked to say the first word, or thought, that comes into their head on hearing the name;
- then by asking consumers to associate kinds of product with the brand names as these are read over;
- and/or by asking consumers to associate the brand names with product attribute statements.

When designing research of this kind three factors need to be taken into account:[11]

- respondents should be given a trial run before the critical names are put to them. This applies in particular to the 'free association' test;
- the order in which names and/or statements are put to respondents should be rotated;
- the time taken to respond must be recorded.

As pointed out in the introduction to this chapter, when a target segment and its wants have been defined, it is possible to work to a clear brief regarding the kind of people who should be recruited for experiments and the criteria for judging the acceptability, or otherwise, of brand characteristics. This applies to the brand name as well as to the other characteristics considered so far, product formulation and packaging.

PRE-TESTING PRICE

7.6 The Right Price

A product's retail selling price is constrained by the cost of materials, company philosophy about returns on investment or contributions to profit, government policy, the cost of competitive products and the cost of marketing it. If the product is out on the market there is little room for manoeuvre. If it is a new product, attempts are made to anticipate what consumers would regard as a suitable price, and to establish a relationship between selling price and product image.

Soundings are taken as the product develops, at the concept stage, when the product is tried, as part of pack tests and (as shown in Chapter 8) during advertising research. The soundings usually take the form of 'intention to buy' questions related to quoted prices.

When the product goes on sale in a store test, or in a full market test, a credible verdict may be delivered depending on the length and sensitivity of the test. *The purpose of taking soundings on the way to a market test is*:

— to see what kind of price consumers associate with the product and how this varies between types of consumer;
— to try out the effect on price perception of changes in the product, its packaging and advertising.

When 'intention to buy' at a stated price questions are regularly asked, companies accumulate normative data. By comparing intentions with eventual buying behaviour it is possible to get close to a correction factor to apply to the experimental findings.

7.6.1 THE BUY—RESPONSE METHOD

The Buy—Response Method derives from the work of Jean Stoetzel, Professor of Social Psychology at the Sorbonne (1960) into price as an indicator of quality. The method has been validated and applied commercially by the Nottingham University Consumer Study Group.[12] The tests are usually carried out in halls, i.e. they are of the 'lab.-type' variety.

The idea of price as an indicator of quality has long been associated with durables and luxury goods. Methodological research has shown it to be relevant to fast-moving consumer goods. Too low a price is risky ('It would be dust at that price' of tea) while a high price may be 'too dear'. The Buy—Response curve (Figure 20) shows the limits within which a selling price would *not be a barrier to acceptance*, while the shape of the curve shows where the most generally acceptable price is likely to fall. In addition, a comparison between the shape of the 'price last paid' curve and the Buy—Response curve may indicate an opportunity: e.g. in Figure 20 it would seem that brands priced at 12p do not enjoy their potential share.

The usual procedure is as follows:

— the range of consumer selling prices in the product field is recorded and not more than ten prices are chosen for testing.
— the respondent is shown the product, its pack or its advertising and is asked 'Would you buy X at . . . ?'. The price first quoted will be near to the average for the product field. The other prices

---

12. Gabor, A., (1977), 'Price as a Quality Indicator', in *Pricing, Principles and Practices*, London, Heinemann Educational Books.

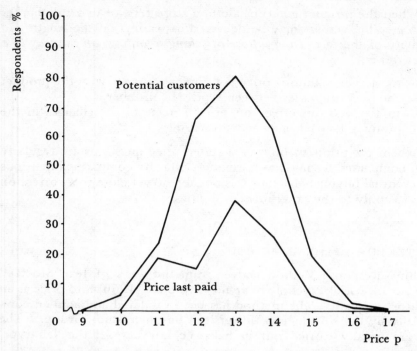

Source: Gabor, Andre (1977), *Pricing: Principles and Practices*, London, Heinemann Educational Books

Figure 20. 'Buy—Response' and 'Price Last Paid' Curves

will be quoted at random so that upper and lower limits are not suggested to the respondent.

Alternatively, if there is a risk of confusing the respondent from the number of possible prices, the sample may be split in half, one half being taken down through the possible prices from top to bottom, and the other being taken up through the list.

— The responses are summed for each price accepted by respondents and the acceptable prices are charted as shown in Figure 20. Respondents are also asked prices last paid and here again the distribution is charted. (There is, of course, only one 'last paid' to a number of 'would buys' for each respondent).

It is possible to use the Buy—Response method to compare the effect on consumer price perceptions of different product formulations, different packaging and different communications.

If a consumer target has not been defined, it is also, of course, possible to compare the responses of different segments of the market.

Conclusion

Much of the content of this chapter applies to services as well as to products. Services have also to be formulated, presented/packaged and priced.

After a review of theory applicable to both lab. and field experiments, the chapter focuses on pre-testing, the object being to bring the best mix of attributes to trial in the real world.

The designer of a pre-testing programme is faced with two dilemmas:

— It is possible to achieve 'internal validity' in lab.-type conditions but the conditions are, to varying extents, unreal and the respondents know they are delivering judgments. Would the results be the same in normal circumstances? Has the experiment 'external validity'?

— In the real world the consumer perceives the whole product, formulation + packaging + price + the 'added value' of advertising. It is, therefore, necessary to devise a programme of experiments which seeks to optimise individual elements, such as formulation, but which attempts to take account of their interaction.

The General Foods procedure summarised in Section 7.4.7 accepts that 'perceptual wholes are more than the sum of their parts'. Two further pre-testing procedures, both designed to get round the 'atomistic/holistic' difficulty, are considered at the end of the next chapter (see Section 8.4.4).

CHAPTER 8

Communications Research: (1) The Message

Introduction

In the last chapter we considered how experiments may be used to reduce uncertainty when Go/No Go decisions have to be made while a branded product is being developed for the market.

We stressed that fact that the brand — the product or service as perceived by consumers — is a mixture of intrinsic qualities (such as colour, taste, consistency) and of the way in which these qualities are packaged and priced.

Consumer perception is, also, of course, influenced by the way in which the brand is presented in advertisements; while whether or not the message is acutally conveyed to the consumer depends on the size of the advertising appropriation and the efficiency with which media choices are made when the advertising schedule is planned.

This chapter focuses on the creative aspect, while media selection is reserved for Chapter 9: but the relationship between the message and the medium used to convey it is necessarily a close one: and the most cost-effective results are achieved when creative work and media planning proceed simultaneously and with joint consultation.

The need to reach target consumers as often and as forcefully as possible within the financial resources available will largely determine media selection. This over-riding consideration may, for example, prescribe use of television to communicate the message, and this decision will have a critical effect on creative thinking. On the other hand, the need to present a benefit, or create an image, as persuasively as possible will influence the length of commercials, the size of print advertisements and the choice of supporting media.

Communications research is a large subject. Figure 21 sets the scene by summarising the stages in the development of an advertising campaign and relating these to the relevant chapters in this book.

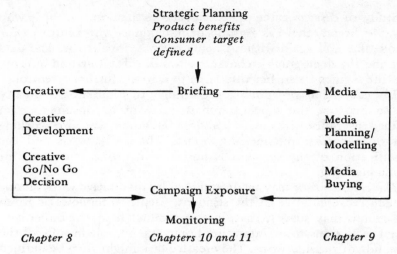

Figure 21. Stages in the Development of an Advertising Campaign

This chapter is concerned with the pre-testing of advertisements but in order to put the subject in perspective it is necessary first of all to:

— distinguish between marketing objectives, advertising objectives and creative tasks;
— review the chronological stages in the advertising research programme (looking ahead to Chapter 9 on Media Selection and Chapter 10 on Experiments in the Field);
— consider some theories as to how advertising works.

8.1 Advertising Objectives and Creative Tasks

We need to distinguish between marketing objectives, advertising objectives and creative tasks. The marketing objective is, in the last analysis, to improve the contribution to profit of a particular brand or to maintain its contribution for as long as possible. The profit contribution can be achieved by improving or maintaining sales value or, but in the shorter term, by reducing marketing costs and this generally means the advertising appropriation. The following made-up case illustrates the relationship between marketing objectives, advertising objective and creative task:

The marketing objective is to increase the market share of the brand by x%. The client's promotional budget, which embraces trade deals and consumer promotions as well as the advertising appropriation, is related to this objective.

Study of disaggregated panel data shows that, among those who buy the brand, there is a group of individuals who return to the brand time and again without being entirely loyal to it. The data describe the demographic characteristics of this group and indicate that the segment is sufficiently large to warrant further attention.

The advertising objective is accordingly to stimulate the loyalty (or to improve the repeat-purchase rate) of a consumer target defined as housewives with children at home who are working full or part-time outside the home. The social class and age classification of the segment is known and this is important for media planning.

The creative task may be determined by qualitative work among women representative of the segment. 'Depth' interviews or group discussions may suggest that, in this product field, the target consumer is anxious to maintain her home-making role in spite of the demands of outside work. The creative task might then be defined as supporting the domestic confidence of these hard-pressed women. There is, of course, more than one way of doing this in an advertising campaign!

If advertising objectves are agreed between client and agency at the outset, and if the creative task is defined at an early stage, there are defined standards for experimental and, finally, monitoring purposes.

8.2 Stages in the Advertising Research Programme

The creative research programme we are going to follow is based on Stephen King's 'The Cycle of Advertising Research'.[1]

8.2.1 THE STRATEGIC PLANNING STAGE

The data considered range from client's sales figures, through trend data derived from subscription to consumer panels and/or retail audits, to repeated attitude surveys tracking consumer responses to brands on the market; tests carried out during the development of the product,

1. King, S. (1967), *Can Research Evaluate the Creative Content of Advertising?*, MRS Conference Papers.

descriptive surveys including segmentation studies and qualitative work on file. This listing does not include the media statistics which we will be discussing in Chapter 9.

The wealth of data made available by electronic data processing has created a developing role for planners in advertising agencies: to help ensure that the available data is effectively digested and to act as purveyors of the relevant and stimulating findings of research. The purveyor role is especially important when it comes to briefing creative people. To do this effectively requires a rare combination of the analytical and creative faculties. *The advertising objective(s) are defined at this stage and the creative group briefed.*

If the marketing company has studied consumers in sufficient detail (if, for example, it has carried out a segmentation study), the *consumer target* and the *benefits to be conveyed to the target* can be sharply defined when media and creative groups in the advertising agency are briefed.

As with product testing, definition of target and benefit(s) specifies the type of consumer to be involved in qualitative and experimental work, and *what perceptions of the product should be used as measures of advertising effectiveness.*

8.2.2 THE DEVELOPMENT OF CREATIVE IDEAS

Let us assume that the creative task has been defined during the strategic planning stage and that the creative group has been effectively briefed. At this early stage of creative development *qualitative work is commonly used to try out ideas.* A limited number of target consumers is shown creative ideas in an unfinished form. The degree of finish is a matter of judgment. The demands of time and cost suggest as rough as possible: what is wanted is response to ideas. These may be conveyed by, say, sketched layout plus headline, or perhaps, typed copy for print advertisements; storyboard or mocked-up video treatment for television commercials.

This material is used as a *stimulus for discussion* in groups or in individual interviews. The discussion or interview is taped so that the creative group (who should in any case be involved in the research work) can play it back. In some agencies, videotape or one-way mirrors are used so that 'body language' may be observed by the creative staff.

No attempt is made to count heads. The numbers taking part in this qualitative work are sufficient to generate a good range of ideas and reactions, but not for statistical analysis. Content of the tapes is analysed in terms of:

- ideas about the product derived from the advertising stimulus, including ideas about the kind of people who might be expected to use the product;

- the extent to which those taking part associate themselves with the product and the context in which it is shown;
- features ignored, which may indicate either that the message is unclear or that those present are disassociating themselves from this aspect.

8.2.3 THE GO/NO GO DECISION STAGE

This is a crucial and contentious stage. Creative ideas have jelled. It may be necessary to give statistical support to the agency proposal; or to choose between, say two, worked-out approaches. The problem has been well stated by Stephen King.[2]

What is now wanted is:

'a quantified measurement of future performance in real conditions'

without incurring the cost of the complete marketing effort and without meeting the competition in the market place. Stephen King makes the point that, while it is impossible to predict sales achievement at this stage (quite apart from the problem of relating sales to advertising, see Section 8.2.4) it *is* possible to measure success in achieving

'the desired responses to the brand of the target consumer'.

The debate centres around discussion as to whether these *intermediate measures* are truly predictive of performance in the market place. Is it possible to *pre-test* advertising effectiveness?

We shall be better placed to answer this question when we have considered some theories as to how advertising works (see Section 8.3) and some of the experimental designs commonly used to test creative work before campaign exposure (see Section 8.4 where we return to the validity of pre-tests).

8.2.4 CAMPAIGN EXPOSURE

Once the creative campaign is out and about in the media it gets difficult to distinguish the effect of the creative work from that of the media selection. After exposure, advertising research is often used to see whether the opportunities to see/hear the creative message, offered by the media selected, are in fact being taken by the target consumers. Results of the recognition checks and campaign penetration studies considered in Chapter 9 are used (a) to monitor performance and (b) to refine future media scheduling: for the process is a circular one.

Of course what we would like to be able to do at this stage is to relate the advertising costs to sales achievement. A simple cause and

---

2. King, S. (March 1968), 'What can Pre-testing Do?', ADMAP.

effect relationship between advertising and sales *can* be observed when response is direct, as in mail order. In most cases *other marketing factors intervene.* Has the sales force, perhaps aided by dealer incentives, been able to achieve not only distribution but 'stand out' value for the brand? What level of competitive activity is the campaign provoking? We discuss the research methods used to help answer questions such as these in Chapter 10.

In the meantime, the grey area is shrinking with the increasing availability of disaggregated data — 'within person' and 'shop by shop' — and the associated development of computer programmes which examine relationships between the brand and media consumption of *individuals* over time: while the availability of 'shop by shop' data will in due course make it easier to establish the effect of distributive, as opposed to advertising, tactics. We return to this subject when considering monitoring procedures in Chapter 11.

The problem of separating the effect of the creative work from the effect of the media planning remains.

8.3 How Advertising Works

It is now generally accepted that there can be no one all-embracing theory because advertising tasks are so varied. To take two extreme cases:

> In *'direct response'* advertising the goods are sold to the consumer in an advertisement and delivery is direct from manufacturer/ marketing company on receipt of cash or credit card number. The Sunday supplements carry many advertisements of this kind.
> In *'corporate image'* advertising the objective may be to protect profit growth from attack by political and social pressure groups; and the advertising task to keep the public informed about technological achievements of benefit to the community. ICI's 'Pathfinders' campaign is an example of 'corporate image' advertising.[3]

In the *direct response* case, sales are substantially attributable to an advertisement in a particular medium (provided the print advertisement, television or radio commercial has a code attached to it, and the purchaser refers to the code!).

In the *corporate image* case, the effect of the campaign is likely to be measured by asking members of the public awareness and attitude questions in ad hoc surveys carried out at regular intervals, say once a year. By asking a standard core of questions in each survey it is possible to keep track of changes in the image of the enterprise held by the

3. Worcester, R.M. and Mansbridge, E. (October 1977), 'Tracking Studies: basis for decision making', *Journal of the Market Research Society*.

general public. *Brand images* are similarly monitored (Chapters 10 & 11).

In the direct response case, advertising can be said *to convert*: in the corporate image case, *to reinforce*. Let us now see how these two conceptions of the advertising task, conversion and reinforcement, arose.

In order to plan advertising research it is as well to have some conception of the different ways in which advertising may work. Some of the concepts are briefly reviewed (see Sections 8.3.1 to 8.3.4) following a more or less chronological order: but there is a vast literature on the subject so some suggestions for further reading are given at the end of the chapter.

8.3.1 THE EARLY MODELS

The earliest model is probably *AIDA*. This model postulates a simple relationship between advertising and selling.[4] Provided the advertising succeeds in attracting attention, arousing interest and stimulating desire, the result is a sale:

Attention → Interest → Desire → Action.

Colley's *DAGMAR* model is more sophisticated in its approach, but the advertising process is still seen as one of *step by step to conversion*. DAGMAR stands for 'Defining Advertising Goals for Measured Advertising Results,[5] the goals being to achieve in the consumer:

Awareness → Comprehension → Conviction → Action

Lavidge and Steiner's 'Hierarchy of effects' model[6] draws on the theory that an attitude embraces three elements or states — cognition (knowing), affect (evaluation) and conation (action): but the advertising process is still seen as one in which, for the potential consumer, a change of attitude will precede a change in behaviour:

Conation	Purchase
	Conviction
Affect	Preference
	Liking
Cognition	Knowledge
	Awareness

The assumption that attitude change precedes change in behaviour ignores the implications of Festinger's theory of *cognitive dissonance*.

---

4. Strong, E.K. (1925), *The Psychology of Selling*, Maidenhead, McGraw-Hill.
5. Colley, R.H. (1961), *Defining Advertising Goals for Measured Advertising Results*, New York, Association of National Advertisers.
6. Lavidge, R.J. and Steiner, G.A. (1961), 'A Model for Predictive Measurement of Advertising Effectiveness', *Journal of Marketing*.

Individuals aim to achieve consonance or harmony in their thinking and feeling. Choosing (as between products, brands and services) threatens a consumer with *post-decisional dissonance*.

> The magnitude of post-decision dissonance is an increasing function of the general importance of the decision and of the relative attractiveness of the unchosen alternative.[7]

It has been shown that car buyers are more likely to look at advertisements for the car they have just bought than for those they did not choose: while Ehrenberg's work on disaggregated panel data has proved beyond a doubt that advertisements for fast-moving brands are more likely to be perceived by those who buy them.[8]

In other words, it is now generally accepted that a change in attitude may either precede or follow action: that the relationship may work in either direction.

Attitude   Behaviour

8.3.2 THE REINFORCEMENT ROLE

Dissonance theory suggests that advertising has a reinforcement role to play, for, by reassuring consumers that they have made a sensible choice, loyalty to a particular model or brand is reinforced.

Ehrenberg's rigorous examination of disaggregated panel data has shown that, in many product fields, 100% loyalty to a brand is rare indeed: on the other hand, choice is not haphazard.

> Let us assume that a typical shopper's short-list is of three brands, E, F, G: that her habitual pattern of buying is E, E, F, G: and our brand is G. It would clearly improve our brand share if this shopper's buying of G were sufficiently frequent in relation to E and F to create an habitual buying pattern of G, E, F, G. The advertising task might then be to reinforce the attraction of G for those who already use the brand from time to time.

For established brands, *sales increases* represent only a *small proportion of total sales* in any one period and reinforcement of the status quo is essential to the maintenance of profit contribution. But consumers die, move out of the country or get too old for the product, and, as Corlett pointed out:

---

7. Festinger, L. (1957), *A Theory of Cognitive Dissonance*, Stanford, Stanford University Press.
8. Ehrenberg, A.S.C. (1972), *Repeat-buying, theory and applications*, Amsterdam, North-Holland Publishing Company.

Brands grow partly through attracting new buyers, partly through increased frequency of buying among existing users.[9]

The relative importance of these two roles, conversion and reinforcement, will depend on the nature of the market and the position of the brand in the market.

New users (converts) are essential to the baby food market. But this is a field in which cognitive dissonance is particularly painful, and reassurance, through reinforcement of the choice made, a powerful weapon for good (or ill, as in some developing countries).

Finally, there are of course situations in which advertising is used to defend a brand's position and the advertiser is satisfied if market share is maintained without any increase in advertising or other marketing costs.

8.3.3 USP AND 'BRAND IMAGE'

These two models were developed in New York advertising agencies in the early 1960s: the 'Unique Selling Proposition' by Rosser Reeves and the 'brand image' concept by David Ogilvy.

The Unique Selling Proposition (1961). In the rare case of a product with a unique, and desirable, attribute, definition of the USP is a straightforward matter. But integral differences between brands in a product field are often marginal and a USP is likely to be suggested by study of consumer habits and attitudes in the product field: to quote a classic example, use of toothpaste + fear of bad breath = 'the Colgate ring of confidence'. The USP, once defined, must be adhered to in every communication about the brand. This is a behaviourist approach to 'how advertising works' and, as with Pavlov's dogs, repetition is of the essence. Time is needed to condition the consumer to associate the proposition with the brand.

'Brand image' (1963). David Ogilvy's concept of the 'brand image' has proved more fruitful in the development of creative advertising. Consumers buy *brands* (not products or services) and by developing a personality for the brand (as opposed to attaching a proposition to it) the brand is made more meaningful to the consumer and this added value strengthens loyalty. The consumer is treated as a rational being with conscious ends in view and a defined self-image. Brand loyalty is strong when there is empathy between the brand's image and the consumer's self-image.

Recall and *awareness* are likely measures to use when assessing the effectiveness of a USP campaign; while *attitude measurement* and the tracking of changes in attitude over time are essential to 'image' studies.

---

9. Corlett, T. (1977), *How can we Monitor the Influences of Advertising Campaigns on Consumers' Purchasing Behaviour?*, MRS Conference.

8.3.4 FISHBEIN AND BUYING INTENTION

'Intention to buy' (or 'try') questions are now accepted as valid indicators of consumer response to products and the advertising associated with them. The answers have been shown to have predictive value. As a result of Fishbein's work on attitude theory and measurement[10] investigations into consumer habits and attitudes now often include attitude questions relating to *the act of purchase*.

Fishbein postulates that *behavioural intention* (BI) is the product of how we feel about the act ('attitude towards the act', Aact) — and in our context the act is buying a brand — plus how we feel about society's attitude towards the act (SN, a subjective norm). In the formula given below w_1 and w_2 are weights representing the strength of our wanting to carry out the act (buying or trying the brand) and the extent to which this might be modified by social considerations:

$$BI = A \ \text{act}_{w_1} + SN_{w_2}$$

There is a lucid and helpful analysis of Fishbein's model in Tuck's *How do we choose?*[11] The Fishbein finding that 'simple behavioural intention can give a good indication of the trend of mass consumer behaviour in the relatively short term' is supported by Unilever experience. Two Unilever subsidiaries have done extensive work in this field, Lintas and Research Bureau Limited.

Lintas asked 'housewives and heads of households' in 492 households whether they would buy/use over the next three years:

more   less   about the same

of a large number of goods and services. '. . . when compared with data later released by the Central Statistical Office, the predicted overall trend was confirmed'.[12]

RBL has long made a practice of asking *'intention to buy'* questions. The data have been systematically filed and (where possible) correlated with actual purchase data. Experience has shown that[13]

> (intention to buy) scores indicate how far the total message effect adds up to a feeling of wanting to buy the brand (as opposed to, say, just enjoying the ad.), and this feeling is related to subsequent sales.

An experimental design used by RBL to assess advertising effectiveness is described in Section 8.4.2.

---

10. Fishbein, M. (1967), *Readings: Attitude Theory and Measurement*, New York, Wiley.
11. Tuck, M. (1976), *How do we Choose? A study in Consumer Behaviour*. London, Methuen.
12. de Groot, G. (1980), *Changes in Consumer Attitudes and Behaviour and its Consequences for Marketing and Research in the 1980s*, MRS Conference.
13. Twyman, W.A. (1973), *Designing Advertising Research for Marketing Decisions*, MRS Conference Papers.

8.4 Measures of Advertising Effectiveness

Before discussing experimentation at the Go/No Go decision stage (see Section 8.2.3) we ought perhaps to remind ourselves that:

- — our concern is with the target consumer's response to the brand and to the kind of people seen as likely to use it: we are not asking for artistic verdicts;
- — qualitative work at the creative development stage (see Section 8.2.2) will have indicated whether or not target consumers understand what the advertising is trying to convey, and how far they associate themselves with this message.

It is unlikely that qualitative work will have been carried out with a sufficiently large number of target consumers to bear statistical analysis, and the reassurance of numbers may be wanted. (Much depends on the nature of the client and the authority of the creative group within the agency.)

The validity of pre-tests is often debated. Experiments are carried out in unreal circumstances. Results are often based on comparison between individual advertisements representing different approaches to the creative task.

Are lab. type experiments which compare the effects achieved by individual advertisements, valid predictors of the response to be anticipated to a series of advertisements appearing in the media over a period of time?

In addition, there is doubt about the validity of the measures used to assess advertising effects whether these be verbal measures such as recall, physiological responses recorded by instruments such as the psychogalvanometer (see Section 8.4.3) or behavioural measures such as coupon redemption. In most experiments, the measures used are verbal ones, and they are often referred to as *intermediate* or *indirect* because they fall short of measuring sales.

8.4.1 VERBAL MEASURES

At the pre-testing stage, i.e. before campaign exposure, the most commonly used measures of creative effectiveness are:

Recall, *Unaided and Aided*
Attitude *towards the product/brand and its likely users*
Intention to Buy

Questions relating to the respondent's habitual BEHAVIOUR in the product field will often help to determine whether the respondent

is a suitable participant in the test. They will also contribute to interpretation of the answers to recall, attitude and intention to buy
questions.

Impact is the result of:

— the information conveyed to the respondent (usually measured
by recall);
— the respondent's emotional response to the brand (measured by
attitude questions);
— the strength of the respondent's desire for the brand (as indicated
by intention to buy questions).

We are close to the hierarchical models with their cognitive, affec-
tive and conative components (see Section 8.3.1) but with two important
differences:

— we recognise that attitude change can be the effect as well as
the cause of a change in behaviour, that it can be *'post' as well as
'pre' action*;
— we distinguish between attitudes towards the brand and those
who might use it, and attitudes towards the act of purchasing or
behavioural intention.

Once the campaign is out in the real world *recognition* is an important measure. Recognition checks whether or not an advertisement has
been noticed. This will, of course, depend on the effectiveness of the
media planning and buying as well as on the creative impact.

Awareness, campaign penetration and salience are other terms used
when discussing advertising research after campaign exposure (post-
testing). Awareness covers a range of responses from mere recognition
to unaided recall of the attributes the advertising seeks to associate with
the brand. Campaign penetration and salience are 'post-testing' (i.e. after
exposure in the media) measures, used when we need to know whether
the opportunities to see, view or hear offered by the media schedule are
in fact being taken.

8.4.2 TESTING BEFORE CAMPAIGN EXPOSURE — THREE METHODOLOGIES

The folder or reel test — a lab.-type experiment. Let us assume that the
creative group has come up with two possible solutions to the creative
task.

The test material: two folders or videotape reels are prepared
containing a selection of advertisements with which the proposed
advertisements will have to compete for attention. The competitive

advertisements are likely to represent a variety of product fields. The two folders/reels are identical except for the test advertisements, assigned one to each, and placed in the same position relative to the rest of the content. It is, of course, important that the test material be of the same degree of finish as the rest of the content.

The design: monadic, using two matched samples of 50—100 members of the target population.

Procedure: The respondents are asked to go through one of the folders or to watch one of the tapes. They are then asked which advertisements they happen to have noticed. Given that the brand is an established one (as is often the case in advertising research) the test advertisement will not stand out as being of special interest to the interviewer. Once *unaided recall* has been recorded, a list of the brands in the test is shown to the respondent as a memory trigger. The respondent may be asked which was most liked and which was liked least, or which 'you would most like to talk about'. Procedures vary but essentially attention is gradually focused on the test advertisement and recall of its content.

Recording of aided recall must of course be differentiated from unaided recall, and the order in which advertisements and product attributes are mentioned is likely to be significant as a measure of salience.

Measurement of results: Applying the notation used in Figure 15 we have an *after only* design based on two matched experimental groups, here E_1 and E_2:

Group	Treatment	Observation	Measurement
E_1	X_1	O_1	O_1 compared with
E_2	X_2	O_2	O_2 in a controlled context.

The basis for comparison is not likely to be limited to recall. Attitude and intention to buy questions may also be asked: while behaviour in the product field will be taken into account.

Testing in the field before campaign exposure. If the brand is on sale it is possible to pre-test in the field by arranging for the run of a publication to be 'split', so that different areas receive issues with different advertisements; or by arranging for different transmitters to put out different commercials. Here again the context is controlled: same television programme, same publication: the independent variable being the advertisement.

Here again the measures used to determine the relative effectiveness of the alternative advertising approaches are recall (unaided and aided), attitude questions, intention to buy (if not already doing so) in the light of experience to date in the product field.

The setting up of this kind of experiment is straightforward enough, publishers and independent television contractors offer standard packages as part of their own sales promotional activity.

The main procedural difficulties are:

— contacting suitable, i.e. target group, respondents;
— matching experimental groups on critical product use and demographic criteria;
— making sure that respondents *have in fact been exposed to the test material*.

A question relating to editorial content of the issue, or, in the case of television about adjacent programmes, is the usual way of establishing that the responses recorded relate to the advertisements whose impact we are trying to assess.

An 'after-only with control' example. When we pre-test the effect of communications we would like to be able to take a 'before' measurement and to base our conclusions on observation of the changes effected by the advertising material on the respondent's awareness, attitudes and intentions with regard to the brand. But we know that questions asked at the first interview are likely to influence responses at the second (see Section 7.2.1).

Research Bureau Limited (a Unilever subsidiary), have validated a procedure which sidesteps this difficulty:

— *two samples* of about 100 target consumers are matched on about two demographic characteristics and, where relevant, on some aspect of brand or product field usage;
— *the experimental group* receives the advertising test material *plus* some other prompting stimulus such as a pack shot;
— *the control group* receives the other prompting stimulus *without* the advertising material;
— *the two samples are questioned about the brand* and the added value of the advertising material is appraised by comparing the responses of the experimental group with those of the control group.
  As we saw in Section 8.3.4, RBL attach considerable importance to the intention to buy measure;[13]
— *the design* (using the notation shown in Figure 15) is, given $X =$ advertising test material and $Y =$ the other stimulus:

Group	Treatment	Observation	Measurement[14]
E	$X + Y$	O_1	$O_1 - O_2$
C	Y	O_2	

---

14. It is possible of course that some of the verbal measures used may not show a positive result for E, the experimental group, and that the overall result may not show value being added by the advertising.

In an 'after-only with control' design sampling error will be greater than it would be if both sets of measurements were taken on the same sample of respondents, as in a before-after design. In order to avoid the possible bias due to the learning effect, communications research relies very often on a comparison of responses from more than one group, whether these be two experimental groups, as in our first example, or an experimental group with a control group. Matching of the groups is critical and it is advisable to ensure that[13]

> test and control samples . . . use the same interviewers in matched locations . . . .

When commercials are being tested, the location is likely to be a van, suitably equipped, or a hall.

8.4.3 PRE-TESTING WITH INSTRUMENTS

There is a good case for using mechanical means of observation when testing the stand-out effect of pack designs (see Section 7.5.2). For a time lab. type experiments using mechanical observation were fashionable in communications research: but the following considerations now count against the use of 'ironmongery' to measure advertising effects:

— use of measuring devices such as the tachistoscope or psychogalvanometer restricts the venue for the experiment to a test centre or mobile van and adds to the cost of data collection, for the ironmongery is expensive and the procedure likely to be time-consuming;
— artificiality of the circumstances in which the advertising material is exposed to target consumers reduces belief in the external validity of their responses;
— it is usually necessary to ask questions in order to interpret the meaning of the physiological observations recorded by the instruments.

We are going to consider three devices: the tachistoscope, the psychogalvanometer and the 'direct eye movement observation system' (DEMOS) developed by the British Market Research Bureau.

The tachistoscope is relevant to the testing of posters for stand-out value, and it could be claimed that the more speedily perceived of two advertisements has the better chance of being noticed in the press or during a commercial break on ITV. But, posters apart, experiments based on verbal measures are likely to produce richer and more actionable data at less cost. It is always possible, of course, to combine the physiological and verbal procedures: to record the speed with which elements in the advertisement are perceived and then to ask the recall, attitude and intention questions.

The psychogalvanometer. The case for physiological measurements rests on doubts about the capacity of researchers to ask meaningful questions and of consumers to give true answers. Response to an advertising stimulus when attached to the psychogalvanometer (or 'lie detector') is involuntary. Electrodes attached to the hands measure sweat levels, an autonomic indicator of emotional arousal. Provided the temperature of the research centre, or van, is kept stable, comparison of fluctuations with a base measurement will show how the respondent reacts to the development of a commercial, or to the sight of a press advertisement or sound of a radio commercial. The emotional responses are duly recorded but the nature of the responses, whether these are favourable or unfavourable, has to be elicited by means of questions.

DEMOS is of particular interest because the system produces both creative and media planning data. The procedure is as follows:

— A member of the target group is invited to a research centre and is ushered into a small waiting room.
— Here there is only one place to sit, face to face with a magazine or newspaper positioned in front of a mirror.
— Concentration on the reading matter is encouraged by the fact that someone is working at a desk in the room.
— Concealed cameras and carefully positioned mirrors make it possible to record on film not only the pages looked at but also how the eyes move over the page. The DEMOS 'set-up' is illustrated in Figure 22.

Creative application of DEMOS. If our test were concerned with only one advertising treatment, we would be left in doubt as to whether the attention gained by the advertisement were due to its creative content or to its position in the publication, and the positioning of advertisements in publications is of concern to media planners.

If we used DEMOS to compare the attention gained by one advertising treatment with that gained by another, and ensured that the two advertisements appeared in the identical position in the same issue of the same publication, we could attribute the observed differences in eye movements to the creative impact of the advertisements: always assuming, of course, that the data were derived from two well-matched samples. (DEMOS can also be used to observe the attention-getting power of different parts of an advertisement.)

Eye movement having been filmed, the respondent may be invited into another room where recall, attitude and intention to buy questions can be asked, as in a folder test. *Verbal responses can then be related to observed behaviour.* The respondent must be told he/she has been filmed:

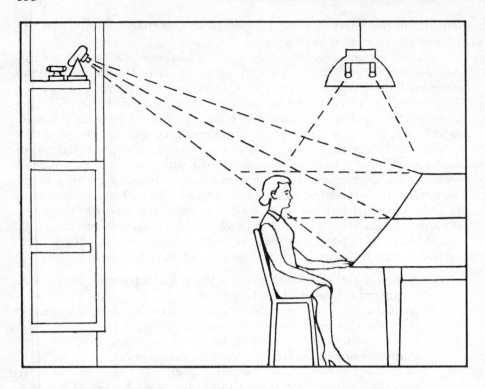

Figure 22. Direct Eye Movement Observation System (DEMOS)

and the film could itself be used as a stimulus in an unstructured interview.

Media application of DEMOS. The procedure makes it possible to compare the attention gained by an advertisement:

— in one print medium compared with another;
— in one position compared with another in the same newspaper or magazine;
— in colour as compared with black and white, or in one size compared with another (e.g. a full page compared with a half page) in the same newspaper or magazine.

In addition it is possible to build up normative data relating to page traffic and to the relationship between advertising and editorial content, subjects of more general interest to media planners. But we are anticipating Chapter 9 and must point out that there are more cost-effective ways of collecting the data on a sufficiently large sample to stand statistical analysis.

8.4.4 PRE-TESTING: COMMUNICATION PLUS PRODUCT

The design considered here moves the Go/No Go decision for a new brand as close to market commitment as is possible in lab. pre-testing conditions.[15]

In Section 7.4.7 we looked at a monadic test procedure developed for General Foods. This type of design, in which the product idea is introduced in some, often unfinished, form before the product is tried, is now a commonly used one.

The communication plus product design developed by Gordon Coulson Associates is of particular interest because:

— the test conditions are made as 'real-life' as possible;
— a 'likelihood of buying' measure is used (see Section 8.3.4);
— concept and 'in use' responses are used, suitably adjusted, to predict *penetration* and *repeat purchase*. (We meet these two important predictors of brand share in Chapter 10.)

The experimental design can also, of course, be used to compare different combinations of communication, pack design and product and price: but, as we shall see, real life simulation must add to research costs; and to avoid the learning effect the design would need to be a monadic one with groups of testers matched.

To get as close as possible to real life:

— advertising and pack are 'finished' — they may not be final but they appear so;
— the pack is of a size it is intended to market;
— the target consumer tries the product where it would normally be used (kitchen, bathroom, garage etc.);
— sufficient time is allowed for a thorough trial by all who might share in the use of the product;
— the brand is introduced as being on the market elsewhere.

In addition to the likelihood of buying question, questions are asked about the product and the kind of people who would use it, how it would be used and its price, both at the concept stage (i.e. before it has been tried) and after trial.

Responses to the likelihood of buying question sort repondents/testers into either three or four groups: three if the trial of the product is limited to those who say they are likely to buy after meeting advertising and pack; four if all those who are willing to try the product are

15. See Coulson, G. (March 1980), 'Total package (or Marketing Mix) Research for a New Brand', in 'New Product Development', supplement to *MRS Newsletter*, London, the Market Research Society; and Clarke, K. and Roe, M. (1977), *The Marketing Mix Test — relating expectations and performance*, MRS Conference Papers.

given the opportunity to do so, even if they have said they are unlikely to buy. As can be seen, extending the trial to those would would be unlikely to buy it has diagnostic value:

	Likelihood of Buying		
Group	Pre-trial	Post-trial	Marketing implications
1	Yes	Yes	All clear
2	Yes	No	Product does not live up to expectations.
3	No	Excluded	'Idea' of the brand does not engender initial buying
If 3 not excluded			
3	No	Yes	Presentation of the 'idea' needs re-thinking.
4	No	No	Brand (as it stands) a non-starter.

If our objective is choice of one advertising creative approach as compared with another, we recruit two matched test samples, vary the communication but hold other elements, such as price, steady.

If we want to predict *penetration* from the pre-trial results and *repeat-buying* from the post-trial results we have to allow for the fact that the consumer's introduction to the brand has been 'hot-housed' in two respects: 100% awareness of the brand and its advertising plus 100% distribution has been achieved.

In a well researched market, given a known advertising appropriation and sufficiently advanced media plans, it is possible to estimate *the probability of awareness being achieved*: indeed, as we shall see in Chapter 9, cost-effective media planning depends on estimation of the likelihood of opportunities to read/view/hear being taken by the target market.

Similarly, given access to trend data relating to retail distribution in the product field, it is possible to estimate *how effective* the *distribution of our brand is likely to be*, given the strength of the competition and the promotional support planned for our entry. This subject is covered in more detail in Chapter 10.

Conclusion

In order to create effective advertising it is necessary:

— to consider how advertising can work to further the marketing objective; and so
— to arrive at a definition of a specific advertising objective.

Given an adequate advertising appropriation, successful achievement of the advertising objective depends on a combination of effective media planning and the capacity to create persuasive advertisements.

Advertising is a substantial marketing cost, especially where branded consumer products are concerned. With considerable sums at stake (see Chapter 9) advertisers are not, as a rule, happy to take creative work entirely on trust; while advertising agents, including their creative staff, seek reassurance that they are on the right lines.

The usefulness of qualitative work to stimulate creative thinking and to try out ideas is generally accepted (see Section 8.2.2). The external validity of creative pre-tests and the reliability of intermediate measures are often debated (see Section 8.4).

A Gallup enquiry among 28 leading advertisers and 26 advertising agencies into pre-testing methods clearly showed the following divergence of opinion. The enquiry was made in 1969, but the divergence still holds good today:

> Research managers of advertising companies want some form of quantitative check on the commercials their agencies produce before they allow media expenditure to be incurred. Agency researchers, however, are sceptical of current pre-testing techniques and tend to limit the role of pre-testing to that of providing diagnostic information for the development of commercials.[16]

It can perhaps be concluded that pre-testing at the development stage serves a useful screening purpose provided experiments are intelligently designed and not too dogmatically interpreted. It is necessary to commit resources to an experiment in the field (see Chapter 10), and to run this for an adequate length of time, to arrive at a definitive answer. And this experiment in the field will be measuring the combined effect of message and medium.

Suggestions for Further Reading

Broadbent, S. (July 1979), 'One-way TV Advertisements Work', *Journal of the Market Research Society*.

Lunn, A.A., Baldwin, A.A. and Dickens, A.A. (November 1972), 'Monitoring Consumer Life Styles', ADMAP.

Twyman, A. (1980), 'Advertising Research in the Eighties, A Research Agency Viewpoint', MRS Conference.

Wells, W.D. (May 1975), 'Psychographics: A Critical Review', *Journal of Marketing Research*, pp. 196–213.

---

16. Gregory, W. and Fanning, J. (1969), 'Researching Research', *The Market for TV Commercials Pre-testing*, ESOMAR.

CHAPTER 9

Communications Research: (2)Media Selection

Introduction

Chapter 8 opened with a definition of advertising, as opposed to marketing, objectives (Section 8.1), reviewed the kind of data consulted when advertising strategies are being planned (Section 8.2.1) and made the point that it is difficult to distinguish impact due to creative work from impact due to media planning once the campaign is exposed in the media (Section 8.2.4).

The close relationship between 'message' and 'medium' is stressed in the introduction to Chapter 8, and Figure 21 is relevant to Chapter 9 as well as Chapter 8. It might indeed be helpful to refer back to Figure 21 before embarking on Chapter 9.

Chapter 9 defines the media planner's task, reviews the research data commonly consulted, considers how these data may be used to reduce uncertainty when making scheduling choices; and considers whether standard measures of 'reading' and 'viewing' indicate that advertisements are, without a doubt, read or viewed, as the case may be.

Advertisers spend over a thousand million pounds a year on display (as opposed to classified) advertising.

About half this expenditure is on print media (newspapers and magazines);
40% on television;
10% on 'support media': posters, radio, cinema.

Given the substantial sum of money involved, it is not surprising that the advertising industry (advertisers + advertising agents + media owners) combines to carry out continuous research into the reading and viewing habits of the UK population. This research is planned and

162

Adults. For press research (JICNARS), this is defined as individuals aged 15 years and over. For television research (JICTAR), the definition is individuals aged 16 and over.

Burst. This is a single period of continuous advertising mainly used in describing television plans. A burst is usually short and a campaign may contain several bursts with gaps between each.

Candidate Publications. These are publications selected for inclusion in a cost-efficiency ranking because the profile of their readers, as shown by published sources, is broadly in line with the profile of the target market.

Cost per Thousand. The cost of the advertisement divided by the number of persons in thousands in the target market which the advertisement reaches. (See *Reach or Coverage*.)

Frequency. This is a measure of how often the advertising is repeated against the target market. It can be measured either by (a) opportunity to see or (b) exposure.

(a) *Opportunity to see* is a chance of seeing the advertising because the individual looks at a publication in which the advertising is printed; or, with regard to television, is in the room during the quarter hour within which the commercial is screened.
(b) *Exposure* is a measure of whether or not the opportunity to see is taken up. It implies eyes open in front of the advertising and is estimated by applying page traffic scores in press and presence scores in television (see Sections 9.3.2 and 9.4.2).

Frequency Distribution. This is a statement of exactly how many people in the target market receive one opportunity to see the advertising, how many receive two opportunities to see and so on.

Market Weight. A numerical weight applied to one part of a target market to show its relative importance when compared with other parts of the same market (see Section 9.2).

Overlap. That part of the country falling within the (reception) boundary of more than one ITV area.

Reach or Coverage. This is the proportion of the target market which will be contacted by the advertising. Contact is defined as having at least one opportunity to see.

Television Rating (TVR). A UK advertiser does not normally buy spots; he buys audiences. The size of the audience is expressed in 'Television Ratings' (TVRs). 1 TVR is equal to 1% of the potential viewing category. Thus, if a spot on London reaches 25% of the London universe, it has achieved 25 TVRs.

Source Ogilvy and Mather (January 1979), 'Media Scene: United Kingdom'

Figure 23. Media Terminology

managed by a series of Joint Industry Committees on which the interested parties are represented:

Joint Industry Committee for National Readership Surveys — JICNARS;

Joint Industry Committee for Television Advertising Research — JICTAR;

with, reporting less regularly:

Joint Industry Committee for Poster Audience Surveys — JICPAS;

Joint Industry Committee for Radio Audience Research — JICRAR.

We discuss the nature of the data derived from these and other sources as this chapter develops, but it might perhaps be as well to familiarise ourselves with the terminology used in media circles before considering the task facing the media planner. The more commonly used terms are defined in Figure 23.

9.1 What the Media Planner Needs to Know

The media planner will, of course, need to know the advertising objectives as agreed between client and agency. He/she will, more specifically, need the following information:

Definition of the target in the market. Demographic characteristics of the target are of first importance because most of the industry data are classified by sex, social grade, age group, whether a housewife and by region.

The JICNARS data include classification of readers by a range of life-style indicators: 'car-owning households', 'chief petrol buyers', 'owners of cheque books', 'holiday takers', etc.

Ownership of a range of durables is also recorded. (The social and marketing richness of the JICNARS data is reviewed in Section 9.4.) The JICTAR data are based on the standard demographics (see Section 9.3). As we saw in Chapter 6 a market segment is not viable unless it is accessible and in consumer markets this means accessible through the media. For media planning purposes it is necessary to translate psychographic classifications and product use classifications into demographic terms. In order to do this, it is necessary to record respondents' demographic and product use characteristics when collecting data about their wants, perceptions and attitudes (see Section 6.6).

Regional strengths and weaknesses. A brand may be more successful in, say, London and South ITV areas than in Lancashire, Yorkshire and the North East. This may be peculiar to the brand or it may apply to the product field as a whole. Given variation in share by area the media planner needs to know whether the advertising objective is to be achieved by building on strength, counteracting weakness or a judicious combination of the two.

The decision will influence the allocation of the media appropriation as between areas and it may determine the choice of media category. Television and the regional press, together with radio, posters and cinema can be scheduled on a regional basis. In general, national newspapers and magazines are not so flexible (though special arrangements can sometimes be made in test markets).

Seasonal nature of the product. Given a product or service with seasonal appeal the tactical decision 'from strength' or 'against weakness' still applies when allocating the appropriation. Should we concentrate expenditure in the high season or seek to extend demand by showing the product (which might be soup or ice cream) to be appropriate outside its season: for example by popularising ice cream as a year-round pudding.

The nature of the creative task. If the product has a demonstrable benefit, use of the television medium is indicated. Television is a 'natural' for the advertising of gas for cooking because, among fuels, gas alone offers the immediate control, up or down, which cooks need on occasion.

On the other hand television is a mass, 'blanket' medium, while print media can be selected for the special interest, authority or ambience conveyed by their editorial content and presentation.

The competitive advertising. How much the competition is spending and in what media can be monitored by subscribing to *MEAL* (Media Expenditure Analysis Limited) and deduced for television from the JICTAR weekly report. Confrontation or guerilla warfare? For a major advertiser the decision is likely to be confrontation: but it may be possible to plan a schedule which sidesteps the competition while offering effective reach, or coverage, of the target.

The size of the appropriation. This is usually determined in advance of media planning but in the rare cases where an unmodified 'objective and task' method is being used to determine the appropriation, the media planner will play an important part in fixing the appropriation. Whether the appropriation is laid down or arrived at in consultation with the media planner, the criterion of success in media planning is the achievement of the optimum mix of

reach (or coverage) X frequency X length/size

the last being influenced by creative considerations (see Section 9.2).

Conversion, reinforcement or both. This basic objective will affect how the appropriation is laid out over time. When a brand is launched, frequent appearances in the media, longer commercials and larger spaces may all be used to achieve penetration of the market in the shortest possible time so that the brand breaks even and makes a profit as soon as possible. With an established brand, reinforcement of existing usage may be more critical and a steady 'drip' rather than a 'burst' be required. Or there might be a case for combining the two, bursts linked by drips. It all depends on where the brand stands in its life-cycle, the size of the appropriation and the advertising task. (One part of the task may be to ensure shelf space for the brand. See Section 6.1 on retail buying power.)

9.2 Achieving Cost-effectiveness

It will help us to appreciate the relevance of the Joint Industry data if we consider what planning for cost-effectiveness involves before summarising the content of the reports and the methods used to collect the data.

It is comparatively easy to program a computer to rank media vehicles according to their coverage of the target market, and to relate coverage to rate-card post.

It is comparatively easy to programme a computer to tell us how many opportunities to see our advertisement can be bought with a given sum of money in a list of possible media.

The task gets more formidable when we seek to take account of *duplication* between, say, television and print media, or between newspapers and magazines, or between the individual publications we are considering for a particular schedule. The National Readership Survey provides valuable input data about duplication as between the readers of different publications, and the survey collects information about ITV viewing and about listening to IBA radio which indicates the intensity with which readers of specific newspapers and magazines also view or listen to radio.

But to achieve cost-effectiveness it is necessary to consider whether the opportunities being given to the target market to receive the advertising message are likely to be taken, and the probabilities will, of course, vary as between the broad media categories and as between the specific publications and viewing times being considered.

Whether or not the opportunities to see are effective and the message is received depends on

the frequency with which the advertisement appears;
the period of time over which it appears;
the frequency with which target readers see issues of publications and viewers view;
the creative impact achieved by the campaign.

If the creative work effectively conveys the product benefit, and if the media planning has been successfully focused on the target consumers in the market, we can expect selective perception to work in our favour.

The model developed by Dr Simon Broadbent may help to concentrate our minds.[1] He uses the expression 'Valued Impressions per Pound' (compare Kotler's 'Rated Exposures').[2]

$$VIP = \frac{\text{coverage of the target} \times \text{market weight(s)} \times \text{media weight(s)}}{\text{cost (£)}}$$

Let us consider the individual inputs in turn:

Coverage of the target: If we are advertising to a middle class ABC_1 audience, we can ignore $C_2 DE$ readers or viewers when relating coverage to cost.

Market weights: We may want to refine our estimate of effective coverage by taking account of the *relative* importance of groups in the target market. A company marketing baby food might well be particularly interested in reaching women aged 15–34. But older women sometimes have babies; also, as experienced mothers, older women may influence the decisions of younger women. Here it would be reasonable to apply a weight of 1 to the prime target, women aged 15–34, but to discount the value of the reading/viewing of older women by applying a weight of, say, 0.5 to the reading/viewing coverage recorded for them.

Media weights. The chance of an advertising campaign attracting the attention of members of the target group is clearly influenced by the readership of the publications on the schedule among members of the target group and, in the case of television, by their viewing habits. We can allow for the frequency with which respondents claim to read, view and listen when programming VIP and can apply weights to this end. (We consider how these data are collected in Sections 9.3 to 9.5.)

As we shall see, however, *reading* and *viewing* are *ambiguous concepts in media research*. Reading a publication can mean anything between reading it from beginning to end and glancing through it (see Section 9.4), while those recorded as viewing during our time slot may well miss our 30-second commercial (see Section 9.3).

We are on debateable ground when we attempt to weight media vehicles according to the probability that they will actually convey the message to the target group. In fact it is only worthwhile attempting to

---

1. Broadbent, S. (1979), *Spending Advertising Money*, London, Business Books.
2. Kotler, P. (1980), *Marketing Management, Analysis, Planning and Control*, 4th ed., Englewood Cliffs, N.J., Prentice-Hall, p. 508 et seq.

apply weights to take account of the probability of opportunities to see being taken if sound normative data are available.

If an advertiser is established in a particular product field, if *campaign penetration* has been monitored (see Section 11.1.3) regularly in terms of recognition or awareness levels achieved, and if it is possible to relate this achievement to individual media vehicles, then there might be a case for giving good carriers of the message preferential weights in the computer programming.

Weighting for ambience and/or authority is even more debateable since the weights are determined by judgment, unless post-exposure campaign monitoring has yielded statistical data sufficiently robust to warrant this refinement.

Cost. This is not necessarily the rate card cost. Indeed for print media it might pay us to run the computer program using market weights only and to use the resultant ranking of newspapers and magazines as a bargaining counter. The demand for television time is such that at present, and before the opening of the fourth channel, the ITV contractors quote prices between wide upper and lower limits and pre-empting is practised. To make *quite sure* of your spot it would be necessary to agree to the top, inflated price: otherwise you might be gazumped.

Total Expenditure

			1978		1979
£ millions			1,242		1,428
per cent			100		100
Print Media	%		%		
National newspapers	32		32		
Regional newspapers	30		30		
Magazines, Periodicals	21		21		
Directories	2		2		
Production	15	100	52	15	100	56
Television			39		33
Support Media					
Posters & Transport			5		6
Radio			3		4
Cinema			1		1

Source: Advertising Association.

Figure 24. Total Expenditure on Display Advertising

There is more satisfaction to be gained from planning and programming a schedule based on print media than one based on television. Booking uncertainties apart, the print media offer variety of choice while the data relating to consumer characteristics are far richer for print media than for television. However a detailed breakdown of print media expenditure shows television to be the dominating medium — in spite of the strike which reduced its 1979 share of total expenditure.

9.3 Television Audience Research

As from July 1983 television viewing statistics are due to be collected for the BBC and the IBA in a combined operation. At present there are differences in the populations sampled and in the data collection methods used so that BBC and IBA results conflict and there is a waste of financial resources.

Whatever the procedure adopted, data are likely to be collected for two different purposes in two different ways. It will be necessary:

— to establish UK reception characteristics, the boundaries of the areas reached by transmitters and stations, standards of reception and the extent to which new technological developments are available to, and used by, viewers, developments such as Prestel, Viewdata, Teletext, video disc, video games and cable linked TV;
— to provide for the continuous monitoring of television audiences for programming and advertising purposes.

The first calls for a large scale survey of households carried out at intervals, say once a year: the second for regular data collection from panels of viewers.

At the present time the BBC collects 'day-after' viewing data using quota samples and recall aided by means of printed programmes. The commercial procedure is summarised below. The independent television companies are, of course, as interested in statistics relating to the popularity or otherwise of programmes as are the BBC. They sell television audiences to advertisers and their agents.

9.3.1 THE JICTAR REPORTS AND SAMPLING PROCEDURES

The Joint Industry Committee for Television Advertising Research subcontracts fieldwork and analysis. The contract is currently held by Audits of Great Britain who have the electronic data processing equipment needed to meet the demand for practically instant *monitoring of the ITV audience*. There are two types of report, weekly and thrice-yearly: together with an annual television reception survey.

Television Buyers rely heavily on the weekly JICTAR report which comes out only eight days after the end of each week. This report logs the audience achieved in terms of TV ratings:

A UK advertiser does not normally buy spots; he buys audiences. The size of the audience is expressed in 'Television Ratings' (TVRs). 1 TVR is equal to 1% of the potential viewing category. Thus if a spot on London reaches 25% of the London universe, it has achieved 25 TVRs. It follows that if an advertiser purchases 10 spots, each delivering 25 TVRs, his total rating delivery would be 250 TVRs.[3]

For ITV homes viewing is recorded minute by minute, and by day of the week within ITV areas: for individuals data are recorded by quarter-hours, by day of the week within ITV areas. The difference in the *reporting interval* is due to the fact that homes viewing is derived from mechanical observation using a Setmeter, whereas individual viewing is recorded in a diary.

The Setmeter automatically records the time during which the set is switched on and the screen lit up. It records the station the set is switched on to. The results are, of course, of programming as well as of advertising interest.

The *Weekly Buying Report* records viewing for broad categories of individuals (as well as for homes): all adults, men, women, housewives and children. A more detailed demographic analysis of the audience is published three times a year (October, February and June) in an *Audience Composition report*. This gives social grade, age group and Terminal Education Age (TEA) of the audience and the report is of particular interest to media planners. The data are smoothed by averaging results over the four weeks previous to the reporting date.

These two reports are based on panels representative of the ITV homes and viewing population in each of the 13 ITV areas. The total number of homes on the panels is getting on for 3,000 and of individuals approaching 8,000. The representativeness of the panels is ensured by the *Television Reception Survey*.

This survey, based on a large probability sample, is carried out once a year. It establishes types of set in use and quality of reception. By asking questions about stations received it confirms ITV area boundaries and defines overlap areas. Knowing where reception areas overlap is, of course, of significance when marketing plans, e.g. market tests, are made and when the reach of television schedules is being considered.

The survey also records the demographic characteristics of the television audience and data are collected about the housewife's average

3. Ogilvy and Mather, (January 1979), 'Media Scene: United Kingdom'.

daily viewing. These data are used to help ensure that ITV homes on the panels are representative of *ITV viewing intensity*. The questions asked are:

During an average week on how many days do you, personally, watch TV?	(Recorded for 7, 6, 5, 3/4, 1/2 or less often)
On a day when you watch TV for about how many hours do you view?	(Recorded for 1 or less, over 1 up to 2, . . . over 9 up to 10)
About how many hours out of every 10 that you watch TV would you say you watched ITV?	(Recorded for None and then as above)

Respondents are sorted into three groups, the third who do the most viewing (heavy ITV viewers), the third who do the least (light ITV viewers) and the middle third (regular ITV viewers).

This questioning procedure is also used in the National Readership Survey (Section 9.4.2) to establish ITV viewing intensity of readers.

9.3.2 THE PROBLEM OF 'PRESENCE'

The minute-by-minute metered record of home TVRs shows what proportion of ITV households had their sets switched on and were receiving ITV when our commercial was transmitted. It does not tell us how many individuals were in the room and whether they were watching at the time. The diary in which individual viewing is recorded is easy to keep: it is merely necessary to mark off time slots, since station and programme details are derived from the metered record on tape.

The problem of establishing actual presence derives from the fact that to ask an individual to record viewing in time segments of less than 15 minutes duration would be unduly onerous, so therefore

a 15-minute segment is marked off if more than half of it has been spent viewing.

Some 70% of commercials are of 30-second length. The JICTAR weekly report gives a valuable record of the fluctuations in the available audience. It does not tell us what proportion of the opportunities to receive our advertising message, represented by the TVRs, was in fact taken.

In order to establish whether an opportunity has been taken an expensive form of survey is sometimes carried out: *coincidental interviewing*. A sample of homes is interviewed between the 'natural break' in which our commercial was screened and the next break. A short questionnaire is used to record what was being viewed, who was viewing and whether the commercial had been seen. Time is of the essence and this type of survey incurs heavy interviewing costs. To make more effective use of the time available between breaks, calls may be made earlier on in the day to establish whether or not the home is an ITV one and to record the household demographics. The respondents are not, of course, told that the interviewer is going to call back: but the fact that contact has been made makes a call during peak time (usually 6—10 p.m.) more acceptable than might otherwise be the case.

In order to gain more mileage from an expensive interview, respondents are on occasion asked about their viewing during the last break and then about the previous ones: this is *coincidental and retrospective* interviewing. In the USA the telephone is used to monitor 'presence'. The case for using the telephone to collect data gets stronger as the number and social range of private households in Great Britain with a telephone increases. (The percentage of households having use of a telephone reached 67.2 in 1979, according to the Government Statistical Service.)

The attention given to ITV programmes in general and to commercials in particular is investigated by large advertising agencies for their clients. Since 1976, for the London non-overlap ITV area, it has been possible to subscribe to an 'on-air' panel which records (a) whether a commercial is seen, and (b) whether it is liked. The trend data syndicated by TABS is considered in Section 11.2.5.

9.4 The JICNARS Data

The National Readership Survey data derives from a meticulously designed probability sample representative of the adult population of Great Britain aged 15 and over. As with JICTAR the fieldwork and analysis is subcontracted, currently to Sales Research Services Limited.

The data are collected throughout the year and care is taken to ensure that seasonal and day-of-the-week fluctuations in the reading of newspapers and periodicals are duly represented in the results. Over 100 newspapers and magazines and other periodicals are covered in the survey, which includes in addition regional newspapers where these circulate.

The NRS objective is:[4]

> . . . to provide such information, acceptable to both publishers of print media and buyers of space, as will be most relevant to the assessment and efficient use of the medium.

---

4. *The National Readership Survey 1979 (1)*, London, The National Readership Survey.

Among possible measures, this requires providing a basis for estimating the numbers and kinds of people likely to receive different patterns of potential exposure to advertisements inserted in individual publications or combinations of publications.

The expressions 'likely to receive' and 'potential exposure' typify the care with which the NRS operation is carried out and remind us that 'reading' can mean anything from 'reading closely' to 'just looking at'.

9.4.1 SAMPLING PROCEDURE

The sampling procedure is described in detail in an appendix to the report which is published twice a year, each report covering a year's data collection. This is a useful source for anyone studying sample design. Briefly:

The NRS uses a probability/random sample drawn in two stages ($n = 30,000$): at the first stage polling districts are drawn within wards, at the second stage individual adults aged 15 and over within polling districts.

First stage: all the wards in Great Britain are sorted into 39 geographical groupings, 'formed by interlacing non-overlapping portions of ITV areas, metropolitan/non-metropolitan counties and Registrar General's Planning Regions'.

The wards are listed within each of these 39 'survey regions' in such a way that, when a fixed interval is applied to a random start, readership of evening newspapers and political complexion are duly represented (see Section 4.2.1) when the p.p.s. draw is made. Some 1,500 wards are drawn with probability proportionate to the size of the electorate at the most recent local government election. Again using p.p.s., one polling district is drawn in each of the 1,500 wards.

Second stage: individuals are systematically drawn from the Electoral Registers for the selected polling districts: and the procedure described in Section 4.2.2 is used to ensure that non-electors have a chance and a known chance of being included in the sample. The non-electors include adults aged 15–18.

9.4.2 DATA COLLECTION

The interviewers carry 'Masthead Booklets' (see Figure 25) to aid recall and minimise confusion as between titles. The order in which the categories of print media are covered is rotated so that the effects of fatigue are spread over the 100 and more publications covered in each interview.

The Masthead Booklet is illustrated in Figure 25. A frequency

PUBLISHED EVERY MONDAY TO SATURDAY

IN AN AVERAGE WEEK THESE DAYS I READ OR LOOK AT THIS NUMBER OF ISSUES

| 6 | 5 | 4 | 3 | 2 | 1 | LESS THAN ONE | NONE |

PUBLISHED EVERY SUNDAY

THE SUNDAY TIMES

IN AN AVERAGE MONTH I READ OR LOOK AT THIS NUMBER OF ISSUES

| 4 | 3 | 2 | 1 | LESS THAN ONE | NONE |

Figure 25. National Readership Survey — 'Masthead Booklets'

PUBLISHED EVERY WEEK

**IN AN AVERAGE MONTH I READ OR LOOK
AT THIS NUMBER OF ISSUES**

| 4 | 3 | 2 | 1 | LESS THAN ONE | NONE |

PUBLISHED EVERY MONTH

**IN THE LAST SIX MONTHS I HAVE READ OR LOOKED
AT THIS NUMBER OF SEPARATE ISSUES**

| 6 | 5 | 4 | 3 | 2 | 1 | NONE |

Source: National Readership Survey 1979 (1)

scale is associated with each masthead and, as Figure 25 shows, the scale varies according to the frequency with which daily newspapers are published compared with Sunday newspapers, weekly magazines with monthly ones, and so on.

The interview opens as follows:

1. 'I want you to go through this booklet with me, and tell me for each paper, roughly how many issues you have read or looked at recently — it doesn't matter where.'

'As you look at each card, will you tell me which of the statements applies?'

ASK Q.2 FOR EACH PUBLICATION CODED OTHER THAN NONE AT Q.1

2. INTRO. 'I would now like to go through some of the publications again and ask you to say, for each one, when you last read or looked at a copy.'

AGAIN EXPLAIN   'read or looked at',
                    'it doesn't matter where', and
                    'any copy'.

'When was the last time you read or looked at a copy of . . . ?'
IF 'TODAY' ASK: 'When did you last look at a copy of . . . apart from today?'

ASK Q.3 FOR EACH PUBLICATION CODED 'YESTERDAY' AT Q.2 (EXCEPT FOR DAILY NEWSPAPERS)

3. 'You say you read or looked at . . . yesterday. Was yesterday the first day you read or looked at that issue of . . . ?'

The first question is designed to establish the average *frequency* with which readers 'read or look at' publications. The second and third establish the *average issue readership* on which the *readership penetration* tables are based.

From the mass of data on file it is possible to derive *duplication of readership* data, i.e. data which show the extent to which publications 'hang together'; the extent to which individuals read, say, *the Sun* plus *the News of the World*, or *the Sun* plus *Woman's Weekly*.

In addition to collecting data about readership the NRS assigns respondents to *ITV viewing intensity categories* according to the number of days in the week and hours in the day they claim to watch ITV (compare Section 9.3.1). Information is also collected about *intensity of IBA radio listening* and *cinema going*. This data makes it possible for the media planner to consider *inter-media relationships*.

9.4.3 CLASSIFICATION OF READERS

The 120 readership penetration tables in the NRS report are categorised as follows:

Readership among all adults
Readership among heads of households/housewives[5]
Readership among men
Readership among women
Readership among housewives

Within these five categories the survey population is classified with a richness of detail which interests sociologists as well as those in marketing. To illustrate this richness Figure 26 shows how three of the five categories are classified. It must be remembered that the NRS is based on a probability sample of substantial size and that the disaggregated data is on tape so that individual records can be correlated in many ways. The reliability of quota sampling in Great Britain owes much to the NRS as a source of quota specification. The social grade classification, so widely used in quota sampling, derives from the NRS data.

9.5 The Support Media

Radio, posters and cinema account for only 8% of expenditure on display advertising. They are often used as local reminders of the national advertising message. As we have seen, the NRS questionnaire makes it possible to sort the population into categories according to the amount of their listening to radio, and to the frequency with which they visit the cinema. Some of the data are included in the twice-a-year report: it is all available on the computer file and this is an important source for the support media.

9.5.1 THE JICRAR DATA

Listening to radio tends to be casual, listeners are not necessarily aware of the source of the background noise, there are a number of stations to choose from and the number is increasing. The JICRAR specification is summarised in the *Consumer Market Research Handbook*[6] as follows:

1. the use of radio-only diaries covering a seven-day time-period;

---

5. They may be one and the same person.
6. Teer, F. (1978), 'Radio, Outdoor and Cinema Research', Chap. 26 in Worcester, R.M. and Downham, J., eds., *Consumer Market Research Handbook*, 2nd ed., Wokingham, Van Nostrand Reinhold.

Readership Among All Adults

Survey region and ITV region
Age, social grade

Employment status (e.g. self-employed, manager)
Occupational status (full-time; part-time; not working: retired; other)
Terminal Education Age

Weight of viewing ITV
Weight of listening to IBA radio

Holiday takers (in GB, abroad, package abroad)
Ownership of cheque book, credit card, stocks, shares, unit trust

Readership Among Heads of Households

Income

Home owning, with and without mortgage
Having moved house in last 2 years
No. of rooms (5 or more, 6 or more, 7 or more)
One or more cars, 2 or more cars, new car

Colour TV	*Deep freezer*
Telephone	*Refrigerator*
Dishwasher	*Player/radiogram*
Washing machine	*Electric polisher*

Full central heating (gas, oil, electricity, solid fuel)

Readership Among Housewives

Survey and ITV region
Age, social grade
With children (0–15 years, 0–4 years, 0–23 months)
Size of household (2 or more, 3 or more, 4 or more)
No. of full time earners (2 or more, 3 or more)
Working full time or part time

Weight of viewing ITV
Weight of listening to IBA radio

Ownership of deep freezer, electric food mixer
Recent acquirers of electric food mixer, automatic washing mashine, twin tub
   washing machine.

Moving house in last 2 years.

Source: National Readership Survey 1979 (1)

Figure 26. Some NRS Classifications of Readers

2. recording of listening to all radio — BBC and commercial;
3. random samples of 1000 or 800 individuals in each area;
4. personal placement and collection of diaries by interviewers;
5. response rates of 65% or more;

6. the collection of listening behaviour quarter-hour by quarter-hour (with the exception of the night hours of midnight to 6 a.m. when half-hourly information was thought to be acceptable);
7. the collection by personal interview, at the diary placement stage, of information about exposure to other media and broad radio-listening claims.

To aid station identification the type of programme broadcast by each station, together with its position on the wave band, is included in the diary which is small enough to carry around in pocket or handbag.

Keeping the diary is simple enough (time slots down the side, stations across the top): it is just a matter of marking off quarter-hours (or half-hours between midnight and 6 a.m.). But keeping a diary does of course make listeners more conscious of their listening.

It would be unreasonable to expect listeners to keep a diary of their listening for more than a week; so it is not possible to adopt the tactic used on consumer panels of ignoring entries until behaviour returns to the normal.

The specification adds up to an expensive research operation. It is accordingly only carried out once a year, with the interviewing and diary-keeping spread over four weeks.

Twenty-four hour recall, the method used by the BBC and by Radio Luxembourg, is cheaper to apply and free from the risk of the conditioning associated with keeping a diary. A sample of the general public is asked to recall its listening during the previous day and recall is aided by means of the programme. Whether or not recall is aided, the data are subject to the fallibility of the human memory and for most people listening is not a memorable activity.

From the marketing point of view, the strength of radio lies in its parochialism. It enables

— national advertisers to make local contact, to support local sources of supply and local promotions; and
— local retailers and suppliers of services to advertise to their catchment areas.

9.5.2 JICPAS OR OUTDOOR ADVERTISING

In terms of expenditure outdoor advertising (posters and transport) is the most important of the support media: but research into the medium has taken the form of a number of ad hoc surveys and it is not easy to apply the findings to media planning.

The methods used were pioneered by B.D. Copland in the 1940s and 1950s. The earliest data collection method, based on what the respondent remembered having seen, was superseded by an 'opportunity to see' technique, also pioneered by Copland; an 'o.t.s.' technique (as described below) is used in JICPAS surveys. The work done in relation to the outdoor medium, and the problems associated with its application to media selection, are well reviewed in the *Consumer Market Research Handbook*[6] where Copland's seminal works on the subject are listed. Difficulties of two kinds arise:

- determining what mix of sites constitutes a representative sample of sites in the area being surveyed;
- applying the results of research carried out in a particular conurbation, town or mix of towns to the *package of sites* offered to the advertiser.

'The majority of British poster sites can be bought only in the form of pre-selected campaigns (PSCs) which are packages of sites. PSCs are available nationally, by ITV areas and by major conurbations'.[1] But, as the O&M report points out, some 63,000 sites of the 169,000 available in the UK are pre-empted by advertisers who have built up their showing over time and hold their sites until they countermand orders.

The interview used establishes the passage past the survey sites by a sample of the population in the area. *Location cards* are used to help the respondent decide whether he/she has passed the site. The survey yields data in the form of o.t.s. and frequency of opportunities to see over a specified period of time.

Whether the opportunities are taken remains open to question. The research findings do not discriminate between the o.t.s. offered to someone strolling past the site and the o.t.s. offered to a driver.

9.5.3 THE CINEMA

Data relating to the number of cinema screens in the UK and the number of annual admissions to cinemas are published by the Government Statistical Service, and these show how cinema-going has declined. *But the medium is still of value for reaching young people*. The 15—24 age group accounts for about a fifth of the total population but for just over half of all cinema goers. The media planner relies on the National Readership Survey data when planning communication via the cinema. There is no JIC for cinema audience research.

Conclusion

This chapter has reviewed the most generally used research sources for media planning in consumer markets. Non-consumer markets are less well supplied with shared cost data. Those engaged in the marketing of industrial or other non-consumer goods tend to rely on an accumulation of readership data collected during the course of questioning about other topics: topics such as how buying decisions are arrived at and who influences the placing of contracts. There is a shared cost source of media data. The Business Media Research Committee collects data from a sample of 2,000 businessmen representative of a universe whose population is estimated at 829,000.[1]

In planning non-consumer schedules the first problem is to locate those who influence the making of decisions, i.e. to define the target. In consumer markets it is comparatively easy to locate the target and to define the opportunities offered by the media categories and by individual vehicles within categories. The challenge comes when attempts are made to assess the probability that the opportunities provided to reach the target will be effective. The same problem arises when planning a non-consumer schedule. Will this professional journal be read, glanced at or passed straight on via the 'out' tray?

Chapter 10 investigates some of the methods used to assess the effectiveness of advertising campaigns after exposure in the media. Recognition and awareness measures are used to define campaign penetration. Provided repeated measurements are taken and normative data are accumulated, then the extent to which a particular vehicle has actually conveyed the message in the past may be used as an indicator for the future.

In Chapter 10 reference is made to the reports published by media owners: television contractors, and publishers of the provincial press, newspapers and magazines. These reports relate viewing and reading statistics to specific product markets. They help in the planning of market experiments as well as in media selection.

The BBC and the ITA are currently investigating the application of new technology to audience measurement. The setmeter may well be superseded and use of new recording devices may lead to a more precise definition of 'presence'.

It will still be necessary for the media planner to exercise judgment (albeit informed judgment) when deciding how best to deploy the selected candidates for the media schedule over time for maximum impact, given financial and creative constraints.

CHAPTER 10

Experiments in the Field

Introduction

Laboratory-type experiments are commonly used while a branded product, and the features associated with it, are being developed for the market. The experiments discussed in Chapters 7 and 8 offer the benefit of *internal validity* but leave us unsure as to whether consumers would respond to the experimental treatment in the same way on meeting the brand in normal circumstances and when unaware that they were taking part in an experiment. We are left wondering whether these laboratory experiments have *external validity*.

This doubt apart, there are important elements in the marketing mix which do not lend themselves to laboratory treatment. Experiments relating to distribution, trade incentives, selling and merchandising strategies need to be staged in the field.

The discussion about experimental design which opens Chapter 7 applies to field experiments as well as to those carried out in the more closely controlled contexts considered so far. In the field control of extraneous variables, 'background noise' is a critical problem. In this chapter we consider:

- obstacles to the achievement of external validity;
- the scope and variety of field experimentation;
- necessary pre-conditions to field experimentation;
- sources of data for measuring effects;
- simulating exposure in the field and the case for simulation;
- the relationship between measuring experimental effects and monitoring in the longer term.

10.1 Obstacles to the Achievement of External Validity

The treatment may be the complete marketing mix (as in an experimental launch) or the manipulation of individual elements, say, adver-

tising or advertising in relation to sales promotion. The following obstacles
to valid results need to be taken account of in most field experiments:

— extraneous variables may contaminate the effect of the treatment,
  e.g. uncharacteristic activity on the part of competitors or the
  effect on consumer purchasing of a local happening such as a
  strike.
— In a laboratory test it is possible to ensure that the treatment is
  introduced to experimental and control groups in exactly the
  same way. This is not always the case with field experiments: for
  example, in an experiment at the point of sale the positioning
  of items, (packs/merchandising material) may well be altered
  unwittingly during the course of the experiment so that experimental and control groups do not receive exactly the same
  treatment.
— It is sometimes difficult to isolate the effect on sales of one particular element in the mix from the effect of others: for example,
  measurement of the effect on sales of an increase in advertising
  weight may be contaminated by differences in the merchandising
  performance of sales representatives, one area being better served
  than another.
— There is a risk of 'hot-housing', particularly in the case of an
  experimental launch when reputations are at stake and there is
  the temptation to show too much management interest, and for
  sales representatives to be unduly zealous.
— The financial commitment is greater in a field than in a lab. type
  experiment. Anxiety to show a return encourages hot-housing
  and may cause the experiment to be stopped too soon. When it
  looks as if an experiment is proving successful considerations of
  'opportunity cost' may prompt too rapid an extension of the
  experiment to the wider market.

It is, however, possible in a well-designed experiment to ensure that
obstacles to a valid result are anticipated and so allowed for. Given an
adequate budget, the research programme will monitor competitive,
and own, activity at the point of sale (see Section 10.4.1). A marketing
intelligence system can be organised to ensure that environmental
happenings are noted. Use of a control group, essential in field experiments, and, where possible, replication of the experiment, make it
possible to calculate margins of error and show how precisely results
may be interpreted.

Whatever the outcome, designing, and interpreting the effect of, a
field experiment concentrates the minds of those involved wonderfully,
so that they complete the operation wiser about the requirements of the
market and how best to meet these.

10.2 Scope and Variety of Field Experimentation

We need to distinguish between:

— experiments related to established brands (which most are) and those related to new introductions;
— experiments in which individual elements in the mix are manipulated and those in which the complete mix is on trial in an experiment launch;
— experiments which can be confined to a limited location (for example, matched groups of retail outlets or of streets) and experiments demanding a microcosm of the real world of consumers, retail outlets and media vehicles.

These alternatives are not, of course, discrete. There are interrelationships between them:

— *experiments related to an established brand* are likely to be focused on individual elements in the mix — on price/packaging/ advertising/sales promotion and so on: or on the relationship between two elements, such as the effect on profit contribution of different ratios of advertising to sales promotional expenditure. (We must not, of course, forget that, once a brand is established, manipulation of elements in the mix takes place in the context of the image created by its marketing history.)

— *For a new introduction* the experimental treatment in the field is likely to be the whole mix: but the experimental launch may be preceded by a pilot launch of, perhaps, the product packaged, named and priced, designed to ensure that the product behaves well between coming off the production line and reaching the consumer.

— *Some elements in the mix lend themselves to field experimentation on a limited scale, whereas others demand a more extended environment.* The effect of a change in pack design can be assessed by comparing sales achieved in two matched and comparatively small groups of retail outlets (see Section 10.3.2). To measure the effect on sales of a change in the level of advertising expenditure may involve comparison between sales achievement in two television areas.

Use of the expression 'test marketing' has been avoided in the preceding paragraphs. Test marketing covers a variety of experimental conditions and this makes for ambiguity.[1] Davis distinguishes between:

---

1. Davis, E.J. (1970), *Experimental Marketing*, London, Nelson.

(a) *the experimental launch* (or test launch) of a new or radically improved product; and

(b) *market tests* in which 'variations are being made only to some parts of the marketing mix of an existing product'.

He further distinguishes:

Within (a) between the *projectable test launch*, an experimental launch designed to yield sales data from which national sales may be predicted; and

a *pilot launch* designed to iron out difficulties before the full experimental launch.

Within (b) between *a specific market test* designed to measure the effect of modifying 'some factor in the marketing mix to a specific new level', e.g. an increase or decrease in retail selling price; and

an *exploratory market test* designed to arrive at a better understanding of the way in which measurable elements in the mix affect consumer buying behaviour.

Most market tests are of the specific type but interest in market modelling has focused attention on exploratory experimentation as a source of input data.

Davis's analysis of the variety of experimental conditions covered by the term test marketing is illustrated in Figure 27.

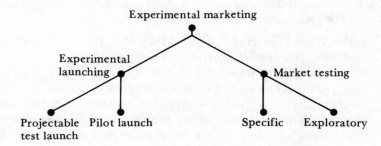

Source Davis, E.J. (1970), *Experimental Marketing*, London, Nelson.

Figure 27. Experimental Marketing Classified

10.3 Necessary Pre-conditions

Before going into the field it is necessary:

— to have formulated objectives and set criteria against which results are to be judged;

- to have decided where the experiment is to take place, on what scale and for how long;
- to have set in motion a research programme designed to monitor happenings in the market as well as to measure effects of the experiment.

10.3.1 FORMULATING OBJECTIVES

In most cases the ultimate objective is increased profit contribution but the immediate objective is likely to be seen in terms of sales. The situation to be avoided is one in which a 'suck it and see' approach is adopted. 'Let's see what sales do.' The product of this approach would be an inadequately controlled, and probably misleading, investigation.

The 'suck it and see' spirit is unlikely to prevail when the experiment is an *experimental launch*: too much is at stake. Predictions of sales achievement, given various levels of marketing cost, will almost certainly have been made at stages on the road to market. It will be known that, for the proposed mix of marketing costs, a specified sales minimum must be passed. Here the main problem is projection to the wider market from the test area (considered in Section 10.4).

Most experiments in the field relate to individual elements in the mix, or to relationships between elements, *market testing*. Before setting up the test we need to have considered the criterion against which the effect of the treatment is to be judged. It is desirable that the possible benefit to be derived from the manipulation of mix elements be estimated in advance for two reasons:

- account has to be taken of two kinds of cost, out of pocket costs and (given success) opportunity costs;
- in order to determine the size of the matched samples we are going to use we need to know not only what proportion of those in the market are likely to respond to the treatment, but also the *precision* with which we are going to want to consider results. The results will be estimates. What margin of error can we accept around the estimates?

These considerations determine the scale of the experiment: in how many retail outlets to put the experimental pack, through how many doors to put the promotional offer, how many people to ask awareness questions and so on. (See Section 4.1.5.)

10.3.2 WHERE AND FOR HOW LONG

Choice of test locations: ITV areas? Sales areas? Test towns? 'In store'? These locations account for most field experiments. Others might be circulation areas of provincial press or reception areas of local radio. The decision as to where to carry out an experiment in the field is influenced by the following factors:

— what element or combination of elements in the mix is being tested (the experimental treatment);
— how the effect is going to be measured (the dependent variable);
— the extent to which consumption and distribution of the product or brand varies in the wider market;
— availability of suitable locations;
— the rigour with which the experiment is designed; and
— the research budget.

There is interaction between these factors but we will attempt to follow this order in considering the influences on choice of location.

The importance of television as an advertising medium means that most experiments related to the complete mix (an experimental launch) or to the advertising element in the mix have to be based on ITV areas. In the US there are many small television stations serving local markets. It is comparatively easy to represent regional differences, and to match experimental and control areas, in the experimental design. In the UK small ITV areas are atypical while larger areas, embracing a wider variety of conditions, represent a considerable marketing investment. It is difficult to design a UK experiment based on ITV areas which mirrors variations in living standards, consuming habits, retailing practices and differences in the regional strengths and weaknesses of brands, the product of past marketing history. But for planning purposes there is available a wealth of marketing information regularly published by the ITV companies.

For an experimental launch to be tested in more than one ITV area (let us say Tyne Tees representing the north of the country and Southern representing the south), the cost is likely to be prohibitively expensive. Going into the second area might, for example, represent the difference between pilot plant production and an extension to the factory, apart from inflating all marketing costs.

It is accordingly common practice to use one ITV area for an experimental launch and to treat the rest of the country as the control area. This is made possible by the availability of syndicated trend data showing competitive brand shares within ITV areas over time, in terms of both retail sales and consumer purchases. These data are used to neutralise the effect of area differences (see Section 10.4).

For an established brand the financial burden is not of the same order as for an experimental launch. It is possible, for example, to conduct advertising weight tests in more than one area or to test a choice of, say, two sales promotions to advertising ratios in two ITV areas: but we still have to take differences between the areas into account when measuring effects.

Turning to the national press, newspapers and magazines, readership statistics are analysed on an ITV regional basis and there is also available syndicated data relating brand and media consumption. (This 'single source' data is discussed in Chapter 11 on monitoring performance). It is possible to compare the effect on brand shares of different combinations of television and press advertising or to consider press alone in an ITV area. The problem is to limit the effect of the experimental treatment to the area of the experiment. It means making a special arrangement to break the print run, or, for magazines, to 'tip-in'. Regional editions cover large areas of the country.

For market tests of elements in the mix other than advertising it is possible to use smaller areas and more rigorous designs. There is a wealth of secondary data available relating to the demographic and retailing characteristics of *test towns* and their catchment areas. These data derive from the Government Statistical Service, the provincial press and the suppliers of syndicated panel services, such as A.C. Nielsen, Audits of Great Britain, Retail Audits Limited and Stats. MR who offer retail and consumer panel services in test towns. In order to sell space to advertisers and to focus their editorial content, the provincial press often carry out their own research within their circulation areas. These data, published in report form, are illuminating when market tests are being designed.

For most field experiments the effect of the treatment is measured in sales. In an area test a retail audit or consumer panel is likely to be used to log brand shares, both before and after the treatment is applied. Certain elements in the mix lend themselves to 'in-store' testing: manipulations of pack and point-of-sale promotion 'ask for' an in-store design.

How are the stores chosen? A company intent on experimentation is pretty sure to have on file a record of ex-factory sales by area, by type of trade customer and by trade customers stratified by the size of their orders. The company is also likely to be subscribing to a syndicated service in order to monitor competitive market or brand shares in relation to its own.

When an in-store experiment is being designed these data will show:

— whether it is necessary to include more than one type of retail outlet in the test;
— whether it is necessary to take account of regional differences in selecting test stores; and
— whether one or more retail organisations are of critical importance.

It may well be that one particular type of outlet (say supermarkets) is so important that the experiment can usefully be confined to this type of store; and to one dominating trade customer (say Tesco). Locations in which to stage the experiment are more likely to be made available if the negotiations are carried on with one retail organisation. In order to measure effect sales have to be recorded both before and after the test and over a period of time. In addition administration of the treatment must be controlled (see Section 10.1). In other words, the experiment depends on the co-operation of head office and of the managers of the selected stores.

There is a statistical reason for basing the experiment on one particular store group, where this is practicable. The selected stores are more likely to be 'like'. This reduces error deriving from extraneous variation. *Randomized Block* and *Latin Square* designs are frequently used in in-store experiments. These designs are described, with examples, in Appendix 2 and Section 7.3, where the reader is referred to Cox and Enis.[2]

The effect of consumer promotions may be measured in interviews with matched groups of consumers instead of, or as well as, by recording sales in matched groups of stores.

Let us assume that a choice has to be made as between two types of promotion. There is no time to set up an in-store operation, or we do not want to discuss our plans with the powerful retail trade just yet: or we might want to introduce a diagnostic element into the experiment, to find out what effect the offer has had on use of the brand and attitude towards it.

In the in-store design we measure the effect of the promotional treatment by *recording sales* for a period *before* and a period *after* the offer is made to consumers, as well, of course, as during this period.

In the design based on consumer interviews, we use *intermediate measures*. We seek to establish levels of awareness of the offer, changes in use of the brand and changes of attitude towards it, but we cannot interview the same respondent before and then again after the offer has been made about awareness, use and attitude. The respondent would *learn* from the first interview and be more likely to notice and act on the offer.

We either use an after-only design and seek to establish past as well as present behaviour at the 'after' interview, *or*, more likely, use a larger number of respondents in matched groups, interviewing one group before the offer is made and the other after. Were we comparing two promotional treatments, the first procedure would need three groups overall — one for each offer and one control —

---

2. Cox, K.K. and Enis, B.M. (1973), *Experimentation for Marketing Decisions*, Glasgow, Intertext.

> while the second would require at least five, preferably six (since the control group may learn): and we have made no allowance for regional differences.

For how long? To measure effects we need to record observations taken before, during and after introduction of the experimental treatment. The period of time to be allowed for in planning and costing a field experiment is influenced by three factors:

— how long to allow for the experiment treatment to begin eliciting a response (penetration);
— how quickly brand loyalty and switching patterns can be expected to develop (repeat purchase); and
— the degree of precision required in the estimate of effects.

In the case of an experimental launch the speed with which penetration is achieved will depend on the nature of the product ('Does it break new ground, like MacDougall's Pastry Mix?', discussed in Section 10.5 under 'micro-marketing'; or is it a 'me too'?); weight and creative effectiveness of the advertising campaign; together with success in achieving distribution and 'stand out' at the point of sale.

But a product can achieve a satisfactory number of triers and then flop: the extent to which triers try again is critical and the time needed to establish *Repeat Purchase* rate in the field depends on the frequency with which the product is bought.

In order to log cumulative penetration and in order to record repeat purchase it is necessary to have available disaggregated records of consumer purchases. Analysis of back data relating to a product field and the brands in it, together with consideration of competitive expenditures on advertising over time, make it possible to predict how long an experiment may have to go on including for how long, and how often, to take observations before putting in the treatment.

Penetration and repeat purchase are discussed in more detail in Section 10.4, together with the use of retail sales as a data source for prediction from experiments.

In an experiment for an established brand we have to allow for *carry-over effects*. The in-store test illustrates the simplest manifestation of this effect. Offers encourage stocking up and stocking up affects repeat purchase. When measuring the effect of advertising for established brands, changes in weight or in creative content, it is important to remember that

> present performance in the test area is influenced by the previous marketing history of the brand. We must give old effects time to die out and new effects sufficient time in which to be felt in the market.

We return to this problem when discussing the computer program developed by Beecham to predict what would happen in a test area if no change were made. (See Section 10.5.2.)

If, as is to be expected, we intend to set confidence limits to our experimental results, we must then ensure that these results are based on a sufficient number of observations. A precise estimate may require that the test runs for longer than would be the case if a more generalised result were adequate: it takes longer to accumulate observations from a retail audit, based on bi-monthly in-store observations, than from a consumer panel reporting back weekly for a four-weekly report. (The statistical significance of experimental effects is discussed in more detail in Appendix 2.)

It is necessary that an experiment be kept in the field for a sufficient length of time and for an experimental launch this is likely to be the best part of a year. During this time the competition is planning (or carrying out) counter-measures and, assuming there is a satisfactory outcome from the experiment, opportunity costs are being incurred in the wider market. We return to the question 'how long?' when considering micro-marketing, The Mini-test Market in Section 10.5.1.

10.4 Sources of Data and Measuring Effects

The dependent variable in most field experiments is sales, and sales are usually reported in terms of brand share. The research programme for a field experiment may provide for the collection of data about other marketing factors such as level of distribution achieved, awareness of advertising and response to an offer, but the critical measurement is likely to be a sales measurement.

Ex-factory sales, however well recorded, suffer from three important limitations as a data source for experimentation in the field:

— they do not tell us how competitive brands are performing in the experimental and control areas;
— the 'pipeline' between the factory gate and the checkout makes it difficult to separate effects due to changes in sales from those due to changes in stocks;
— it is difficult to isolate the volume and value of sales ex-factory attributable to the experimental and control areas.

These limitations may be overcome but subscription to a continuous service is common practice.

10.4.1 RETAIL AUDIT: CONSUMER PANEL

Retail audit, consumer panel or both types of data sources will be used to monitor brand shares. In a test area it may well be necessary to enlarge the regular, on-going samples of retail outlets or of consumers, or to set up special ad hoc ones. It depends on the choice and the size of the test area. In addition, the standard reporting interval may be shortened, but the data collection procedures are standard.

Figure 28 compares the data yield of these two types of syndicated service whose main raison d'être is, of course, the continuous monitoring of marketing performance so that we are in effect anticipating Chapter 11. Figure 28 shows the strengths and, by implication, the weaknesses of the two data sources.

The procedures used to predict national or broad-scale shares from area tests are similar whichever form of panel is used, but the consumer panel has certain advantages in brand share prediction (see Section 10.4.3). However, before comparing predictive procedures there are some further details to be filled in:

- in both cases the client specifies the brands he wants to see recorded, usually major competitors plus an 'all others' group together with the client's brand;
- the brand characteristics to be classified individually in the regular report are also agreed in advance — type of pack, size, flavour, etc.

We are going to consider how retail audit and consumer panel data may be used to indicate what the effect of the experimental treatment would be if it were applied to the national or broader market. We first need to distinguish between *projections*, which assume that all other things remain equal, and *predictions*, which attempt to take account of factors which vary between the experimental area and the broader market.

- The retail audit is based on samples of retail outlets which represent the volume of business going through different categories of outlet, not the number of shops in each category (see Section 4.3.1). The sample may represent one type of outlet such as grocers or chemists (as in the Nielsen Food Index and the Nielsen Drug Index) or, where distribution is through a variety of outlets (as with razor blades or soft drinks), the sample may be constructed to represent this variety.[3]
- The consumer panel will represent either private households with data collection via the housewife, or individuals. (In addition to panels representing consumers in general, there are a number of specialist panels such as the Motorists Diary Panel operated by Forecast (Market Research).)

3. Hughes, B. (1978), 'Trade Research', Chap. 7 in Worcester, R.M. and Downham, J., *Consumer Market Research Handbook*, Wokingham, Van Nostrand Reinhold.

RETAIL AUDIT	CONSUMER PANEL
Consumer sales and brand shares:	Consumer purchases and brand shares:
Units	*Units*
Sterling	*Sterling*
Average per shop handling	*Brand penetration*
	Consumer typology*
	Demographic characteristics
	Psychographic characteristics
	Buying behaviour
	x amount bought
	x loyalty/switching
Retailer purchases	Where purchase made
Units (not *sterling*)	*Type of outlet*
Brand shares	
Source of delivery	
Direct/via depot/other	
Retailer stocks and brand shares	
Units	
Average per shop handling	
Stock cover	
Days, weeks, months	
Prices	Prices
Average retail selling prices at time of audit	*Average purchase price*
Promotion	Promotion
Display at point of sale	*Offers associated purchases*
Special offers	
	Advertising*
	Media consumption by panel-members ('Single source' data, see Section 11.2.2)
BY TYPE OF RETAIL OUTLET	
BY ITV AREA	BY ITV AREA
Reports	Reports
Bi-monthly	*Four-weekly*

* Quarterly or special

Figure 28. Data Yield — Retail Audit and Consumer Panel Compared

— The retail audit is a demanding but straightforward operation:

Past Stocks + Deliveries − Present Stocks = Sales[3]

'Past stock' is stock left for sale at the close of the last audit, usually two months ago: 'deliveries' means stock coming in since the last audit. The formula is simple, but the procedure is infinitely detailed.

— The consumer panel data derive either from a diary, designed as a pre-coded check-list, or from an audit of household stores.

The retail audit is valuable in the experimental situation because, in addition to recording retail sales and brand shares, it monitors distribution achieved and signals the danger of 'stockout' (a particular risk in an experimental launch dependent on pilot plant production).

The consumer panel describes the types of consumer responding to the experimental treatment and makes possible the calculation of repeat purchase rates.

10.4.2 PREDICTION BY STANDARDISING BRAND SHARES

Taking a simplified example, if a new brand were to achieve £100 consumer sales in an experimental area where sales of all brands in the product field totalled £1,000, it would be naive to assume that, on going national, the new brand would achieve £10,000 in a national market worth £100,000. Simple projection of the 10% brand share from experimental area to total market is to be avoided because even nationally distributed and consumed brands show regional variation. The field as a whole may show little variation but individual brand shares are the product of past achievement on a number of fronts — selling and sales promotion, distribution, advertising — and it is unlikely that the marketing histories of the brands in the field will have followed, in each case, a uniform course in all areas.

The effect of marketing history up to and during the experiment is taken into account by standardising brand shares, a technique developed by Davis.[1] When a new brand is introduced into an area market, achievement in brand share is made at the expense of other brands already there. Assuming a positive result for the new entry, some brands will resist more successfully than others. If the experiment is allowed to run long enough (see Section 10.3.2) and provided that a competitor does not succeed in muddying the water,

an estimate of national share is arrived at by applying the changes to brand shares observed in the experimental area to the shares held by competing brands in the national market.

The procedure is spelt out in the following example which assumes an experimental launch (brand T) into a product field of four brands $(A - D)$.

	Experimental Market				National Market, Projected		
	Brand Share (%)		Lost	Loss as % of	Brand Share (%)		
	Before	After	to T	Pre-test Share	Before	After	
A	30	27	−3	−10%	35	35−3.5 = 31.5	
B	15	10	−5	−33.3%	9	9−3 = 6	
C	25	25	n.c.	—	31	31 n.c. = 31	
D	30	27	−3	−10%	25	25−2.5 = 22.5	91.0
T	—	100	11	100	11	—	100−91 =	9.0
							100.0

Had the target set for T been a 12% share, the difference between the 11% achieved in the experimental area and the projected 9% arrived at for the national market would have been critical.

This example relates to an experimental launch. The standardisation procedure could also be used when predicting the effect of changes to the marketing of an existing brand, but the impact on market testing of individual elements in the mix is likely to be less noticeable than the impact of an experimental launch. It will be more difficult to achieve statistically significant results. The AMTES (Area Marketing Test Evaluation System) econometric model is designed to meet this problem and it is further discussed in Section 10.5.2.

Brand shares are the product of the historic working of the mix variables at certain fixed points in time, i.e. when the observations are taken. These data may show the relationship between area brand sales and national sales to be a volatile one. In this case the underlying relationship is revealed by averaging the readings over a period before and after the introduction of the treatment. The length of this period will depend on the frequency with which the product is bought.

10.4.3 BRAND SHARE PREDICTION

The brand share data used when taking the standardisation approach can derive from either a retail audit or from a consumer panel, i.e. from shares of retailer sales or from shares of consumer purchases. We are now going to consider a predictive model for which *disaggregated* consumer panel data are necessary inputs. This procedure, developed in connection with the Attwood Consumer Panel[4] can be applied to any

---

4. Parfitt, H.J. and Collins, B.J.K. (1967), *The Use of Consumer Panels for Brand Share Prediction*, MRS Conference Papers.

continuous series recording purchases by housewives, individuals, motorists, mothers or pet owners, provided the product concerned is re-purchased often enough.

The brand share prediction model is based on three statistics:

Penetration: buyers of the test product as a percentage of all buyers in the product field, as they accumulate during the period of the test (P);

Repeat purchase rate: triers of the test product buying again as a percentage of all buyers in the product field (R);

Buying rate factor: a weighting factor which allows for the finding that buyers of the test product consume more or less than the average — a weight of 1 — for the field (B).

The predictive strength of the model has been proved in field experiments using generally available panel data and in the micro-market testing approach exemplified by the Mini-test Market operated by Forecast (Market Research), a Unilever subsidiary (see Section 10.5.1).

$$\frac{P}{100} \times \frac{R}{100} \times B = predicted\ brand\ share$$

- After a time the cumulative penetration of the brand, i.e. the number of people buying the brand for the first time, shows a declining rate of increase. Once the shape of the curve is determined and a declining rate of increase is observed, it is possible to make a reasonable estimate of the ultimate likely penetration.
- The repeat purchasing rate is calculated by taking the total volume of purchases in the product field made by people who have tried the brand under study and expressing the repeat purchases of the brand as a proportion of these total purchases. This repeat purchasing rate usually declines in the early weeks after a first purchase and eventually begins to level off. When this levelling-off occurs it is possible to calculate what the equilibrium market share of the brand will be.[5]

In the now classic case of Signal toothpaste, P was finally estimated at 37% twenty weeks after the launch when R was levelling off at 40%. (At that time B had not been introduced into the formula.) The predicted share of the toothpaste market was 40% of 37%, i.e. 14.8%. Signal achieved this share some three or four months after the prediction was made and the brand held a share of 14% to 15% until the toothpaste market was radically changed by the introduction of the fluoride toothpastes.

The predictive power of the $\frac{P}{100} \times \frac{R}{100} \times B$ model is shown most

5. Parfitt, J. (1978), 'Consumer Panel Research', Chap. 8. in *Consumer Market Research Handbook*, 2nd ed., Wokingham, Van Nostrand Reinhold.

dramatically when an experimental launch is being observed, but the model is also applicable to field experiments involving the manipulation of elements in the mix.[5]

10.5 Simulating Exposure in the Field

When a brand is exposed to the market, risks are incurred:

- Unless the field experiment is conducted on a limited scale, as in an in-store test, substantial production and marketing costs accrue.
- The competition is alerted and may respond by:
  - (a) going national with a copy of the product;
  - (b) confusing experimental results by a counter-attack more intensive than would be possible on a national scale;
  - (c) quietly monitoring the experiment while developing plans designed to spoil the national launch when it comes.
- Retail buying power is increasingly concentrated in few hands so that securing effective distribution depends on the decisions of a few individuals. Failure to perform well in the experimental area not only handicaps the brand on test, it also affects 'the manufacturer's track record'[6] and so does longer-term damage.
- Given that the sales/brand share targets set are achieved, for the duration of the field experiment opportunity costs are being incurred. Generally speaking, to arrive at a valid estimate it is necessary to remain in the field for nine to twelve months.

There is, therefore, a need for procedures which get closer to the verdict of the market than is possible in the 'hidden' lab.-type experiment. The lab.-type experiment depends on such intermediate measures as intention to buy. What is wanted is a sales or brand share measure without exposure to competitors and retailers. We are going to consider two approaches to this problem both now broadly available:

- (a) Micro-market testing, the Mini-test Market (developed by Unilever);
- (b) Area Marketing Test Evaluation System or AMTES (an econometric model developed by Beecham).

10.5.1 MICRO-MARKET TESTING, THE MINI-TEST MARKET

This procedure uses the brand share prediction model discussed in Section 10.4.3. The critical measurement is 'repeat purchasing', 'repeat buying'

---

6. Pymont, B.C., Reay, D. and Standen, P.G.M. (1976), *Towards the Elimination of Risk from Investment in New Products*, Amsterdam, ESOMAR.

in the Mini-Market context: but, instead of diary, or audit, recording of the purchases of individual panel members, the Mini-test Market data are *the purchases of panel members from a door-to-door retail grocery service*.

The Mini-test Market was set up ten years ago to eliminate potential loss-makers before products went on trial in the market. It was limited to product testing and stood as an additional research stage between lab.-type testing and an experimental launch. It is now being used to help resolve problems associated with individual items in the mix, such as the right recommended retail selling price: to reduce the period of time during which products need to be exposed in the open market and, when exposure is particularly hazardous, to take the place of an experimental launch.

The method. The data are collected from two consumer panels representing households in the North (Manchester) and the South (Southampton). There are 500 housewives on each panel so that the panels are large enough to split. When comparisons are being made, a Latin-square design is used to take account of possible regional difference (see Section 7.3).

The panel members are invited to join a Shoppers' Club. They receive a *monthly catalogue in full colour* featuring some 1,500 lines representative of supermarket stock. Prices are kept in line with local supermarket prices and there are 'own-label' lines. Every other week the shopper gets a *promotions bulletin* featuring special offers and up-dating the more volatile commodity prices.

The van man calls once a week to collect the housewife's order. The order is met from the stock in the van. The order form lists all available items, together with their prices, and all the shopper has to do is to tick her requirements. Optical Character Reading ensures rapid processing of the data on the order form.

The monthly catalogue carries full colour advertisements and, by splitting the panel, it is possible to compare response, in terms of repeat buying, to different advertising approaches. The promotions bulletin makes it possible to compare the effect of different types of promotion while prices can be manipulated without upsetting the retail trade.

The Mini-test Market shoppers must not, of course, be asked diagnostic questions if their shopping behaviour is being used for predictive purposes. The operation does, however, include a separate panel of 400 shoppers who are asked use and attitude questions as the need arises.

In due course *a mobile supermarket* or automarket may take the place of the catalogue + mobile stockroom: a procedure being used in West Germany and Sweden. Panel members are *card-carrying shoppers* and their purchases are electronically recorded at the checkout. Use of

Automated Front End electronic models is on the way to being ubiquitous in the retail trade, and the Automart anticipates what will be a common research procedure (see Chapter 11).

Validity and applications. The procedure ensures 100% distribution so that penetration accumulates and levels out more rapidly than would be the case in market conditions: but the predictive value of the procedure was thoroughly tested at the pioneering stage[7] and it is, of course, continually under test as products and strategies cleared by the Mini-test Market enter an area or national market. Three cases are of particular interest as examples of marketing problems, apart from the Mini-test Market application:

Problem: *to determine the optimum recommended selling price for a new introduction.*

Product: Sunlight Lemon Washing-up Liquid

The product was designed to be better and more expensive than Fairy Liquid. Two prices X two areas in a Latin Square design.

Results:	*Higher Price*	*Lower Price*
Cumulative Penetration (of product field buyers)	42%	50%
Repeat Buying Rate	13%	18%
Buying Rate Index	1.0	1.0
PREDICTED BRAND SHARE	5.5%	9.0%

The 3.5% difference in predicted brand share 'represented approximately £1.5 m at retail value in the national market place'[6] at the time.

Appearance of a competitor prompted a national launch straight from Mini-test Market.

National brand share peaked at 14% after 24 weeks, settled at 9% in the 48th week.

Problem: *to measure the threat launched by a competitive product undergoing experimental launch.*

Product: Carousal Margarine

The product was bought in the competitor's test area (Midlands ITV). The advertising was monitored and translated into print advertisements for the Mini-test market catalogue.

7. Paymont, B. (1970), *The Development and Application of a New Micro Market Testing Technique*, Barcelona, ESOMAR.

Results: (after six months on Mini-test)

Cumulative Penetration	
(of product field buyers)	32%
Repeat Buying Rate (volume)	4%
Buying Rate Index	1.10
PREDICTED BRAND SHARE	1.4%

After launch by Kraft, consumer panel data showed volume brand shares of Carousal, predicted at 1.4%, fluctuating as follows:

1973	AUG	SEP	OCT	NOV	DEC	JAN	FEB	1974
%	1.4	0.8	0.7	0.6	0.6	0.8	1.2	

Problem: *To avoid being copied.*

Product: MacDougall's Pastry Mix

This was a brilliantly simple, easily copied, product concept — just add water to flour in which the other necessary ingredients had been incorporated.

It was accordingly decided to 'go national' after only 24 weeks on Mini-test Market, and this paid off.

Micro-market testing provides valid estimates of potential brand shares: but an experimental launch has logistical purposes which demand real-life exposure. An experimental launch is a dress-rehearsal. 'What brand share can we expect?' is a critical question but other questions need to be answered: will the product travel unspoilt from factory to the point of sale? Is the sales force geared to sell-in effectively? Are distributive and re-stocking arrangements satisfactory? Will the retail trade be moved to display the product effectively?

Questions such as these can be answered before the conventional nine to twelve months' long experimental launch is half-way through. It is the building-up of penetration and the settling down of the repeat-purchase rate that take time. Micro-marketing hot-houses penetration and makes it possible to establish repeat buying behaviour fairly rapidly. There may be a case for treating the area test as a logistical exercise.

10.5.2 AREA MARKETING TEST EVALUATION SYSTEM, AMTES

Before embarking on an experiment in the market it is important to decide how precisely we are going to want to interpret the effect of the experimental treatment (see Appendix 2). An experimental launch may be expected to make a significant impact on a test area, but manipulation of one element in the marketing mix may well produce an effect which cannot be measured precisely enough to give a clear verdict once confidence limits have been attached to the statistical estimate. A result of *marketing* significance may not be *statistically* significant.[8]

In area tests ITV areas are frequently used with the rest of the country standing as a control. Examination of historic retail audit data at Beecham Products has shown that:[8]

> . . . sales in one area as a percentage of national sales fluctuate considerably even when no area test is being carried out.

Sales of Beecham Foods' largest brand (Lucozade) in the largest ITV area (London, with one in five of all UK homes), expressed as a percentage of national sales, fluctuated within a range of between 16.2% and 21% during the year to March/April 1979 (Nielsen). Many experiments relate to less popular brands tested in smaller ITV areas.

Such a volatile relationship between area market and national market indicates that, when only a small effect has marketing significance, it is necessary:[9]

> either to record a large number of observations, i.e. to go into a large test area for an unduly long period of time;

> or to remove from the estimate 'the effects due to various uncontrolled but measured variables affecting sales'.

AMTES is an econometric model, i.e. it uses aggregated data unlike the Brand Share Prediction Model (see Section 10.4.3). The model makes it possible to establish in advance of going into the field and without alerting the competition:

> what would be likely to happen, nationally and in the test area, if the status quo were maintained.

By comparing what actually happens during the course of the experiment with what would have happened had no change been made it is possible to interpret the experimental effect more narrowly without staying unduly long in the field, i.e. longer than about a year.

The method. The procedure has been crystallised by Michael Stewart as follows:[8]

> 1. Draw up a list of all the variables which might have a different effect on brand sales between the test area and the control area. (The control area is usually the rest of the country.)
> Examples of such variables would be own and competitors'

8. Stewart, M.J. (March 1980), 'Measuring Advertising Effects by Area Tests', ADMAP.
9. Bloom, D. and Twyman, W.A. (April 1978), 'The Impact of Economic Change on the Evaluation of Advertising Campaigns', *Journal of the Market Research Society.*

prices, distributions and advertising weights, temperatures and levels of sickness.

2. Extract the data for sales and explanatory variables in the test and control areas for at least 20 periods before the start of the test — for example four years of Nielsen or Stats. MR data, or two years of TCA, TCPI or PPI data.

3. Calculate, for sales and explanatory variables, the ratios of the test to control figures.

4. Perform all possible subset Multiple Linear Regressions in order to obtain an equation relating the fluctuations in the sales ratio to fluctuations in the ratios of the explanatory variables.

5. As each period's data during the area test become available the actual values of the ratios of the relevant explanatory variables are put into the equation to yield an estimate of the expected ratio of sales in the test and control areas if the test had no effect. This estimate is then compared with the actual ratio of sales in the test and control areas. The difference between the two measures is the estimated effect of the area test.

A test is applied to see if the difference is statistically significant, and confidence limits about the estimated sales effect are also calculated.

The AMTES procedure is therefore based on a combination of econometric modelling and experimentation in the field.

A large number of observations is required at the modelling stage (see 2, above). For retail audit data (Nielsen, Retail Audits and Stats. MR) it is necessary to go further back into the past than for the consumer panel data (for example, the Television Consumer Audit recording housewife purchases) because the consumer panel data is reported more frequently (every four weeks) than the retail audit data (bi-monthly). Where sufficiently extensive back data is not on file, this can often be bought from the suppliers.

The most commonly used inputs are retail selling price (the prices actually charged to consumers), advertising weight (amount spent or TVRs) and distribution (percentage of retail outlets stocking) for the test brand and its competitors, in the test area and nationally.

In a number of product fields, weather (mean temperatures, hours of sunshine) and levels of sickness will be taken into account in the equation.

An application and its validity. AMTES was developed in 1973. Since then some eighty AMTES exercises have been carried out. Many of these relate to changes in advertising copy, to changes in the weight of advertising or to the effect of different mixes of television and press.

Horlicks: Yorkshire TV Area Copy Test

Sales in Test Area as a Percentage of Sales in Control Area

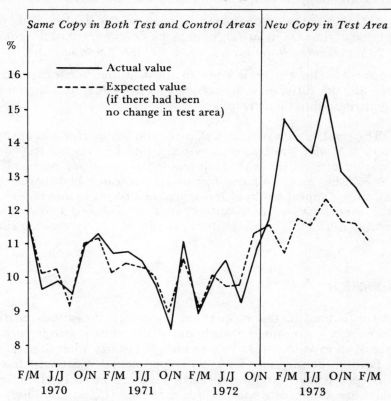

Source: MRS Conference Papers, 1976

Figure 29. An Application and its Validation

But the procedure can be applied to all the marketing variables. It has been shown that changes to the creative communication have a quicker and more marked effect on sales than changes to advertising expenditure. The Horlicks case illustrates the effect of creative change.

Problem: *to predict the effect on consumer sales of changing the creative concept from an association of* Horlicks *with a good night's sleep to an association with relaxation.*

Method: Before 'relax' was exposed in the Yorkshire ITV area, the relative importance of all possible combinations of measurable variables which might account for differences between the Horlicks performance in Yorkshire and its performance nationally was scrutinised by AMTES, and an equation which explained most of the difference was arrived at.

The AMTES prediction compared with sales as shown by Nielsen over the period of time taken into account in the development of the equation. *The 'fit', as Figure 29 shows, validated the AMTES equation.*

Results: The effect of new copy in the test area is clearly shown in Figure 29, the difference between 'expected value' and 'actual value' being attributed to the new 'relax' copy.

The creative change to 'relax', proposed by the Horlicks advertising agency, J. Walter Thompson, was prompted by concern lest the long association of Horlicks with sleep had led to 'wear-out' in the effect of the advertising on consumers. Exploratory research had suggested that 'relax' might appeal to those less concerned to get a good night's sleep. In the event, a usage and attitude study established that 'relax' was increasing sales by increasing the regularity of use by existing Horlicks users.

Conclusion

We have focused in this chapter on the critical measure of marketing performance — consumer sales/brand shares: but research during the course of an experiment is likely to include criteria other than sales.

Before, during and after an experimental treatment has been introduced, repeat surveys are carried out to measure the effect on product *use* and on *attitude* towards the brand (U and A studies) of the proposed change, whether this relates to a new introduction or to an established brand.

In advertising media experiments, changes in brand *awareness* are likely to be recorded, while syndicated services **which** relate *media exposure* to product and *brand consumption* **help** to validate media planning.

The main raison d'être of shop audits and consumer panels (see Section 10.4.1) is the *continuous monitoring of market performance*. They are described in this chapter because an appreciation of the nature of the data is necessary to an understanding of the projective and predictive techniques discussed.

We are, however, reserving discussion of the ancillary measures mentioned above for Chapter 11, because their main use is to keep track of consumer response to the brand after it has been launched.

Evaluating Performance
and Predicting

Introduction

This chapter considers how performance may be monitored and suggests how the data collected by the monitoring procedures may be used to plan ahead. The monitoring/predicting process should be a continuous one; while the system adopted should, of course, relate marketing costs to sales achievements.

The marketing research procedures used to measure the effects of an experimental launch (see Chapter 10) are substantially the same as those used to monitor performance after the brand has 'gone national'. Accordingly Chapter 11:

— first discusses the contribution of marketing research to the monitoring of important mix activities;
— then reviews the components of a marketing information system before
— suggesting how the output of the MIS may be used in forecasting.

The chapter concludes with a summary of the technological developments encountered during the course of the book, including the means to process disaggregated data and the value of these data as inputs in micro-behavioural modelling.

11.1 Marketing Research Data Used in Monitoring

We considered the use of consumer panel data to monitor consumer sales and brand shares in Chapter 10 on Experiments in the Field. This section focuses on the kind of marketing research data used to monitor:

— selling and distributing activities;
— media planning effectiveness;
— impact of the advertising campaign as a whole, including the tracking of brand and corporate images.

11.1.1 MONITORING SELLING AND DISTRIBUTING ACTIVITIES

A company's own records and feedback from the sales force have, of course, important contributions to make. We are going to concentrate on the use of syndicated trade research in the assessment of own performance as compared with that of competitors. A marketing company may subscribe to a full retail audit (see Figure 28), a distribution check or to both: but in all trade research the following sampling requirements need to be taken into account:

— We have to decide whether the product is such that one type of retail outlet predominates so that we can draw out conclusions from a sample based on say, the grocer or chemist trade (e.g. Nielsen's Food Index and Drug Index).

If the product is sold through a wide variety of outlets, none predominant, it is necessary to use a panel reflecting this variety[1] or to rely on the limited distributive data generated by a consumer panel (see Figure 28). Razor blades exemplify this type of product.

— In trade research as in industrial research (see Section 3.8) the sample is designed to represent the trading importance of each category (e.g. 'multiples') rather than the number of shops or establishments in each category.

In a continuous panel operation information regarding total turnover is more readily available than is the case with distribution checks, where repeated surveys are likely to be used. Here, as in most non-consumer research, it is necessary to assess turnover (or output) on the basis of such measures as rateable value (see Section 4.3.1) number of staff employed, floor area, number of checkouts.

The basic stratification by turnover is, of course, provided by Government statistics relating to production and distribution.

The scope of the full retail audit is shown in Figure 28. Distributive and, by implication, selling effectiveness can be monitored against the following criteria:

— own unit sales to retailers compared with those made by competitors;

---

1. Hughes, B. (1978), 'Trade Research', Chap. 7 in Worcester, R.M. and Downham, J., *Consumer Market Research Handbook*, 2nd ed., Wokingham, Van Nostrand Reinhold.

— whether these goods reach the retailer direct, via a depot of the chain to which the retailer belongs or by some other means (such as a Cash and Carry);

— share of the total retail trade done by retailers stocking our brand compared with those stocking competitive brands (£-weighted distribution);

— own stock cover, given the rate at which our brand is selling, compared with the competition;

— the amount of shelf space and the display support given to our brand compared with competitors.

The data are shown for each category of outlet within ITV areas, so provided that a company's sales areas can be related to ITV areas it is possible to evaluate sales force achievement in the light of these criteria as well as the distributive and merchandising policies being followed. The following Nielsen case[2] shows how retail auditing can improve selling/distributive performance:

Product: Showering's BABYCHAM.
Problem: Out of stock at the end of the Christmas season, in spite of a forceful selling policy.

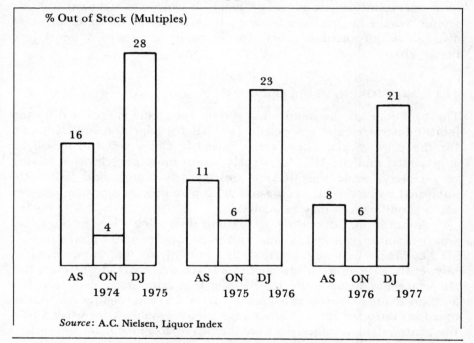

Source: A.C. Nielsen, Liquor Index

2. Wallis, C.J. (1981), 'Shop Audit Research, What it is and What it Does', in Bradley, U. (ed.), *Applied Marketing and Social Research*, Wokingham, Van Nostrand Reinhold.

Shops which were without stocks of Babycham in the first weeks of January would not in most cases have been out of stock by the end of the peak selling weeks of Christmas and New Year . . .

Solution: The 'source of purchase' tabulation added to the Nielsen Liquor Index at the end of 1976 showed 'just how substantial was the impact on total sales of outlets which received their deliveries via Multiple Group depots. It became obvious that Showerings' problem lay not in convincing the head office buyers to take higher quantities of stock, but in ensuring that Babycham flowed out of the depots and into the stores evenly throughout the pre-Christmas period'.[2]

A number of research suppliers include *distribution checks* among the services they offer. The scope is narrower than the full retail audit, being limited to what is visible at the point of sale, presence of the brand and its main competitors, shelf space allocated, promotional offers, selling prices.

The distribution check may be used because a full audit cannot be afforded, because the need to monitor distribution is felt to be a short-term one, to investigate a local problem for which the standard auditing sample would be inadequate when broken down, or to supplement distributive information from, for example, a consumer panel (see Figure 28).

11.1.2 MONITORING MEDIA PLANNING

The backbone of the monitoring system for media is provided by the joint industry research, especially JICTAR for television and JICNARS for the print media. These are reviewed in Chapter 9 and it will be appreciated that the JICTAR weekly report monitors television buying very closely, while the JICTAR thrice-yearly reports and JICNARS, published twice a year, keep a watch on planning decisions and suggest where modifications may be advisable.

In addition, advertising agents and their clients buy into services which monitor own and competitive expenditures across all media (c.f. MEAL, Media Expenditure Analysis Limited), so that comparison of own costs with those of competitors is relatively straightforward. But allowance has to be made for the fact that rates are subject to offers and bargaining so that there is a margin of error around figures necessarily based on rate-card rates. Also, ambiguities inevitably arise when advertisements relate to more than one brand, or to more than one variety of a brand.

From the monitoring/planning point of view, the industry data leave two important questions unanswered:

- are the opportunities to receive the message being taken? and
- is media selection based on the demographic characteristics of buyers/users as closely 'on target' (and therefore as cost-effective), as is desirable?

The o.t.s. problem is ventilated in Chapter 9, and we return to this vexed question when we consider ways of monitoring the impact of the advertising campaign as a whole in Section 11.1.3.

The second question brings us to *single source data*. There are three ways in which a marketing company can seek to relate product/brand use to media consumption:

- via a consumer panel;
- via the Target Group Index;
- by adding media questions to surveys about the habits and attitudes of brand users.

The Attwood Consumer Panel and the Television Consumer Audit (both now owned by Audits of Great Britain) provide, from among panel members, samples for questioning about media consumption. A good deal is known about the buying behaviour of panel members and by drawing samples from the 5,000 or so on file it is possible to establish a 'single source' relationship between buyer behaviour and media consumption. Fresh samples are drawn at regular intervals. In the case of the Attwood Panel (diary-based), housewives are asked to keep a media diary for seven days; in the case of the TCA (audit-based), housewives are asked about their media consumption during the previous seven days, a seven-day aided recall survey.

This procedure can, of course, be applied to any panel designed to record buyer behaviour. The questions asked follow the National Readership Survey as closely as time permits. As we saw in Section 9.4.2 the NRS includes a significant inter-media section designed to relate viewing, listening and cinema-going habits to exposure to print media.

The Target Group Index, a syndicated service operated by the British Market Research Bureau, relates product and media data across a wider product field than that covered by the TCA and Attwood panels. The TGI is rightly defined as a National Survey of Buying: 'buying' embracing, for example, leisure and financial activities.

The sample is drawn using the random location procedure described in Section 3.6.2. The data collection is designed to produce annual reports on specific product fields. In many fields these annual reports

We've worked out a simple way for you to tell us what products you buy. You will see that for each of the products listed in the following pages, there are three questions:

1. Do you ever use (or buy, serve, drink, take, smoke, etc.) the product?

   If you DO, code the box for "yes"

   Yes   No

   In this case you should then go to questions 2 and 3.

   If you DON'T, code the box for "no"

   Yes   No

   In this case you can ignore questions 2 and 3, and go straight on to the next product.

2. If the answer is "yes", you are asked how often you use it, or how much you use. Please code the box for the most appropriate answer. (An example of a completed set of questions is given on the right of the page: you can see that the person uses Adhesives about once a week.)
   CODE ONE BOX ONLY. If you can't give an exact answer, please give an approximate one.

3. You are then asked which brands you use. Please code in the first column the brand you use most often. (In the example, Airfix is the brand of Adhesive the person uses most often.) If the brand you use most often is not listed, please write it in on the lines provided at the bottom of the last question, and code it in the "most often" column. But before you do so, please make sure it's not listed. You may, in a few cases, wish to code in the "most often" column more than one brand if you use them about equally.

   Then code in the second column any other brand or brands you have used in the past six months. Again, if there are any such brands which are not listed, write them in at the bottom of the page and code them in the "others" column. You can see that this has been done with Pritt in the example.

If the product is one which you use more at some times than at others, please tell us how often you are using it, or how much you are using it at the present time. If you are a housewife, please tell us — when you are answering questions on food and household products — what is bought by you or on your behalf for you and your family. For the other products, it is normally your own personal use of them which we would like to know about.

By the way, it will help us, if you do not write on the questionnaire itself, apart from coding boxes and writing in non-listed brands. You will find a sheet for "Notes" at the end of the questionnaire if you want to comment, or add to any of your answers.

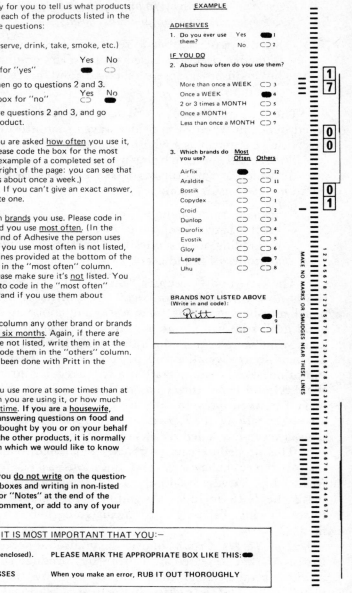

IT IS MOST IMPORTANT THAT YOU:—

USE PENCIL ONLY (a pencil is enclosed).   PLEASE MARK THE APPROPRIATE BOX LIKE THIS:

DON'T MAKE TICKS OR CROSSES   When you make an error, RUB IT OUT THOROUGHLY

Figure 30. TGI: 'How to Tell Us'

are supplemented by half-yearly summaries. The sample is large (25,000), and the self-completion questionnaire long (70 pages). The questionnaire is placed by interviewers and an effective response rate of 60% plus is recorded. The introduction to the 70-page questionnaire, 'How to tell us' (in answer to the title, 'What do you buy?'), explains how to answer the pre-coded questions and shows what sort of data are being collected (see Figure 30). The media questions follow the NRS design.

The following table (Figure 31), reproduced from material used to validate the service when it was first introduced, illustrates the sensitivity of the relationships revealed by the 'single source' approach. In this table the data base is 'all adults'. It could of course be, for example, all those who buy brand X 'most often' (see Figure 30) or, say, readers of the Daily Express who buy brand X sometimes; the first being of interest if the advertising objective were to reinforce brand loyalty, the second if the objective were to persuade 'switchers' to be less changeable.

Product Field	Wine (use)	Slimming (trying to)	Laxatives (once a week or more)
Base, all adults	28.5%	19.0%	20.2%
Index	100	100	100
Readers of Daily Express	118	111	90
Readers of News of the World	79	100	115
Average daily viewing of ITV:			
less than one hour	207	79	60
six hours or more	75	116	145

The index shows that among readers of the Daily Express (to take an example), the proportion of 'wine users' and of slimmers is higher than the national average, for which the index is 100; while Daily Express readers use laxatives 'once a week or more', less than the national average.

Figure 31. Selectivity of the TGI Illustrated

These examples show how the TGI helps to determine the selection of (a) media category and (b) media vehicles within categories: the data are also, of course, used in 'post-campaign evaluation'.

In industrial and other non-consumer markets it is common practice to attach media questions to surveys designed to establish the requirements and attitudes of those who influence buying decisions. The data are stored and used when making, and evaluating, media plans.

Media questions may also be attached to the use and attitude surveys regularly carried out by marketing companies.

Many of our clients already commission consumer surveys into their markets. By a simple step we can sometimes double the value of these surveys at very small additional cost: by adding media questions.[3]

3. Segnit, S.S. and Broadbent, S. (1970), *Area Tests and Consumer Surveys to Measure Advertising Effectiveness*, ESOMAR.

This approach is appropriate when media alternatives are being compared (as in the examples quoted above), but for planning/monitoring purposes it is usually advisable to consider data drawn from the broad field of media choice, using the standard NRS questions.

11.1.3 MONITORING THE ADVERTISING CAMPAIGN

At the end of the road the critical measure of advertising effectiveness is sales and the measurement of sales achievement is discussed in Chapter 10. But sales are, of course, dependent on factors other than the advertising campaign, and in order to monitor the effectiveness with which the message is conveyed to target consumers those 'intermediate measures' employed at the pre-testing stage (see Section 8.4.1) are again used, but in a different, 'real-life' context. We are going to consider three commonly used monitors — *recognition, salience* and *attitude* change. We are then going to review the system pioneered by TABS (Television Advertising Bureau (Surveys) Ltd.), whereby responses to on-air commercials are scored by a panel from which trend data is derived.

Recognition. Recognition is more relevant to post- than to pre-testing. It attempts to measure whether or not the opportunity to see the advertisement has in fact been taken by the respondent (see Sections 9.2 and 9.3.2). This depends, of course, on both the media selection and the creative work. In a recognition check the object is first and foremost to find out whether the respondent recognises the advertisement: not what is remembered about it, nor the respondent's attitude towards the subject of the advertisement, just *whether the respondent happened to see it*.

If the respondent knows the subject of the enquiry, he/she may oblige by recognising the advertisement. It is therefore necessary to use a procedure which either conceals the subject of interest, or one which makes it easy for the respondent to say 'No'. Examples of both approaches to this problem are given below.

We have also, of course, to take account of the fact that memory is fallible. The respondent may forget having seen the advertisement (but memory may in due course be triggered off at the point of sale): or claimed recognition may in fact relate to previous advertising for the brand.

The two procedures described here aim to make it possible for the respondent to recognise without inflating the recognition score.

For print media: A sample drawn from the target group is shown a current issue of the newspaper or magazine. The respondent is taken through the whole issue, page by page. If the respondent happens to have looked at the page, items on the page (editorial as well as advertisements), are scored for having been looked at.

This procedure was pioneered in the US by Daniel Starch and developed in the UK by The Gallup Poll. Regularly used, as in the Gallup Field Readership Index, norms are arrived at for major publications and for different product fields and the probability of an advertisement being (a) noticed, and (b) read, given its position and size, may be calculated; and the result used in building a media model (see Section 9.2).

There is a logistical problem: it is necessary to have a sufficient number of copies of the publication on hand for marking up — one to each respondent. And it is not applicable to television.

For television: The following procedure, developed by Communication Research Ltd., aims to encourage a true answer while making it possible for the respondent to say whether or not he or she recognises a particular commercial:[4]

> Here are some pictures from a television commercial for (PRODUCT). Please look at them carefully and read this short description of the commercial. (INDICATE.)

> This particular commercial has only been shown in some parts of the country. It may not have been shown here. Have you seen it?

The recognition scores measure *campaign penetration*, 'the extent to which a campaign succeeds in penetrating its target audience'.[4] Most advertising research relates to established brands and 'confusion claiming' may arise — usually because respondents assume that they must have seen advertising for a well-known brand (even if they haven't), or assume that they must have seen it in one medium (usually TV) when in fact it was in another. The above question type is specifically designed to minimise such 'confusion claiming'. The level of confusion can be tested by using matched samples from the target audience and going through the procedure with one sample *before* the commercial is actually screened and the other *after*.

Any procedure regularly and systematically used generates normative data against which recognition (or 'campaign penetration') scores may be assessed.

Salience: 'One of the principal objectives of advertising will be to bring a brand to the top of people's minds or to keep it there — to improve or maintain brand salience'.[4]

When a brand is first introduced we are concerned with the impact achieved by the advertising. Once this has been established the aim is to reinforce its position vis-à-vis the competition in the potential consumer's mental shopping basket (see Section 8.3.2 on the reinforcement role).

---

4. Caffyn, J.M. (1977), *Measuring Effects of Advertising Campaigns*, MRS Conference Papers.

'Thinking now of just chocolate blocks and bars, please will you tell me what products come into your mind?'

The brands are recorded in the order in which they surface and their positions are ranked, the first mentioned out of, say, five possibles scoring 5, the second 4 and so on. Salience scores are aggregated for own brand and for main competitors, and mean scores are calculated by dividing the aggregates by the number in the sample. Trend data based on the mean scores:

indicate salience standing relative to the competition over time;
help to measure the effect of advertising changes in scheduling, weight and creative content.

Attitude and brand image. The attitude measures used to monitor the effect of an advertising campaign on brand image are less 'cut and dried' than recognition as a measure of campaign penetration and salience as a measure of the 'stand-out' effect on the consumer's mind achieved for the brand by the campaign.

The extent to which marketing companies deliberately cultivate images for their brands, the strength of their belief in the added value of an appropriate image, varies with the product field, the management philosophy of the company and the way in which the advertising agency working on the brand approaches its task.

If advertising is being used to create and then reinforce a brand image, with a view to strengthening consumer loyalty, resisting pressure from the retail trade and extending the brand's life cycle, then there is a strong case for continuously monitoring consumer attitudes towards the brand.

If the market has been segmented (Chapter 6), if consumers have been consulted about their needs, beliefs and perceptions, and if consumers and/or brands have been sorted into groups according to the attitudes which express these needs, beliefs and perceptions, then there will be little doubt as to which attitude measures to use when monitoring the brand image.

The data are best collected for the product field as a whole, or for all substantial brands, not only for the purpose of comparing the image of our brand with those of competing brands, but also to avoid the 'friendliness effect' which questions about one particular brand might evoke.

As we have seen, being asked attitude questions is likely to increase a consumer's awareness of brand attributes. To avoid this learning effect, the population of interest is sampled afresh each time but standard questions are used.

These questions can take three forms:

- association of a list of attributes with a list of brands, a simple checking-off operation — e.g. Persil ticked for whiteness;
- a ranking of attributes — e.g. Persil first out of x brands for whiteness — the data being processed in the way described for salience scores;
- a rating of attributes using either Likert or Semantic Differential scales (see Section 5.5) — e.g. Persil whiteness shows, or (inconceivably!) it does not.

When collecting brand image data it is, of course, advisable to establish what brand(s) the respondent is using/has used/is aware of (see Section 5.1).

Attitude questions can be a component in a marketing company's own 'usage and attitude' survey, carried out, say, once a year to add flesh to panel data: or a marketing company may subscribe to a 'shared cost' service such as the Advertising Planning Index operated by the British Market Research Bureau. (For companies marketing food products, shared cost data about how commodities and brands are actually used is available from, for example, the Taylor Nelson Family Food Panel. Members of the panel keep an exhaustive diary for a short period of time.)

11.1.4 MONITORING THE CORPORATE IMAGE

With the development of consumerism, of public concern for the environment and of doubt as to whether big is really beautiful, multi-nationals such as Philips and ICI have become increasingly aware of the need to keep track of the relationship between their corporate image and demand for their products.

This book is about the marketing of branded products and the following example[5,6] is chosen with this in mind: for one of the encouraging features of the present time is the extent to which government departments, public bodies and local authorities are seeking to monitor the response of the general public to social campaigns on stopping smoking, using seat-belts, using the postcode and saving water.

---

5. Worcester, R.M. and Mansbridge, E. (October 1977), 'Tracking Studies: Basis for Decision Making', *Journal of the Market Research Society*.

6. McIntyre, I. and Worcester, R.M. (1981), 'Strategic Decision Research, its communications and use at ICI', in Bradley, U. (ed.), *Applied Marketing and Social Research*, Wokingham, Van Nostrand Reinhold.

Subject: The General Public's image of ICI

Method: Subscription to the MORI Corporate Image Survey from 1969 to 1977

Sample: 4,000.   Survey: annual.

Questions re. attitude towards:

— industries in which ICI is active, e.g. chemicals, textiles, paints, plastics:
— ICI and its main competitors.

Example of questioning procedure: [6]

'I would like to read out to you some statements which people have made about large companies. For each one, I would like you to tell me whether you agree or disagree.'

READ OUT STATEMENTS IN GRID BELOW

IF INFORMANT IS UNCERTAIN, PROBE: 'Do you lean more towards agreeing or disagreeing?'

IF, EVEN AFTER PROBING, INFORMANT HAS NO OPINION, RING NO OPINION CODE

	Agree	Disagree	No opinion	
(a) Large companies are essential for the nation's growth and expansion.	1	2	3	
(b) It is in the country's interest that the big industries should be nationalised.	5	6	7	
(c) In many of our largest industries one or two independent companies have too much control in the industry.	9	0	X	41[7]
(d) Companies' profits in Britain are too high.	1	2	3	42[7]

Results: Awareness of the 'Ideas in action' campaign: [5]

1974: 30%   1975: 35%   1976: 41%

---

7. Column numbers, see Figure 10.

The 4,000 sample large enough to allow responses of special interest groups, such as ICI's immediate customers, to be considered separately.

In 1975 attitudes held by communities local to ICI factories compared with those held by the public in general.[5]

People living near ICI plants 'were both more familiar and more favourable'. Compared with the generality:

	% + or −
Say they 'know' ICI well	+ 8
'Favourable' towards ICI	+ 6
Think ICI shows an interest in people as well as profits	+ 6
Think ICI has excellent benefits for employees	+ 12
Think ICI is fair in the wages it pays	+ 9
Think ICI has good relations in communities where it operates	+ 7
Think ICI makes too big a profit	− 9

As with brand image studies, there is a choice of either subscribing to a syndicated service (as in this case) or 'going it alone'. With forethought in the timing of the survey in relation to the campaign, it is possible to relate image results to the media selection, weight of advertising and creative approach used in the campaign (see the article by Worcester and Mansbridge[5] for data relating to Philips 'Simply years ahead' campaign.)

11.1.5 THE TABS 'ON-AIR' PANEL

TABS (Television Advertising Bureau (Surveys) Ltd.) began its 'on-air' panel operation in 1976 in the 'non-overlap' London ITV region'.[8] By the end of 1981 the service will be both 'multi-area and multi-media'. Related to television TABS:

- Provides truly *objective* and *quantitative* scores for each of the key aspects of a TV campaign.
- Monitors consumers' responses to commercials in the *real life natural in-home viewing situation*.
- Measures a campaign's effectiveness *continuously*, i.e. not only when it's on-air but also the subsequent *'decay'* rate *after* it has ended.

8. 'TABS ON-AIR PANEL', TABS brochure, 1980.

— Links *real* exposure to commercials with actual brand/product field *usage*.
— Uses a *large representative panel* of respondents — gross size 2,000 housewives and 1,500 men.

Members of the panel are 'active reporters' for one week out of four.

The *Derivation of the Basic TABS scores* is clearly shown in Figure 32. 'Baseline' scores are recorded during the weekend prior to the week's viewing which starts on a Wednesday. The questionnaire instructs panel members to:[8]

> Watch the programmes you want to watch whether they are on BBC or ITV. Don't change your viewing because you are filling in this booklet.

In the booklet the Goodwill visual 10-point scale (Brand for me . . . not for me) is described as a ladder; the Visibility scale (Advertised on

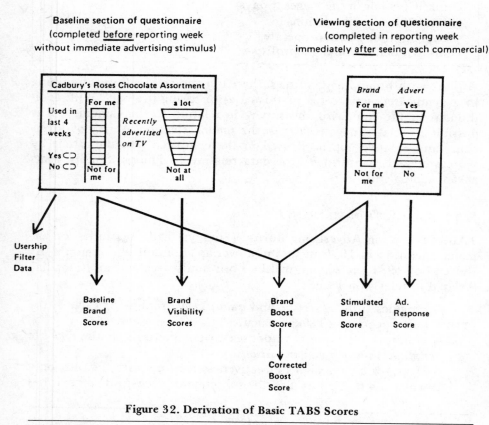

Figure 32. Derivation of Basic TABS Scores

9. Hoyes, P. (January 1981) 'The Case for TABS — towards a validation', *ADMAP*.

TV a lot . . . not at all) as a flower pot and the Advertisement response scale (Advert. Yes . . . No) as an egg-timer.

Use of these distinctive shapes makes it possible to score for Goodwill and Advertisement response in the two to three seconds between commercials without confusion. As with the JICTAR diary (see Section 9.3.1), it is not necessary for respondents to write in brand names: *Time* of the commercial break ('This set of adverts. began at . . . ') identifies brands seen on-air.

Use of the 'Brand for me . . . not for me' scale as a measure of Goodwill towards the brand has been validated by computing correlations between Goodwill and Market Share scores for a number of brands in each of the following product fields:[9]

> *1977*
> Washing Powders (high suds, 9 brands)   .99
> Washing-up liquids (4 brands)   .97
> Toilet soaps (8 brands)   .92
>
> *First half of 1977*
> Deodorants (3 brands)   .98
> Toothpastes (8 brands)   .92
> Shampoos (6 brands)   .87

Validity of the TABS Visibility scores has been assessed in the light of the JICTAR TVRs. This is not a simple matter because of the 'presence' problem (see Section 9.3.2), but for brands whose advertising weight shows variation over time (most do) 'there is evidence for a correlation averaging about 0.9 between mean visibility scores among product group users and lagged TV rating points for its campaign as measured by JICTAR'.[9]

11.2 The Marketing Information System

We have been considering the use of marketing research procedures to monitor important components of the marketing mix. Let us now see where marketing research procedures fit into the marketing information system as a whole. Marketing research data are important MIS inputs, especially those data collected continuously (trend data) or at regular intervals as in tracking studies (see Section 11.1.4): but effective assessment of current performance in order to plan for the future requires information from sources other than marketing research. The Components of the Marketing Information System are represented in Figure 33:[10]

---

10. Kotler, P. (1980), *Marketing Management, Analysis, Planning and Control*, 4th ed., Englewood Cliffs, N.J., Prentice-Hall, p. 602.

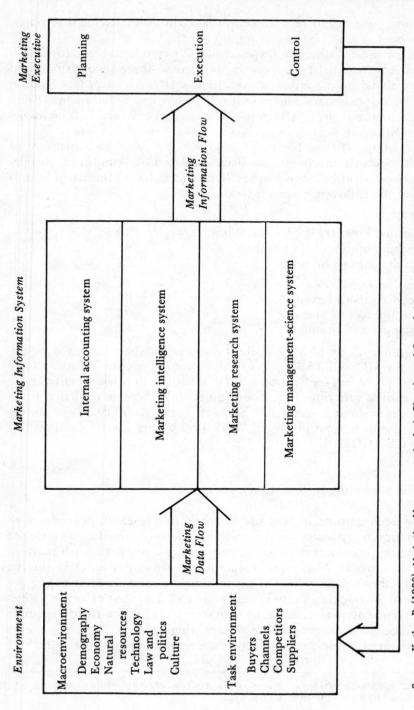

Source: Kotler, P. (1980), *Marketing Management, Analysis, Planning and Control*, 4th ed., Englewood Cliffs, N.J., Prentice-Hall, p. 602.

Figure 33. Components of the Marketing Information System

- we are reminded that the Marketing Information System should be designed to keep management in touch with environmental trends and happenings relevant to the market in which the company is operating (Kotler's 'macro-environment'), as well as monitoring own and competitors' performances in the market place (the 'task environment');
- the inclusion of the 'Internal Accounting System' as a component in the MIS underlines the fact that it is advisable to set marketing costs against sales performance;
- the system is shown as part of a continuous process which has a planning function as well as a controlling one.

Let us now briefly review the components in turn.

11.2.1 INTERNAL ACCOUNTING SYSTEM

The importance of the internal accounting system as a data source is ventilated in Section 2.3 where it is stressed that:

the relevance of a company's accounting system to the marketing of its products indicates the strength of its orientation towards the market.

Once a brand has been successfully launched it is required to make a contribution to profit. In the course of operating in a market, companies (especially those marketing fast-moving branded products) arrive at a norm for profit contribution often expressed as a percentage of sales revenue.

The established brand is required to generate sufficient revenue from sales:

- to make the required contribution to company profit;
- to cover costs associated with the production and marketing of the brand (variable costs);
- to make a contribution to company overheads (fixed costs).

The formula:

$$\text{Sales Revenue} = \text{Variable Costs} + \text{Contribution to Fixed Costs} + \text{Contribution to Profits}$$

involves critical decisions:

The procedure for determining the contribution to fixed costs is likely to be a simple but rather arbitrary one — the bigger the brand's sales the larger the share of fixed costs allocated to it.

The allocation of variable costs to individual brands is facilitated by electronic data processing, but the allocation of production, warehousing, transport and selling costs to specific sizes, scents, flavours, types of packaging may still demand judgmental decisions. In addition it is, of course, necessary to relate costs to sales areas if sales performance is to be properly assessed.

Allocation of advertising costs, often a substantial variable cost, is more straightforward; provided that the company's sales areas can be related to the ITV areas used in media planning, and provided that not more than one brand, or brand variety, is included in the campaign. Perhaps the simplest marketing activity to cost is a trade or consumer promotion.

The most critical relationship is that between the sales target and the marketing support required to achieve the target. If support were increased, would this heightened marketing activity generate sufficient additional sales revenue to more than offset increases in other variable costs (such as production costs), in contribution to fixed costs and profits? And vice versa? The Internal Accounting System records and attributes own costs. In order to make decisions of this kind, data are required from marketing intelligence and marketing research sources.

11.2.2 MARKETING INTELLIGENCE SYSTEM

Readers are referred to Chapter 2, where secondary data sources are reviewed, since these are an important component in an intelligence system.

Deciding what information should be regularly recorded, for example which of the economic indicators published by the Government Statistical Service to watch, is straightforward enough: but in designing an intelligence system there are two critical areas:

- determining to whom information should be circulated, in what detail and how frequently;
- providing for the feeding back — from the sales force, from technicians, trade unionists, suppliers — of news about significant happenings, such as the kind of happening which might contaminate the results of a marketing experiment.

Intelligence relating to the 'macro-environment' is required by both consumer and non-consumer companies. For intelligence relating to the 'task environment', companies marketing consumer goods tend to rely on shared-cost marketing research services such as consumer panels and retail audits, but for some consumer markets, e.g. durables, the data published by trade associations are important MIS inputs. The need to provide for news of happenings remains.[10]

Companies operating in industrial and other non-consumer markets rely on their own intelligence gathering and on information supplied by the manufacturing, trade or professional association to which they belong.

11.2.3 MARKETING RESEARCH SYSTEM

Most of the data sources and procedures commonly used to monitor and predict can be classified under one of two heads:

- trend data derived from retail audits and consumer panels, i.e. data collected time and again from the same sample of retail outlets, households and individuals (in so far as this is possible given drop-outs);
- repeated sampling of a specified population, using the same questionnaire each time, or one with a core of standard questions, but selecting the individuals for questioning afresh ('tracking studies').

Data for a tracking study may be collected and financed in one of three ways:

- subscription to a series of shared cost surveys specifically devoted to the tracking of images, e.g. the British Market Research Bureau's Advertising Planning Index (API) or the Market & Opinion Research International's Corporate Image Survey;
- by buying space in the questionnaire of an Omnibus survey (in this case the context in which the questions appear on the questionnaire will vary from one survey to another);
- by 'going it alone', say once a year, carrying the full cost.

Marketing research data are essential to the building of most marketing models.

11.2.4 MARKETING MANAGEMENT SCIENCE SYSTEM

Among the decision-making techniques associated with 'management science', the use of models to help solve marketing problems is being stimulated by:

- developments in information technology which facilitate the generation and manipulation of data;
- desire to extract more mileage from the wealth of data available to marketing companies, much of it derived from marketing research sources.

Syndicated services and segmentation studies (see Chapter 6) make a substantial demand on increasingly scarce budgetary resources. Panel data, and use and attitude data can make a big contribution to model building: marketing management and research specialists have a common interest in putting these data to work. In addition, if the model building is a shared activity, research specialists and marketing managers are brought closer together.[11]

We return to the subject of model building in Section 11.4. In the meantime we ought perhaps to remember that:

— 'A model is a set of assumptions about the factors which are relevant to a given situation and the relationships which exist between them.'[12]

— Design of a survey is in effect a model-building exercise for, when determining the parameters of the population to be sampled and of the data to be collected, assumptions are being made — albeit informed ones — about 'the factors which are relevant' and 'the relationships which exist between them' (see Chapter 2, Exploring the Market).

— We need to distinguish between micro-models built on disaggregated data and macro- (econometric) models built on aggregated data. Parfitt and Collins's Brand Share Prediction model is based on disaggregated data, while Beecham's AMTES is based on aggregated data (see Chapter 10).

In Chapter 8 we met a number of models including Ehrenberg's NBD/LSD model and Fishbein's 'buying intention' model.

11.3 Forecasting Procedures Reviewed

The sales forecast is basic to the marketing plan whether the forecast be one for the coming year or for, say, the next five years. Management will not make resources available to a brand unless its sales target, together with the marketing support needed to achieve the target, are cogently argued, with the case for the allocation of company resources being supported by financial and market data.

This book is particularly concerned with the marketing data which companies collect and analyse in order to make plans, to monitor the effects of these plans and then to look ahead to the future. There is of

11. Westwood, P.A., Lunn, J.A. and Beazley, D. (July 1974), 'Models and Modelling', *European Research*.

12. Rothman, J. (1978), 'Experimental Designs and Models', Chap. 3 in Worcester, R.M. and Downham, J., *Consumer Market Research Handbook*, 2nd ed., Wokingham, Van Nostrand Reinhold.

course no end to the process: it may well prove necessary to modify the current operational plan while most forward plans are treated as rolling plans, subject to the forces at work in the macro- and micro- environments (see Figure 33).

Here we briefly review forecasting methods in common use, with interest in the marketing research inputs likely to be used. For a more exhaustive treatment of the subject readers are referred to Green and Tull.[13]

There are four main forecasting techniques: (a) extrapolation techniques, (b) correlation techniques, (c) econometric techniques, and (d) polling techniques.

11.3.1 EXTRAPOLATION TECHNIQUES

Trend data are required and the observations need to have been recorded over a period sufficiently long to span seasonal and (where relevant) cyclical changes. The internal accounting system provides data relating to own performance: but the forecast is, generally speaking, more soundly based if own strength/weakness relative to the competition is taken into account.

Most consumer markets are well served with data which express own performance as a brand or market share. In non-consumer markets the data are not so readily available, but industry/trade shares may be estimated from data published by the Government Statistical Service and by trade associations.

The time-series may either be plotted and projected in a naivé way (and for a short-term forecast this may well be adequate), or the recorded observations may be weighted according to their recency using the technique of *exponential smoothing*. This attaches greater importance to more recent results. A third way of treating trend data is *time-series decomposition* technique. It is assumed that a time-series is composed of a trend (which we are trying to isolate), a cyclical component, a seasonal component and an 'irregular' component. We examine the series with a view to separating these components from each other so that we can more easily see their individual characteristics and patterns. Clearly, the more perfect our information about the market, the more alert will we be to the significance of fluctuations in the trend data.

11.3.2 CORRELATION TECHNIQUES

Correlation techniques are particularly interesting in the marketing context because they can take account of the interaction of the mix elements.

13. Green, P.E. and Tull, D.S. (1978), *Research for Marketing Decisions*, Englewood Cliffs, N.J., Prentice-Hall.

They also take account of factors in the macro-environment relevant to the market concerned.

We are looking for variables which have been shown over time to have a sufficiently close relationship to sales to act as predictors of sales. These predictor variables may be found in the marketing mix or in the macro-environment. The size of the 'baby population' is likely to predict demand for baby foods, or demand for durables to correlate with 'new housing'. These are simple one-to-one correlations. The correlations between brand shares and shares of advertising expenditures (with or without allowance for sales promotional expenditure) are often studied when brand sales are being forecast. It could be that an increase in brand share due, say, to more effective distribution, leads to a decision to increase expenditure on advertising; i.e. that the sales increase precedes the advertising increase. It is as well to be alert to spurious correlations such as this when using a correlation technique in order to forecast.

11.3.3 ECONOMETRIC TECHNIQUES

These differ from the simpler correlation techniques in complexity of inputs. Choice of variables and decision as to how the variables are to be weighted are influenced by theories as to how the economy works, or as to how consumers behave or advertising works. AMTES is a comparatively simple econometric model (see Section 10.5.2). A good deal of effort is being devoted to the development of econometric models by manufacturing and marketing companies, research and advertising agencies. Most of this work is specific to individual brands and procedures and results are rarely published.

11.3.4 POLLING TECHNIQUES

These are of two kinds: the respondents may be informed or they may be consumers or opinion-holders without special knowledge of the market. Sales representatives are often asked to make sales forecasts. The forecasts are aggregated by the area manager (if the company's sales force is structured in this way) and the area forecast is forwarded up the line. Suppliers may be asked about costs: industrial customers about the total industry demand as they see it developing. (They will be more forthcoming about their industrial market as a whole than about their own anticipated demand.)

Polls of this kind draw on the respondent's experience. The resultant forecast may usefully be compared with one based on more objective methods.

It is common practice to take polls of business opinion at regular intervals. Taylor Nelson's Business Opinion Study is a well-known example. The Gallup Poll carries out a monthly attitude survey of the British public. One thousand adults are asked the following standard questions:

> Do you think that unemployment will go up, decrease or remain the same during the next six months?

> Do you expect that prices will go up, decrease, or remain the same during the next six months?

> Do you get the impression that your (your husband's) firm is busier now than it was this time last year, not so busy, or just about the same?

> Over the next twelve months do you expect to increase or decrease your income?

> Over the next twelve months do you expect to increase or decrease your financial commitments such as mortgage and hire-purchase?

Heald has shown that an Index of Consumer Confidence based on data derived from these questions predicts consumer purchasing of cars and other durables in the shorter term.[13]

The data derive from polls but the questions asked and their multi-variate processing blur the distinction between 'polling' and 'econometric' (see Section 11.3.4) when labelling this forecasting technique.

In conclusion: (a) All forecasts assume a certain stability in market forces, that past trends and relationships will hold sufficiently well in the future to make forecasting worthwhile. (b) The forecast sets performance standards for all the elements in the marketing mix and for production. (c) Technological developments in data processing (see Section 11.4) have made a considerable contribution to the practice of forecasting.

11.4 Technological Developments

11.4.1 EFFECT ON THE COLLECTION AND PROCESSING OF DATA

Most market research data are collected using well-tried methods long associated with survey research (see Chapter 3) and experimentation (see Chapter 7). However, electronic developments have had a profound

14. Heald, G. (October 1971), 'Consumer Confidence and its Effect on Expenditure for the British Economy', *Journal of the Market Research Society*. (See also: Heald, G. (September 1980), 'Marketing Predictions: Crystal Ball Gazing and Looking Through a Glass Darkly, *Marketing Week*.)

effect on the processing of data, for example in the use of multi-variate statistical techniques to sort consumers into types and products into groups as consumers perceive them (see Chapter 6); and in the quantification of macro- and micro-models. We have, on the way through this book, had evidence of the effect of technological development on data collection:

— questionnaire administration by computer is considered in Section 3.5 on 'conveying questions to respondents';
— automatic recording of the purchases of panel members at scanner checkouts in the Mini-test market operation in Germany and Sweden (see Section 10.5.1);
— provision for optical reading together with detailed pre-coding, designed to speed data processing, makes it easy for respondents to fill in diaries.

The retail trade's gradual adoption of scanner checkouts is particularly significant:

— output of the Automated Front End electronic checkout will in due course supersede the traditional retail auditing method described in Chapter 10.
— It is also likely to supersede the collection of consumer panel household purchase data in the home. If members of a shopping panel are provided with a card carrying a reference number, the Automated Front End electronic checkout can be programmed to attribute the purchases to an individual panel member whose characteristics are on file.
— In the meantime, the big suppliers of retail audit data, A.C. Nielsen, Retail Audits, and Stats. MR, are developing computer programs which make it possible to combine disaggregated 'store by store' results in a variety of ways: e.g. to group stores according to the variety of selling prices given to a brand by retailers to measure the extent to which this factor influences its brand share.[15]

The day is fast approaching when marketing executives will have direct access to computer files, the computer will be 'on line' and the required data will appear on a Visual Display Unit.

Clearly, if fruitful advantage is to be taken of this facility, a good deal of education is going to be needed. One way in which marketing management is acquiring understanding of the opportunities and hazards inherent in the data resources is by taking part in market modelling activities (see Section 11.4.2).

---

15. Bloom, D. (1980), *The Renaissance of Retail Auditing and its Implications for Research in the 1980s*, MRS Conference Papers, and 'Point-of-Sale Scanners and their Implications for Market Research', *Journal of the Market Research Society*.

11.4.2 MARKETING RESEARCH AND MODELLING

It is possible to build a model without statistical data. There are 'theory-based' as well as 'data-based' models. The former utilise concepts about the working of the economy and about consumer behaviour derived from the study of economics and of the social sciences. Theory-based models feature in books on consumer behaviour. They suffer from the weakness that they cannot be proved wrong.[16] The early models of 'how advertising works' (see Section 8.3.1) were theory-based. Models based on statistical data can be proved wrong and so they are susceptible to being tested. Survey research makes an important contribution to the building of marketing models.

This input may be aggregated ('macro') or disaggregated and individual ('micro'). Broadly speaking, macro models are used to describe and predict total movements in the economy or in a particular market, while micro models are used to describe and explain the consumer behaviour influencing these movements.[17] Beecham's AMTES (see Section 10.5.2) uses aggregated data, while Parfitt and Collins's brand share prediction model (see Section 10.4.3) is based on disaggregated data.

Models may be described as 'descriptive', 'diagnostic' or 'predictive'. As we have seen, these market research functions are related to each other and this relationship is exemplified in Ehrenberg's NBD/LSD model (see Section 8.3.2). Ehrenberg's rigourous examination of 'historic' panel data led him to the formulation of laws governing the buying and media habits of consumers. This diagnosis aids prediction by establishing normal behaviour.[18]

A distinction is sometimes drawn between 'behavioural' and 'statistical' models. Here again, in the marketing research context the distinction is by no means a hard and fast one. Fishbein's model (see Section 8.3.4) is based on 'underlying assumptions about how the individual behaves', but the behavioural inputs (as when 'behavioural intention' is 'intention to buy') are the product of survey research. The development of both micro and macro models has, of course, been stimulated by the application of electronics to data processing.

In order to build a *predictive model* of the behaviour of an individual in a marketing situation, it is necessary to have access to *descriptive data* such as:

— the behaviour, beliefs and attitudes of consumers in the product field;
— the extent to which they are aware of the choices available to them;

---

16. Tuck, M. (1976), *How do we Choose? A Study in Consumer Behaviour*, London, Methuen.
17. Lunn, (1978), 'Consumer Modelling', Chap. 20 in Worcester, R.M. and Downham, J., *Consumer Market Research Handbook*, 2nd ed., Wokingham, Van Nostrand Reinhold.
18. Ehrenberg, A.S.C. (1972), *Repeat-buying, Theory and Applications*, Amsterdam, North-Holland Publishing Company.

- the importance they attach to different product/brand characteristics,
- the constraints on their buying behaviour — disposable income, social and cultural pressures, availability of the brand whose future we are trying to predict.

Psychologists have developed a number of theories to explain the way in which choices are made by individuals,[17] and some of these theories are referred to in Chapter 8. Development of the computer has stimulated interest in The Information Processing Theory of Consumer Behaviour.[19] This theory

> aims to describe and explain the means by which people absorb, structure and utilise information.

> In the marketing context, it is based on the recognition that consumers are constantly exposed to more information than they can meaningfully cope with.

> Consequently, they adopt decision rules — or strategies — in order to simplify the choice process.

Four decision rules have been defined (see Figure 34). For any one product field it is possible to classify consumers according to the rule they follow. An individual is unlikely to apply the same rule to all product fields (though consistency of decision-making style may emerge from the data).

If a company has disaggregated data on file about the habits and attitudes of the consumers in its market, it has ready access to a sample of 'electronic consumers' whose responses may be predicted, provided the data are rich enough and attributable to individuals.

Given a knowledge of how these consumers choose, which decision rules they follow, it is possible to *simulate* their individual responses to a new introduction or to the changing of an element in the mix of an established brand.

Apart from the main objective — improved decision-making — micro-behavioural modelling brings other benefits to a marketing company:

- *It is cost-effective*. The data on the computer file can be re-worked and the 'electronic consumers' questioned time and again (though not, of course, for ever since habits and attitudes change, and much marketing activity is directed to that end).

---

19. Palmer, J. and Faivre, J-P. (November 1973), 'The Information Processing Theory of Consumer Behaviour', *European Research*.

— *It brings together marketing managers and research specialists.* The marketing manager, or brand manager, asks 'What if we . . . ?' Raised the price? Introduced an aerosol pack? Extended the range? Introduced a new brand? He/she gets involved in the modelling process and thereby develops a better understanding of the research data and of how these data may be used.

Threshold rule: Brands with unacceptable features are eliminated from further consideration, 'irrespective of any favourable features they may be thought to possess'.

A too-high price (extravagant) or a too-low price (shoddy) might eliminate a brand from further consideration. (See Section 7.6.1 on the Buy-Response Method).

Disjunctive rule: 'A single overwhelming advantage may determine choice'. If this advantage is associated with a particular brand, the consumer will be brand loyal.

In the margarine field the single overwhelming advantage for cholesterol shunners would be 'high in polyunsaturates, contains no cholesterol'.

Lexicographic rule: At the point of sale, 'The first brand to demonstrate an advantage on a sub-set of key attributes, considered in order of importance, is chosen'. Ehrenberg's analyses of panel data have shown that, in most product fields, consumers make their brand choices from a limited number of candidates. Few are 100% 'brand loyal'.

In the toilet soap field, the advantages looked for by an individual might be scent, a luxury look and price, in that order of importance: if the purchaser is a mother, the sub-set of key attributes might be price, large size, healthy smell in that order.

Compensatory rule: Choice is made after a weighing up of pros and cons, and 'the option chosen will be one which is perceived to have the best overall balance of favoured characteristics across all attributes'.[16] This decision rule is likely to be followed when a substantial or durable purchase is being made, e.g. a packaged holiday or a television set: but its application is not limited to these. This rule is followed in the 'Trade-Off' model.[17]

Figure 34. Four Consumer Decision Rules

Conclusion

This chapter defines the kind of marketing research data used to evaluate the effect of planning decisions. It places marketing research in the context of the marketing information system and shows how the planning—monitoring—planning process is continuous.

The critical importance of profit contribution is stressed and the

relationship between sales revenue, provision for variable costs, contribution to fixed costs plus profit contribution is faced. Commonly used
techniques for forecasting sales are reviewed together with their data
requirements.

The chapter comments on technological developments which have
already affected data collection and analysis, or are likely to do so in
the near future. These have made possible the processing of disaggregated
data and the chapter ends with a view of micro-behavioural modelling.

Postscript
on the
Marketing Research Functions

This book has been written with the object of relating marketing research to the functions of marketing. The marketing considerations come first, and the research procedures follow.

Having come to the end of the marketing research process it is clear that marketing research has its own specific functions of description, explanation, evaluation and prediction.

Description is a wide-ranging function. It embraces the channels through which products and services reach consumers, and the ways in which consumers use them, as well as the perceptions and attitudes which lead to the making of consumer choices.

Explanation of consumer behaviour derives from diagnosis of the relationships between attitudes and perceptions as expressed, and behaviour as recorded. Both qualitative and quantitative data supply explanations, the latter in the form of statistical associations.

Evaluation is a critical function when products and services are being developed, the cost-effectiveness of marketing decisions assessed and plans made for the future. It embraces experimentation and the application of forecasting techniques.

Prediction depends on the availability of trend data, collected during the monitoring process, together with the results of experimentation. The functions of evaluation and prediction are closely associated. The evaluative function is exercised to the limit of available data when predictive models are built.

At the end of the day there can be no exercising of the functions of explanation, evaluation and prediction unless relevant and sound descriptive data are available.

233

Appendix 1
Introduction to Sources
of Secondary Data

GUIDES TO SOURCES

Guide to Official Statistics (A), Central Statistical Office

Government Statistics, a brief guide to sources (A), free from the Central Statistical Office, CO:CSO Section, Great George Street, London SW1P 3AQ.

Business Monitors give you the facts about your industry, free from the Central Statistical Office, address above.

Sources of United Kingdom Marketing Information, Tupper, E. and Wills, G. (1975), Benn.

Review of Consumer Research Sources for Products and Media, 2nd. ed., Twyman (1976), Institute of Practitioners in Advertising.

GOVERNMENT STATISTICAL SERVICE

Monthly Digest of Statistics (M), *Annual Abstract of Statistics* (A)

Economic Trends (M)

British Business (M)

Population Trends (Q) England and Wales only. For Scotland and Northern Ireland see estimates of the Registrars General for Scotland and Northern Ireland.

Population Projections (A)

Business Monitors (prepared by the Business Statistics Office):
   Production Monitors (A, Q, M)
   Service and Distributive Monitors (A, Q, M)
   Miscellaneous Monitors, e.g. *Motor Vehicles Registrations* (M), *Statistical News* (Q), *Cinemas* (A), *Overseas Travel and Tourism* (Q)

Transport:
   Transport Statistics (A)
   National Travel Survey 1975—76

Family Income and Expenditure (from the Office of Population Census & Surveys)
Family Expenditure Survey (A)
General Household Survey (most recent report 1977)

Visit: Government Bookshop, 48 High Holborn, London WC1V 6HB; and the Statistics and Market Intelligence Library, 50 Ludgate Hill, London EC4M 7HU.

COMPANY INFORMATION

KOMPASS Register. Companies listed geographically and by Standard Industrial Classification (UK and other countries).
Who Owns Whom (A), Dun & Bradstreet
Guide to Key British Enterprises, Dun & Bradstreet
Stock Exchange Yearbook (A), Thomas Skinner Directories

INTERNATIONAL SOURCES

UN Statistical Yearbook
Main Economic Indicators (Organisation for Economic Control and Development)
General Statistical Bulletin, EEC
Overseas Trade Analysed in Terms of Industries (Q)

INFORMATION PUBLISHED BY MEDIA OWNERS

(for example IPC: *Woman and the National Market* (A);
UK Spending Patterns, ed. Critchley, 1975).

BANK REVIEWS

(published regularly by Barclay's, Lloyd's, Midland and National Westminster).

PERIODICALS

Campaign (W)
Economist (W)
Retail Business (M). This is a useful source of information about markets and marketing. Expert appraisal of 'trade' and published sources. Consult the index. Photocopies of articles are available.

A = annual, Q = quarterly, M = monthly, W = weekly.

Appendix 2
Statistical Tests

by
E.J. DAVIS
Henley: The Management College

The Null Hypothesis

When dealing with the results of experiments or surveys carried out on samples of people, shops, or whatever, it is seldom possible to *prove* results. Instead, we usually attempt to assess which of two mutually exclusive hypotheses is more likely to be true on the basis of our observed results. The general forms of these two hypotheses and the symbols attached to them are:

H_0 the hypothesis that our results do not show any significant differences between population groups over whatever factors have been measured; and

H_1 the hypothesis that differences shown in our results reflect real differences between population groups.

The first of these hypotheses, H_0, is known as the null hypothesis. If it is true it indicates that our results show nothing except chance differences between our measurements. If we can obtain sufficient evidence to refute this hypothesis with an acceptable level of confidence, then we are justified in accepting the alternative hypothesis, H_1.

In effect we begin by assuming that any difference between two sample measurements is not significant and is due to chance until we can find a good basis for rejecting this assumption. If we can reject the null hypothesis we say that our result is 'significant'.

Errors of the First and Second Kind

In addition to setting down our hypotheses, we need also to decide on the degree of risk we can accept of being wrong in taking a result as

236

significant when it is not. For most market research purposes we work with a level of risk of 1 in 20 of being wrong, often referred to as the 95% limit or the 5% level of significance. In terms of the experiments discussed in Chapter 7, this means that we devise our experiments so that we can apply tests of significance such that if they indicate a real difference, this will be a correct evaluation 95 times out of 100. As we do not normally carry out our experiments often enough to be able to think in terms of being right on 95% of occasions we change the words slightly, and say that we have a 95% chance of being right. From this it follows that we have a 5% chance, or probability, of being wrong, and our tests are operating at the 5% or 0.05 level of significance.

The level of significance here indicates the level of risk of our being wrong in rejecting the null hypothesis when it is true, and thus of accepting our experimental difference as real when it is not. Being wrong in this way is known as a Type I Error.

There is a converse risk — that of failing to detect or to accept a positive experimental result because our experimental measurements are too crude. If, say, a change in some measure, such as consumption of some food product from 30 grams per head to 35 grams per head per day would show a profitable return on some marketing expenditure, then an experiment capable only of showing a change of 10 grams or more as significant will leave the company open to such a risk.

An opportunity to take profitable marketing action may be lost because an experiment is set up which is not powerful enough to measure results with the precision needed in the particular situation. Being wrong in this way is known as a Type II Error.

Two further elements which should be taken into account when assessing the levels of significance to be used are the size of the benefits expected if successful action is subsequently taken, and the penalties expected from taking a wrong decision. In situations such as the final stages of the development and launch of a new brand, the potential benefits and potential losses resulting from decisions based on the experimental results are high. This normally calls for the design of experiments giving high levels of precision and low risks of wrongly rejecting the null hypothesis — such as 1 chance in 100 (the 1% level), as opposed to the one chance in 20 (the 5% level). But such experiments are themselves costly, and should not be used in less risky situations where the costs would not be justified. Initial testing of ideas and products is often better undertaken based on the use of significance levels of 10% or more, simply because in the early stages of testing it is often unreasonable (and probably unprofitable) to insist on the more rigorous levels of significance appropriate to high-risk situations.

The problems then of interpreting the statistical results of experiments are by no means simple, nor confined merely to the use of prescribed formulae yielding magic numbers to be labelled 'significant' or 'not significant'. However, with these reservations the following statistical tests can be applied with care to a range of statistical results.

Differences Between Sample Measurements

The range of uncertainty surrounding a measurement obtained from a sample is indicated by the 'standard error' of that measurement.

To calculate the standard error of a measurement, such as the mean price respondents say they would pay for a new product, their mean foot measurements, and so forth, we first calculate the arithmetic mean and use that as a basis for calculating the standard error. The standard error of a mean can then be calculated from this formula:

$$se_m = \sqrt{\frac{\Sigma (x - \bar{x})^2}{n^2}}$$

where n = sample size (assumed here to be at least 30);
x = each individual measurement taken in turn;
$\bar{x}$ = the mean of all values of x; and
Σ indicates all values of $(x - \bar{x})^2$ added together.

When dealing with attributes such as whether a person smokes or not, whether they like the test product or whether they think they would buy the test product in preference to their usual brand, we can use a more simple version of this formula. In these cases we can put $x = 1$ whenever the respondent smokes, prefers, would buy, or whatever, and $x = 0$ if he or she does not. It is then easy to show that under these conditions the standard error of the percentage having the stated attribute can be calculated by the formula below:

$$se_p = \sqrt{\frac{p (100 - p)}{n}}$$

where p = the percentage scored 1 (preferably between 10% and 90%), and
n = sample size (assumed to be at least 30).

(When using proportions instead of percentages substitute $(1 - p)$ for $(100 - p)$ in the formula.)

Testing Experimental Differences Involving Percentages

Experimental designs such as those used for rating new products (see Section 7.4.2) may involve monadic tests using independent matched samples each reporting on one variant, or comparative tests where the same sample of people report on two or more variants of the product. The procedures for testing the results vary, and are described separately.

Monadic Results from Independent Samples

The hypotheses:

H_0 that any difference between readings p_1 and p_2 from two independent random samples of n_1 and n_2 respondents is the result of chance alone.

H_1 that the difference between the readings must be attributed to the experimental conditions.

Note that these hypotheses do not stipulate any direction for any difference, i.e. whether p_1 or p_2 is the higher percentage. Hence a two-tailed test is used, and finding a significant difference in either direction would lead to the rejection of H_0.

First calculate p, the overall percentage given by combining both samples, on the assumption that they are both drawn from the same population. This is given by

$$p = \frac{n_1 p_1 + n_2 p_2}{n_1 + n_2}$$

Then calculate the standard error of the difference $(p_1 - p_2)$

$$se_d = \sqrt{p(100 - p) \left(\frac{1}{n_1} + \frac{1}{n_2} \right)}$$

In the special case where $n_1 = n_2$

$$p = \frac{p_1 + p_2}{2}$$

$$se_d = \sqrt{p(100 - p) \frac{2}{n}}$$

Now calculate the absolute value of the test statistic, t, ignoring its sign, where t is defined as:

$$t = \frac{p_1 - p_2}{se_d}$$

If $t \geqslant 1.64$ the difference is significant at the 10% level; if $t \geqslant 1.96$ the difference is significant at the 5% level; and if $t \geqslant 2.58$ the difference is significant at the 1% level.

If a significant difference is found at the required level it suggests that the difference between the readings p_1 and p_2 is not simply due to chance, but reflects a real difference in preferences for the test items.

In some circumstances the direction of any difference is important, as in experiments with a new version of a product expected to be preferred by more people than the old. Here we are not testing whether there is a difference in *either* direction, but whether there is a difference in *one* direction only. In such cases a one-tailed test is used and rejection of H_0 only follows if the test is significant in the appropriate direction.

Assume that p_1 measures acceptance of the old product, and that p_2 measures acceptance of the new version when they have been tested on two independent samples. Then our hypotheses become:

H_0 that p_2 is no greater than p_1, and
H_1 that p_2 is greater than p_1.

We calculate se_p and t as before, but now we are only interested in t if p_2 exceeds p_1. The test is now concerned with only one tail of the distribution of error, and the values of t associated with different levels of significance are changed.

If $t \geqslant 1.29$ the one-way test is significant at the 10% level, and if $t \geqslant 1.64$ the one-way test is significant at the 5% level, and if $t \geqslant 2.32$ the one-way test is significant at the 1% level.

Comparative Readings from the Same Sample

If we measure preferences for *A, B, C,* etc. in the same sample, then there are problems of correlation. As p_a increases so p_b may well diminish, and vice versa. Now to establish whether any difference is significant we have to take account of correlation in our formula for se_p. Our hypotheses become:

H_0 there is no difference between the proportions p_a and p_b preferring *A* and *B*, measured within a single sample.
H_1 there is a difference between preferences for *A* and *B*.

Now the formula for the standard error of the difference becomes:

$$se_d = \sqrt{\frac{p_a(100 - p_a) + p_b(100 - p_b) + 2p_a p_b}{n}}$$

$$t = \frac{p_a - p_b}{se_d} \quad \text{as before,}$$

and the values of t apply as before for either one-tailed or two-tailed tests.

More Complex Tests of Preference Scores

Sometimes we wish to examine more complex situations, such as a preference test where the sample is broken down by some other attribute such as social class. Then the χ^2 or chi-squared test is a more useful way of proceeding.

Suppose we have the following results from a sample of 195 housewives who have each tested products X and Y and stated their preferences. Information on social class has also been collected from each respondent. The results were:

	ABC_1	C_2D	
Prefer X	60	40	100
Prefer Y	30	65	95
	90	105	195

A t-test on the overall split between preferences for X and Y has shown that this is not significant. It appears that there may be differences in preferences between social classes. While it would be possible to carry out a t-test for each class a χ^2 test is more powerful and economical. Here:

H_0 there is no difference between the pattern of preferences by social class.

H_1 the pattern of preferences differs between the two social classes.

If there is no difference between classes, then we would expect the same proportion of housewives in each class to prefer X, and the same proportion to prefer Y. The overall estimate of the preference for X is 100 out of 195. Applying this ratio to the 90 ABC_1 housewives, we would expect 46.2 to prefer X, i.e., $100/195 \times 90$. Similarly we would expect $95/195 \times 90$ ABC_1 housewives to prefer Y; $100/195 \times 105$ C_2D housewives to prefer X, and $95/195 \times 105$ to prefer Y.

In fact, once we have calculated one of the four expected values in a 2 × 2 table such as this one, the other three values are fixed because of the need for columns and rows to add to their original totals. In technical terms we have only 'one degree of freedom' in such a table.

For each cell we now have an observed (O) and an expected (E) value. We then calculate $(O-E)^2/E$ and add.

	Observed	Expected	$O - E$	$(O - E)^2$	$(O - E)^2/E$
X/ABC_1	55	46.2	8.8	77.44	1.68
Y/ABC_1	35	43.8	−8.8	77.44	1.77
X/C_2D	45	53.8	−8.8	77.44	1.44
Y/C_2D	60	51.2	8.8	77.44	1.51
	195	195.0	0		6.40

We can now consult a table of values of χ^2 for our number of degrees of freedom and level of significance, and see whether our sample value exceeds the tabulated value or not. If it does the differences are significant at that level.

		Degrees of freedom		
	1	2	3	4
10%	2.7	4.6	6.3	7.8
5%	3.8	6.0	7.8	9.5
1%	6.6	9.2	11.3	13.3

Some values of χ^2.

Comparing the calculated value of 6.40 with the table for one degree of freedom, the results are seen to be significant at the 5% level but not quite at the 1% level.

In general, when using χ^2:

— use frequencies, not percentages;
— cells should preferably contain five or more cases;
— degrees of freedom = (rows − 1) × (columns − 1), e.g. a table of two rows and three columns has $(2 − 1) \times (3 − 1) = 2$ degrees of freedom.

Differences Involving Variables

The same general procedure is followed for comparing means of variables as for proportions. In these cases, for independent samples calculate a pooled estimate of the se thus:

$$se_d = \sqrt{\frac{n_1}{n_2} \cdot se_{\bar{x}_1}^2 + \frac{n_2}{n_1} \cdot se_{\bar{x}_2}^2}$$

$$t = \frac{\bar{x}_1 - \bar{x}_2}{se_d}$$

Null hypotheses and alternative hypotheses are set up as before, and the links between values of t and levels of significance for one-tailed and two-tailed tests are the same as for testing proportions.

Where pairs of readings are taken from the same sample, such as numbers of cigarettes smoked by individuals before and after an experiment or weights of slimmers before and after treatment, etc., the situation is most easily handled by calculating the difference, d, for each individual and $\bar{d}$, the average value of d. Then calculate se_d:

$$se_d = \sqrt{\frac{\Sigma (d - \bar{d})^2}{n}}$$

Then our hypotheses become:

H_0 that the value of d is not significantly different from zero; and
H_1 that the observed differences are significant.

and the tabulated values of t at different levels of significance and for one-tailed and for two-tailed tests apply as before.

For More Complex Situations 'Analysis of Variance' is Used

Consider the experiment described in Section 7.3 with results in volume of sales by outlets in three areas, North, Midlands and South and with three pack designs or treatments on test.

	Shop sales in a pack test				
	T1	*T2*	*T3*	*Total*	*Average*
N	150	220	180	550	183.3
M	90	100	110	300	100.0
S	60	70	70	200	66.7
Total	300	390	360	1050	
Average	100	130	120		116.7

The regional differences in sales are clearly seen, and on visual inspection they appear to be greater than the differences in sales between the experimental packs. It therefore becomes logical to try to separate the variation or 'variance' between treatments (pack designs in this case) from the variance between regions. Hence we undertake an analysis of variance.

Now the overall variance is given by:

$$s^2 = \frac{1}{n - 1} \Sigma(x - \bar{x})^2$$

where n = number of cells in the analysis
$\bar{x}$ = the average sales level over all stores in all regions, i.e:
$$\bar{x} = \frac{1050}{9} = 116.67.$$

Within the total variance some part will be due to:

— variations in sales between areas;
— variations in sales between pack designs; and
— chance variations in sales between stores.

The statistic F is used to assess whether any observed differences in the variance contributions are significant, or probably due only to chance, and hypotheses H_0 and H_1 are set up as before.

The calculations necessary to analyse the overall variance from the experimental results into the parts due to each of these sources are as follows:

r = number of rows (areas)
t = number of treatments (packs).

Add up total sales and calculate average sales ($\bar{x}$).
For each area find total sales and average sales (rows) — $\bar{A}_i$.
For each pack find total sales and average sales (cols) — $\bar{P}_j$.

Calculate $\sum\limits_{1}^{r} \sum\limits_{1}^{t} (x_{ij} - \bar{x})^2$ = Sum of Squares Total (SST).

Calculate $r\sum\limits_{1}^{r} (\bar{A}_i - \bar{x})^2$ = Sum of Squares, Areas (SSA).

Calculate $t\sum\limits_{1}^{r} (\bar{P}_j - \bar{x})^2$ = Sum of Squares, Packs (SSP).

As a check on arithmetic one more figure may be calculated:

$$\sum\limits_{1}^{r} \sum\limits_{1}^{t} (x_{ij} - \bar{A}_i - \bar{P}_j + \bar{x})^2 = \text{Error/residual Sum of Squares} = \text{(SSE)}.$$

Calculate degrees of freedom (d.f.) as follows:

Total d.f. = no. of areas × no. of treatments − 1
= $(r \times t) - 1$.
Between areas d.f. = no. of areas − 1
= $(r - 1)$
Between treatments d.f. = no. of treatments − 1
= $(t - 1)$
Residual/Error d.f. = $(r - 1)(t - 1)$

Note that the degrees of freedom between areas + between treatments + residual = total degrees of freedom. Then complete the following table:

Source of Variance	Sum of Squares	d.f.	Mean Square	Value of F
Between Packs	SSP	$t-1$	$MSP = SSP/(t-1)$	MSP/MSE
Between Areas	SSA	$r-1$	$MSA = SSA/(r-1)$	MSA/MSE
Error/Residual	SSE	$(r-1)(t-1)$	$MSE = SSE/(r-1)(t-1)$	
Total	SST	$rt-1$		

Analysis of Variance for random block design.

For the shop sales data from the pack test:

r = areas = 3
t = packs = 3

$$\sum_{1}^{r}\sum_{1}^{t} (x_{ij} - \bar{x})^2 = 24,400.0$$

$$r \sum_{1}^{r} (\bar{A}_i - \bar{x})^2 = 21,666.7$$

$$t \sum_{1}^{t} (\bar{P}_j - \bar{x})^2 = 1,400.0$$

$$\sum_{1}^{r}\sum_{1}^{t} (x_{ij} - \bar{A}_i - \bar{P}_j + \bar{x})^2 = 1,333.3$$

The table then becomes:

Source of Variance	Sum of Squares	d.f.	Mean Square	Value of F
Areas	21,666.7	2	10833.3	32.5
Packs	1,400.0	2	700.0	2.1
Error	1,333.3	4	333.3	
Totals	24,400.0	8		

We can now consult tables of the values of F to test whether either of the F values is significant. We enter the tables with 2 d.f. for areas and 2 d.f. for packs (the numerators in the F ratios) and 4 d.f. for the Mean Square Error (the denominator). In tables of the values of F the degrees of freedom for the numerator are denoted by v_1, and those for the denominator by v_2.

Using $v = 2$ and $v = 4$, the tables show the following significant values for F:

1% level $F = 18.00$
5% level $F = 6.94$
10% level $F = 4.32$
25% level $F = 2.00$

This result shows, as we suspected, that there are very strong area differences, with the between-areas value of F being significant well beyond the 1% level. The value of F for the packs however is only significant at the 25% level — that is we could expect such observed differences in the sales of the different packs in one experiment in four, just by chance even if the packs had no differential effects on sales levels.

The action to be taken on this result would depend on other factors in the situation, such as the relative costs of the three packs, the time pressures for a decision, and so forth. Broadly we could:

— adopt pack 3, accepting the low level of significance of the experimental result;
— continue with the existing pack (if there is one); or
— carry out further experiments to get a more specific indication of the effects of packs on sales.

Analysis of variance is such a widely used method of assessing the significance of experimental results that it is included in most computer statistical packages. The programs vary in detail, but the raw data are fed in as responses to promptings by the computer program, and the completed calculations printed out or displayed in a form similar to the table above. Some programs stop at the calculation of the F values, but others go on to indicate the associated levels of significance.

It is important to appreciate what calculations are taking place to produce the analysis of variance from a set of data, but seldom necessary to carry through the arithmetic by hand.

The facilities are also normally there for handling the calculations arising from more complex experiments quickly and accurately, for taking account of more factors, and for investigating possible interactions between levels of factors. At each stage of increasing complexity the calculations expand, but following the patterns shown above.

For example, the Latin Square design discussed in Section 7.3 leads us to this final table:

Source of Variance	Sum of Squares	d.f	Mean Square	Value of F
Between Packs	SSP	$t-1$	MSP $= $ SSP$/(t-1)$	MSP/MSE
Between Areas	SSA	$t-1$	MSA $=$ SSA$/(t-1)$	MSA/MSE
Between Outlets	SSO	$t-1$	MSO $=$ SSO$/(t-1)$	MSO/MSE
Error/Residual	SSE	$(t-1)(t-2)$	MSE $=$ SSE$/(t-1)(t-2)$	
	SST	$t-1$		

Analysis of Variance for Latin Square.

The similarity in structure between the tables is seen, with the inclusion of an additional line in the Latin Square results. The error/residual calculation is now

$$\sum_1^t \sum_1^r (x_{ij} - \bar{A}_i - \bar{P}_j - \bar{O}_k + 2\bar{x})^2$$

where the $\bar{A}_i$s are the averages of the Areas;
where the $\bar{P}_j$s are the averages of the Packs; and
where the $\bar{O}_k$s are the averages of the Outlet types.

Worked Example of the Use of a Latin Square

This example follows the design set out in Section 7.3, with three packs being tested in three outlet types in three areas. The sales figures are shown below.

	Type of retail outlet				
Region	Grocer	Chemist	CTN	Total	Average
North	122^2	114^3	139^1	375	125
Midlands	108^1	115^2	104^3	327	109
South	91^3	110^1	114^2	315	105
Total	321	339	357	1017	
Average	107	113	119		113

Raw sales data from pack test.

The indices against cell sales indicate the pack version used.

To facilitate the calculation of the pack averages the figures may be rearranged thus:

				Total	Average
Pack 1 sales	139	108	110	357	119
Pack 2 sales	122	115	114	351	117
Pack 3 sales	114	104	91	309	103

It is now possible to calculate all the sums of squares required and to fit them into the analysis of variance table.

Source of Variance	Sum of Squares	d.f.	Mean Square	Value of F
Packs	456	2	228	25.3
Areas	672	2	336	37.3
Outlets	216	2	113	12.6
Error	18	2	9	—
Totals	1362	8		

These values of F can be compared with the tabulated values for v_1 and v_2 both at two degrees of freedom:

at the 5% level $F = 19.0$, and
at the 1% level $F = 99.0$.

Hence both pack figures and the area figures show significant differences at the 5% level.

The fact that the figures show significant variations by pack needs careful interpretation, and reference back to the averages by pack indicates that the variation arises from one pack performing less well than the other two. There is still doubt about which of the three packs may sell best — but some progress has been made in finding that one version sells less well than the other two.

Suggestions for Further Reading

Cox, K. and Enis, B. (1973), *Experimentation for Marketing Decisions*, Glasgow, Intertext.

Harris, P. (1978), 'Statistics and Significance Testing', Chap. 12 in Worcester, R.M. and Downham, J., *Consumer Market Research Handbook*, Wokingham, Van Nostrand Reinhold.

Montagnon, P.E. (1980), *Foundations of Statistics*, Cheltenham, Stanley Thornes.

Glossary of Abbreviations

The page references are to the earliest appearance of the abbreviation in the text.

Index